ECONOMICS FOR THE TWENTY-FIRST CENTURY

Economics for the Twenty-first Century

The economics of the economist-fox

ANDREW M. KAMARCK

Routledge
Taylor & Francis Group

LONDON AND NEW YORK

First published 2001 by Ashgate Publishing

Reissued 2018 by Routledge
2 Park Square, Milton Park, Abingdon, Oxon, OX14 4RN
711 Third Avenue, New York, NY 10017, USA

Routledge is an imprint of the Taylor & Francis Group, an informa business

A Library of Congress record exists under LC control number: 00054302

ISBN 13: 978-1-138-72024-4 (hbk)
ISBN 13: 978-1-138-72023-7 (pbk)
ISBN 13: 978-1-315-19510-0 (ebk)

Contents

List of Tables

Acknowledgements

John Train, a noted investment adviser, when asked what is the best training for making investment decisions (i.e. the allocation of scarce resources), stated, *To start with, I am quite sure what isn't: majoring in economics.... Investment success requires above all a knowledge of business...; a feeling for how people function; and a wide and deep judgment of affairs in general.* [1994] On the contrary, economics, when it is not the desiccated subject of Train's scorn, provides the broad knowledge which Train considers necessary for investment success.

My colleagues during my career, particularly in the World Bank, demonstrated how economic training enabled one to take full advantage of all pertinent knowledge and experience to make wise investment and policy decisions. All of us, prior to joining the Bank, had held top positions in governments, central banks, investment banks, and other private sector businesses in countries throughout the globe. In coping with the new unique problems we were faced with in the initial years of the Bank, there was an intensive learning process profiting from the rich experiences available. It is impossible for me to identify exactly who was responsible for particular strands of my present fabric of thought. These were spun in a synthesis of discussion and experience.

I was fortunate in the last five years to participate in several workshops, organized and directed by Armand Clesse of the Luxembourg Institute for European and International Studies, as part of a series of a long-term project on "The Vitality of Nations". This project investigates, using a multidisciplinary and multinational approach, the issue of the rise and decline of countries. The project has produced a number of insightful studies—from which my own text has profited. The project fits precisely my interest in how economics needs to be approached and used to be valuable. Dr. Clesse accordingly included a workshop at the Harvard Faculty Club on 24 April 1998 on a draft of this book. A summary report on the workshop is annexed to this book. As is evident from references found throughout the book, the workshop was invaluable to me in validating and clarifying some of my thoughts, suggesting new ideas, and finally saving me from some errors that I had stumbled into. I also benefited from an additional critique that Jack Powelson was kind enough to undertake.

I am most grateful to my World Bank colleagues and Dr. Clesse, his collaborator, Anemone Thomas, and the participants in the workshop for all the benefit I derived from their association, assistance and guidance. If I have gone astray in some respect, it is, of course, my personal responsibility.

1   Introduction and Overview

A person is not likely to be a good economist who is nothing else. J. S.
Mill.

Isaiah Berlin, in his essay on the hedgehog and the fox, depicted the chasm
between thinkers who relate everything to a single system, a single
organizing principle, and those who see the world as too various to be
caught by any single universal absolute. Conventional economics has been
dominated by hedgehog theorists. Michael M. Weinstein described it this
way:

> On my first day as a graduate student in economics ..., the professor
> introduced the discipline by intoning, "All of economics is a subset of
> the theory of separating hyperplanes."...
>
> I...muttered, only to myself, that I had thought economics was
> about the plight of people living in sub-Saharan Africa or the impact of
> technological change on living standards. ...
>
> Decades later, I find economics graduate students asking
> themselves the same question: where is the economics substance in
> graduate economics programs? [2000, 1]

Scholars have been expressing their dismay for a generation at the
state of economics. In 1982, Wassily Leontief complained that the
theorists producing mathematical models and econometricians fitting
algebraic functions did not advance in any perceptible way a understanding
of a real economy (Letter to *Science*). And Mark Blaug commented that
economics is becoming *...an intellectual game played for its own sake and
not for its practical consequences*, creating models which are
...scandalously unrepresentative of any recognizable economic system.
[1997, 2-4; quoted in Sugden 2000, 28-9]

The Economist puts the economy's view of economists this way:

> Is it any wonder that businessmen cannot stand economists? The typical
> manager never seems to face the same problem twice, always says
> exactly what he means, expletives included, and is certain that the people
> he deals with are not even remotely rational. He could not have less in
> common with the typical economist, who is always searching for
> universal solutions, cannot articulate them even when he finds them, and
> bases his entire view of the world on the principle that people are
> rational to a fault. [1997, June 14, 67]

To provide the explanatory power and useful guidance needed for people in the economy and government, economics has to be mature enough to recognize the extraordinary complexity of the real world. As Hicks insisted, "What we want. in economics, are theories which will be useful, practically useful." [Hicks 1983, 15 cited in Hutchinson 1996, 208]

My last book, *Economics and the Real World,* laid out the limitations confronted by economics in grasping that part of the real world that economic theory is assumed to cover. Most important is recognizing the roughness of the accuracy that is attainable in comprehending the real world. The sources of data often have their own agenda to exploit. Most economic phenomena are *continua,* categories are arbitrary, and the accuracy attainable is rough and imprecise. Further, there are major defects in some existing economic concepts and other necessary concepts do not yet even exist. Discovering or knowing a fact is without much meaning if one does not possess the necessary concept to understand it.

There is a growing consensus that for the third millennium we need to go beyond the ruling theories of the last century.

> The economists of the twentieth century, by pushing the neoclassical model to its logical conclusions, and thereby illuminating the absurdities of the world which had been created, have made an invaluable contribution to the economics of the coming century; they have set the agenda, work on which has already begun. [J. E. Stiglitz 1991, 136]

In the twenty-first century, economists need to approach the subject in the spirit of Ronald Coase, the 1991 Nobel laureate, who believes that assumptions should be realistic, that economists can learn from observing reality, and that this is particularly necessary when we need to break our existing habits of thought. [Coase 1991,11]

Conventional economics neglected or overlooked large areas of the economy.[1] Much of positive value in contemporary economics came mostly from the results of empirical work and research. Progress in the next century towards making economics a more useful branch of learning will continue to come from focusing on the real economy.

Appreciation of how a modern economy works requires a richer, more varied knowledge than that taught by formal twentieth century theory. There is nothing sacred in maintaining traditional disciplinary habits and bounds when they cripple the effectiveness of a discipline. Twenty-first century economists need to be foxes rather than neoclassical hedgehogs. As David Cutler perceptively observed, *If you think only as an economist, you'll produce silly answers. And if you don't consider economics at all, you'll produce silly answers.*

---

[1] George A. Akerlof's useful series of essays illustrate the profitable consequences of adopting non-conventional economic assumptions. Guy Routh's *Alternative Text* provides another economic world view that makes much of the economy more intelligible. [Akerlof 1984; Routh 1984]

This book is designed to help economists to be economic foxes by increasing the range of economist's tools, drawing on the knowledge and experience of other disciplines, to cope better with the extraordinary complexity of the modern economy. Economics as a real science must concern itself with empirical matters. To be effective, it must take into consideration the complex nature of human beings and the contextual, institutional, social and historical factors at play in the economy.

Involvement with strange economies and unfamiliar disciplines exposes the unconscious assumptions one has been nourishing. To give a homely example: before visiting Britain, an American may assume that driving on the right is natural behavior. Rather than accepting the imperialistic claim that economics can explain all human behavior, economists should rather realize that other disciplines can help in explaining economic behavior. In Viner's words,

> ...crossing the boundary lines into other disciplines tends to provide mutual stimulation and safeguards...against degeneration of the individual disciplines into formal and lifeless academic systems whose original organs of contact with the problems of real life ... have become atrophied through more or less deliberate disuse. [Viner 1937, 594-5]

Human beings (and human institutions) cannot be understood fully by a simple one-size-fits-all theory. Some parts of economics (opportunity cost, comparative advantage, the importance of economic incentives, for example) are useful in all disciplines. However, to fully understand behavior in a market, in an enterprise, in the public sector, one has to go beyond the conventional belief that one theory fits all.

The argument may be clearer by analogy. Benjamin Rush, a signer of the Declaration of Independence, was the most prestigious teacher of medicine of his time. He believed that the body had to be in equilbrium and taught that all diseases are, in the final analysis, the same, fever caused by overstimulation of the blood vessels. The cure was to bring the system back to equilibrium by bloodletting and purges (the treatment suffered by George Washington in his final sickness). With greater knowledge, medical science has learned that there are many different classes of diseases requiring different kinds of cures. There are diseases caused by: (1) bacteria, (2) rickettsia, (3) viruses, (4) heredity (genetic origins) (5) environmental causes, (6) nutritional deficiencies. There are also immune system diseases like MS and diseases like Alzheimer's whose causes are still not completely understood.

To be live up to their important role in society, economists need a broad vision, a wide-ranging intellect, and a rich assortment of tools drawn from many disciplines. Adam Smith, Marshall, Schumpeter, and Keynes were great economists because they were much more than just hedgehog economists. The economist-fox requirements were clearly put by Keynes:

The amalgam of logic and intuition and the wide knowledge of facts, most of which are not precise, which is required for economic interpretation in its highest form is, quite truly, overwhelmingly difficult for those whose gift mainly consists in the power to imagine and pursue to their furtherest points the implications and prior conditions of comparatively simple facts which are known with a high degree of precision. [Essays in Biography, 191-2]

The objective in this book is to help to provide the same kind of revelation in understanding an economy that an artist possesses in the visual arts. A beginner looking at a still life sees a green bottle, a red apple and a yellow cloth on a table top. An artist, however, can point out to him:

The bottle's not green, though there's green in it. See the blue and the yellow. There's also blue in the shadows, purple on the shadow side of the apple, yellow reflections.

When the amateur truly opens his eyes, he is like a blind person suddenly given sight; all he views is ablaze with nuances of color. Similarly, if this book succeeds, the reader will be able to grasp better how richly complex an economy is in its structure and in its operations.

Chapter 2 makes a rapid dissection of the canonical hypotheses of contemporary economic theory. We then go on to an analysis and review the pertinent theories useful for the different sectors of the real economy: Chapter 3, The Corporation; 4, Corporate Governance; 5, Services; 6, Public Sector; 7, Civil Society; 8, Professions; 9, Social Capital; 10, National Cultures; and 11, The Tropics. By bringing in richer knowledge from other disciplines major important aspects of the economy are perceived that neoclassical economics tends to overlooks.

A central theme of the book winds through these analyses: *The essence of the economy is not logic; it is life. It is shaped by the complex drives of human beings, by their social capital—their institutions, customs and cultures. The attempt to find some order in the economy as in the world—the social construction of reality—has to take account of the richness, complexity, and the constant flux that confronts us. It cannot be cramped into a neat tidy structure poised on a few simple logical axioms.*

Grau, teurer Freund, ist alle Theorie
Und grün des Lebens goldner Baum.[2]—Goethe

---

[2] Gray, dear friend, is all theory
And green is the golden tree of life.

2 Canonical Hypotheses

...the self is not a unified, simple, rational entity that an individual ... controls. It is, instead, a cauldron of conflicting impulses, some rational, some irrational, some power-seeking, some self-sacrificial.— Reinhold Niebuhr.

Walras, in trying to construct an economic theory on the analogy of Newtonian physics, confronted the problem of how there could be any regularity when humans have the richness of emotions, motives, expectations, and uncertainties which affect all of us. Walras solved his problem by limiting human beings to a single drive, infinite selfishness. This—under the modern more palatable guise that human beings rationally maximize self-interest—is still the *fundamental assumption* on which neoclassical economic theory rests. In Milton Friedman's words: the assumption takes *profit maximization as a central element* and treats *human beings as rationally directed toward the maximization of profit.* [1983, 172-3] The assumption turns out to be both normative and positive—people should and do always act in their best interests. The assumption is necessary to make possible the mathematical modeling of economic problems. [Samuelson 1947, 21]

A remarkable aspect of the fundamental assumption is that it lacks substantiation. There is no *a priori* guarantee that this assumption is true. No body of research validates the assumption, on which the whole formal conventional structure rests. It has never been established empirically that individuals always act in a rational calculating self-interested manner. Nor has it been established that when an individual does show calculative–rationality in pursuing his self-interest, that this behavior derives from inherent human nature rather than from acculturation or a personal quirk.

But, this assumption together with equilibrium, in Robert Solow's characterization, are the canonical hypotheses of economic theory.[Kreps 1997, 59]

Virtually all economic theories have as primary desiderata that the behavior described must be consistent with some notion of equilibrium. ...among social scientists, only economists insist on a physical-sciences-style equilibrium as part of the analysis. [Lazear 2000, 101]

The argument in this chapter will probably be most difficult for many economists to accept since it goes so directly counter to the mathematical mind-set economics graduate training instills. Often, the difficulty in such circumstances is, as Dr. William Osler commented on the slowness of the acceptance by doctors of the need for aseptic treatment of wounds, it was ... "a long and grievous battle, ... with the opposition of men who *could not*—not who would not—see the truth". [emphasis added, quoted in Horton, 2000, 38]

Self-interest

William James distinguished between the *I* and the *Me*. The *I* is the ultimate thinker which decides on actions, the *Me[1]* is the object of all of one's selfish concerns. The *I* can make decisions benefiting the *Me*, that will benefit others, or even that harm the *Me*. The economics assumption, however, is that the *I* always acts to benefit the *Me*. This implies that humans do not have *free will*. To have *free will*, you have to be able to choose your self-interest or make some other choice. If in every circumstance, the path of self-interest is inevitably chosen, then, you have no *free will*.

Sometimes, the assumption is defended on the basis that altruism, our choosing to help others, is in our "self-interest". This is the logical fallacy, *petitio principii* (begging the question), i.e. assuming what needs to be proved. One cannot include altruism in self-interest. In this case, our action taken by our *I*, is directed not towards the *Me* but the *Other*.

The behavior of every person, of every *I*, is the nexus of a large number of acting causes. No single cause determines the life of the individual. It is this evolving structure of multiple causal pathways that makes the actions of a living creature so difficult to understand. We often do not know why we prefer one outcome to another. One likes to have a reason for what one does even when there is none. Economic theory, in contrast, assumes that each individual *has stable and coherent preferences, and that she rationally maximizes those preferences.* [Rabin 1998, 11]

The conclusion drawn, however, from experiments and studies, which is also intuitively correct, is that people do not normally have a complete set of preferences for every situation. People decide their preferences when they have to, or decide to, make a choice or judgment. The context and procedures involved in making choices influence what preferences are chosen. [Tversky & Thaler 1990; Smith 1994,124]

Experimental tests, also, suggest that consumers betray an inability to make coherent and consistent consumption decisions.[Johnson, Kotlikoff, and Samuelson 1987] "People misjudge the probabilistic consequences of their decisions. ...even when they correctly perceive the

---

[1] Stephen Bergman, a Harvard clinical instructor describes the *Me* this way: *The ego is insatiable. If you are into your ego, you can never get enough—not enough drugs, sex, money, alcohol, ..., not enough anything. ...The only thing that helps is getting beyond yourself.* [Lambert 2000, 65]

physical consequences of their decisions, people systematically mis-perceive the well-being they derive from such outcomes." [Rabin 1998, emphasis in original, 33] Our choices may be unstable over time; we choose and then regret we didn't choose differently; we make choices that are counter to our interests in the long run.[2]

The rationality-optimization assumption depends on the belief that the individual's choices are his own; that preferences are not influenced by what others do. If people change their choices following on others' actions, the demand curves dance around and become indeterminate. The pervasiveness of advertising and the large amounts of resources devoted to it gives considerable weight to the belief that companies are convinced that they can influence consumers' choices. Some companies even spend more on advertising their products than they do on producing them.

The existence of conspicuous consumption and advertising testifies that individual preferences are not completely internal to the individual.

Beliefs and emotions drive action as much as self-interest. Human beings live in a society. From birth, our individual personalities are affected and modified by the social practices, attitudes, educational experience, we are immersed in. This socialization process is internalized to some degree by us and is externally expressed in more or less conforming social and economic behavior. We learn very early to tap into the collective wisdom and experience of our society—both to inform us as to what is proper behavior and to what is acceptable or desirable consumption and investment.

Darwin perceived that the success of many species, including human beings, is based on cooperation and altruism in helping one another.

> It must not be forgotten that although a high standard of morality gives
> but a slight or no advantage to each individual man and his children over
> the other men in his tribe, yet that an increase in the number of well-
> endowed men and an advancement of morality will certainly give an
> immense advantage of one tribe over another. [Darwin 1888, 132]

Our species succeeded in surviving and becoming dominant on earth through cooperation. The field studies of our relatives, the primates, and post-Darwinian scholars have identified this characteristic as present in our evolutionary history. [Ridley 1997] Recent research on social capital is indicating that societies with high levels of trust and cooperation tend to have the most successful economies. (See Chapter 8)

Cooperation and competition are the twin forces that drove, and drive, evolution from the first beginnings of life on this earth. Cooperation is as essential for evolution as competition in natural selection. Cooperation creates more complex structures, competition among them through

---

[2] Gene Heyman, lecturer in psychology at Harvard states flatly: "Humans are inconsistent. Their preferences change with the setting." [Lambert 2000, 67]

natural selection chooses which ones will survive. [Coveney and Highfield 1995, 232]

The history of corporations in modern capitalism replicates the evolutionary chronicle of life.

Human beings can as easily be other-regarding as self-regarding. W.V. Quine states that we must recognize that altruism is a drive that people have and that we should nurture it in the formative years in order to fan the sparks of fellow-feeling into a perceptible flame. [1987, 3-5]

Altruism, in fact, is one of the innate drives in primates like the apes, the monkeys, and ourselves. One of the early classics in primate studies relates how the males of a troop of baboons which was preyed on by a leopard, organized an ambush and killed the leopard, with one of the male baboons dying in the battle. [Marais 1939, 33-8]

Psychologists emphasize that to be mentally healthy an individual should have self-love but this requires more than being driven by selfishness. A person who is self-absorbed in his own desires is often a mentally ill person. To become whole, such an individual has to learn to relate to others. This is fundamental in human biology,

> ..there is one central, universal aspect of human behavior, genetically set by our very nature, biologically governed driving us along. ...[this is] the urge to be useful. This urge drives society along, sets our behavior as individuals and in groups... [Thomas 1980, 21]

To be happy, we must live for something more than selfish ends. This is a truth discovered and repeated across the centuries by the great thinkers and philosophers. This is central in Christian theology—the individual is taught to submit to and find his center in a power or principle outside of himself. Greed is condemned. The teaching is put strongly:

> ...those who desire to be rich fall into temptation, into a snare, into many senseless and hurtful desires that plunge men into ruin and destruction. For the love of money is the root of all evils... [Timothy 6:10]

The theme that fulfillment lies in renunciation is so prevalent in religion that it must correspond to some deep part of human nature.

> We have lost the power even of imagining what the ancient idealization of poverty could have meant: the liberation from material attachments, the unbribed soul, the manlier indifference, the paying our way by what we are or do and not by what we have,...in short, the moral fighting shape....There are thousands of conjunctures in which a wealth-bound man must be a slave, whilst a man for whom poverty has no terrors becomes a freeman. [William James 1902, 333-4]

In a Buddhist or Hindu culture, a rich man may give up all his possessions and become a beggar. The Buddhist belief in reincarnation suggests that you do not have to get everything in this life—you will have more lives and more chances. It is not unheard today even in Christian cultures for such a person to become a monk, priest or minister.

Happiness does not come from great possessions, enormous income, or great success. To be happy, one must have something to do that one knows is useful to others, someone to love, and something to hope for. Work must give more than a money reward—a sense of contribution, of pride in accomplishment, of joy in using one's special talents. Marshall commented that true happiness depends on self-respect, and that self-respect comes only from endeavoring to live to promote the progress of the human race. (Eighth ed. fn.,15]

Human beings are motivated by what they think and believe and by how they have been socialized. For Smith, self-interest had a crucial moral component. We are social animals, and social virtues such as trustworthiness and a willingness to cooperate are essential to our well being. In our market economy, most of us have to make a living and hence have to pay attention to the economic motive. This is required by our economy and not necessarily by human nature. Yet the economic motive does not demand the single-minded selfish self-interest of theoretical economics. One does not have to be greedy or insensitive to others—even though some people do go that far.

Valuable results through empirical research can be secured by concentrating on the regularities of the *what* and *how* of economic behavior. It is not necessary to assume unmitigated selfishness to find reasonable consistency and regularity of behavior in particular situations. This requires focusing on material welfare results rather than on the unmeasurable individual psychological benefits. From these findings, as in other historical sciences, we can infer causes, solidly based on having studied the process in action and the results. In this way, with a focus on material welfare, economics becomes a relevant science.

Rationality[3]

The second part of the fundamental assumption is that every individual acts rationally in making choices to maximize his self-interest. The assertion that people always act rationally is regarded by many theorists as an axiom—in Aristotle's definition, "a proposition that neither can nor need be proved." *Axioms...constitute claims about this world so widely agreed as to make further argument unnecessary.*[Wiles 1983, 84; Hahn 1985, 5]

Note that it is assumed:

---

[3] Comments by Michael Ambrosi, David Colander, Peter Doeringer, and Jan S. Hogendorn helped clarify my thinking on this particular aspect of the subject.

1. that people have full knowledge of what is in their best interest,
2. that they *should act rationally* if they wish to optimize their well-being, and, finally,
3. that they really *do act rationally* to optimize their well-being.

Whether "rationality" is regarded as an assumption, an axiom, a self-evident proposition, or as an *a priori* truth, as such it is *exempt* from having to be tested empirically.

But what exactly is acting rationally? A good working definition is that it is the most effective, most logical, behavior of an agent towards attaining a desired goal or purpose. "Irrational behavior" is that which frustrates or does not contribute to attainment of an agent's goal or purpose. Note that "rational" or "irrational" behavior is not necessarily that which the agent believes to be such, but rather that which can be so characterized by an objective observer.

The idea that one can explain everything on the basis of a simple assumption about human behavior—which is not scientifically provable and which excludes most of what we do know and can observe about humanity—does not stand examination. Certainly, human beings can and very often do act rationally. But the notion that people always demonstrate fully rational, optimizing, calculating behavior is not supported by empirical observations in any social science. Nor is it supported by psychological analysis of human behavior.

The external influences upon people from institutions, history and and relationships are manifold and pervasive. Actions can be motivated by emotion, impulse, faith, authority. The inner drives and emotions that motivate people are infinitely complex. As a result, it is highly probable that most motivations that people regard as reasonable would fail the extreme economic rationality test. Very few people are calculatingly rational.

Past experience and the phenomenon of transference all play a part in motivating present behavior. Carl Jung observed that the great decisions of human life are far more motivated by instincts and other mysterious unconscious factors than by "conscious will and well-meaning reasonableness". Human motivation is, in short, a highly complex and difficult subject and psychological and psychoanalytic theories are far from having established a solid basis on which one can rely in trying to explain the *why* of human behavior.

The idea of human beings as basically rational was inherited from the Age of Reason. It took the First World War to destroy this belief for many. John R. Commons, influenced by the slaughter of millions in the senseless conflict, put his verdict strongly: *Man is not a rational being as the Eighteenth Century thought: he is a being of stupidity , passion, and ignorance, as Malthus thought.* [1961, 682] Keynes agreed that the *a priori* view that human nature is reasonable is *disastrously mistaken,* overlooking *the insane and irrational springs of wickedness in most men.* [1949, 98-99]

Most of us would admit that we make many decisions on less than a completely rational basis. Every economist who makes New Year's resolutions is confessing that the preceding year's behavior has been less than optimally rational.

Astrology, originating five thousand years ago in Babylon, has millions of believers. Newspapers carry astrology columns. Astrology is pure irrationality. Yet, if success in the market-place is the result of choice made by rational consumers, then, astrology is superior to economics. Many more people consult their horoscopes regularly for advice than consult economic advisors. President Reagan was notoriously reluctant to take advice from Martin Feldstein, his Chairman of the Council of Economic Advisers, but the scheduling of his Presidential activities was determined by an astrologer.[4]

Very few people can truly claim to be completely free from belief in some kind of irrational nonsense—the Bermuda Triangle, poltergeists, levitation, U.F.O.'s, communication with the dead, clairvoyance, mediums— or from superstition. Owners build hotels and office buildings that skip having a thirteenth floor. Newton, Napier, Tycho Brahe, all devoted much of their time to what we regard as irrational pursuits.

As Adam Smith noted, people *overvalue* their chances of winning in lotteries and *undervalue* their chance of loss. [107-8] The same is true of gambling in casinos.

Millions of addicts persist in self-destructive habits at the cost of health, money, jobs, family ties. They often know full well that they should quit in their own best interests but, against reason, are unable to do so.

We play various commitment tricks on ourselves to control our actions and to prevent ourselves from succumbing to some temptation that we know we will not be able to resist. Ulysses and the sirens is the usual example. People visiting a gambling casino will deliberately restrict the amount of money they take to ensure that they not yield to temptation and risk losing more.

I would venture that there are few people whose actions and decisions are *always* fully determined by rational calculation in making economic choices. There are times when there is pleasure from throwing caution to the wind and doing something completely foolish and irrational.[5]

Most of us buy some commodities from habit and some from impulse.

---

[4] The President's Chief of Staff, Donald Regan, complained: *...the President's schedule is the single most potent tool in the White House, because it determines what the most powerful man in the world is going to do and when he is going to do it. By humoring Mrs. Reagan we gave her this tool—or, more accurately, gave it to an unknown woman in San Francisco who believed that the zodiac controls events and human behavior and that she could read the secrets of the future in the movements of the planets.* [Regan 1988, 74]

[5] For example, when the time arrived when we no longer felt financially constrained, my wife and I derived considerable satisfaction from giving up any idea of living by a budget. That is, we gave up trying to be calculatively rational in allocating our income.

An overwhelming majority (nearly 70 percent) of American income-taxpayers make interest-free loans ($114 billion in 1998) to the U.S. Treasury each year by overpaying their taxes and then receiving refunds on filing their returns with the Internal Revenue Service. This money they could have easily kept by adjusting their withholding or changing the amounts paid in estimated tax. Then, there are the people, who owe taxes but file early, losing the interest they could have earned by waiting until April 15 to mail their returns. Both categories, over-payers and too early-filers, are clearly not rational maximizers.

The classic case of the "Winner's Curse" illustrates the often irrational basis on which buyers make their decisions. Numerous experiments have demonstrated that the winner of an auction where the commodity's value is not accurately known, more often than not, finds that in winning, he lost: the commodity he bought is worth less than his bid. Corporations can also become swept up by competitive fervor.

The future is largely *uncertain,* it is not reducible to a series of outcomes to which an economic agent can attach calculable probabilities on which he can rely.

Substituting expected utility or subjective probability into a model does not eliminate the fact that the real world uncertainty still remains. The outcome then is not likely to be optimal but, hopefully, second-best. [Fusfeld 1996, 310-11]

Beliefs play an important part throughout the economy.

> The way the economy does work can depend on the way agents believe the economy to work.
>
> ...the way the economy responds to a policy move by government can depend on the interpretation that other agents place on it, and therefore on their beliefs about the way things work. ..If participants believe that every increase in the money supply will be fully translated into the price level, irrespective of any other characteristic of the situation, then they are likely to behave in ways that will make it happen. [Hahn and Solow 1997, 150]

In short, there are many influences on people's behavior. Some part of our behavior is hereditary, some the result of our deliberate intention, some results from customs, traditions, rules, institutions—all these produced by social evolution, the result of human action. The assumption does not stand examination that people always know and have established stable, well-defined preferences ordered in a rational scale on which they act rationally in making their choices.

Science has not yet produced a model of the self that can be fully relied on as a firm base for a science of any realm of human action. But it is accepted that people possess multiple intelligences. Individuals differ from one another in the ways in which they perceive, retain and use information. Each individual constructs his/her own amalgam of intelligences.

Rational, logical intelligence is only one component. It is presumptuous and unjustified for economic theory to assert that calculative rational logic is the dominant factor controlling everyone's behavior.

The conventional theory describes how hyper-rational completely selfish people should and would behave in a non-existent world of complete certainty and knowledge in logical time, but not how real people in fact do behave in real, historical time in the world that we do inhabit. Accepting this, there are two fall-back positions used to defend the rationality hypothesis. The first is that perfect *economic men* influence other people to follow their example. Such behavior then becomes so widespread that one can assume it applies to most people and, therefore, there is little error in assuming such behavior is universal. The second position, is that calculative rationality becomes dominant through natural selection. People who are rational maximizers succeed and those who aren't, perish. This argument has been explicitly applied to analysis of firms and behavior of investors in security markets.

If either were true, it should prove itself in the well-organized security markets where the incentive is purely monetary and a large number of participants are experienced, sophisticated professionals. Alas, the informed consensus now is that the earlier efficient market theory is no longer viable in this regard.

> ...one would have to be extremely committed to rationality not to agree that in the area of financial economics, the heart of traditional economics, a number of important market phenomena are well explained by assuming that not all behavior is fully rational. This raises questions for other areas of economics where the preconditions for rationality are not so well established. [Russell 1997, 90,]

Reality appears to be consistent with cognitive science theory: The ultimate human scarce resource is mental energy (and time). It is reasonable to develop stereotypical models to call upon. When processing input from the senses, the mind tends to choose the model most readily available that seems to fit the situation. It looks for others or tries to create new ones only if the first model clearly fails. The mind employs decision heuristics and rules of thumb as another way to economize. There is a *deliberation-cost* to be paid. [Conlisk 1996] In making decisions concerning our own welfare, there is also the problem of *will*—people have imperfect strategies of self-managment. A person can know perfectly well what he *should* do but be unable to do it. [Gazzaniga 1985; McCain 1992; Schmid 1994; Thaler 1991]

Similarly, whereas standard theory assumes that economic agents make an exhaustive search of all possible decisions and then optimize in picking the best, Herbert Simon observed that people adopt the reasonable course to "satisfice" by picking the first satisfactory commodity they find or making the first satisfactory decision they arrive at. Decision-makers often consciously pursue a policy of sub-optimizing: they make a decision, try it out, and improve it on the next go-round.

The closeness of behavior in a transaction to perfect rational maximization, *ceteris paribus,* is likely to be vary directly according to:

1. the size (or importance) of the stake;
2. the degree of professionalism or specialization of the agent;
3. the degree of impersonal relationships among the parties;
4. the pressure of competition;
5. the availability of useful pertinent knowledge;
6. the simplicity of the transaction.

These are largely self-explanatory. If a large amount of money is involved in a simple transaction and the negotiators are professionals, etc. then, it is highly likely that self-interest will be rationally maximized.[6]

It is probably accurate to observe that most people are trying to pursue personal gain in their economic life, bearing in mind all the limitations of knowledge (including self-knowledge) and of rationality, and the social and ethical norms they respect. This does not necessarily mean being exclusively driven by selfishness or greed and disregarding the interests of others. The fact that actions may be less than fully rational does not mean that behavior is not reasonable, that regularity may not be present or that one cannot identify a pattern of behavior that describes what the majority of economic agents tend to do in specific situations. One could also observe that many people do reasonably well in this pursuit and many do poorly. Even though most agents in an economy are not rational maximizers as long as there are a substantial number that are operating at the margins, while the economy could not be said to operate Pareto-optimally, some of the results might come more or less close to it.

In considering the "self-interest" component of the fundamental assumption, one conclusion was that as a normative prescription, it should be interpreted not as selfishness but in Adam Smith's sense of including regard for others. In the "rationality" element of the fundamental assumption, one must conclude that it falls short of describing much of economic behavior. However, as a normative prescription, it is useful in emphasizing end-means rationality as an approach to policy.

Equilibrium

While computers, the internet, biotech, globalization, are revolutionizing every aspect of the economy, economists largely still perceive the economy through the lens of a concept that denies change. "Equilibrium" is still, as Robert Solow observed, a fundamental, canonical, hypothesis of economics.

---

[6] This approach owes much to Thomas Mayer. [1999]

"Equilibrium" is a condition in which all acting influences cancel each other out, resulting in a stable, balanced, or unchanging system. Equilibrium is a polar word—there is more than a whiff of something desirable about it.

In stark contradiction, the most important characteristic of our capitalistic market economy is *change* and this is the very essence of the system. *It is the economic system itself that generates the forces which incessantly transform it.* [Schumpeter 1912, 159]

The assumption that the economy is a stable system that returns to equilibrium values after any disturbance, frustrates the capability of theory to arrive at a correct understanding of the real dynamic economy.

The genesis of the dominance of the equilibrium concept in economic theory, was perhaps understandable in light of the cultural and intellectual environment of the past. Well into the twentieth century, it was taken for granted that the universe itself was in an unchanging state of equilibrium which either was created at some point in the past or had existed forever just as it now is. But with science since then correcting our concept of reality, most people now realize that day-by-day we move on into the new world of the future. We are not, as the concept of equilibrium implies, at, or continually returning to, a destination. We are instead on a journey into the unknown. It is now more difficult to deny Schumpeter's thesis that changes ...*are theoretically and practically, economically and culturally, much more important than the economic stability upon which analytical attention has been concentrated for so long.* [255]

Physics, itself, has abandoned the idea of a universe in equilibrium. The universe is no longer timeless; it has a beginning and drastic change over time. In biology, Darwin's theory is now supreme. Species are not immutable, new ones develop, others disappear. The ability to reproduce and evolve is the essential characteristic of life. The process is open-ended and stochastic. No individual is a perfect copy of its predecessors, mutation is constantly taking place. Change is vital. As Darwin said, *It is not the strongest species that survive, nor the most intelligent, but the ones most responsive to change.*

Social and demographic changes impact the economy. For most of human history, population numbers grew very slowly. Then, in modern times, the rate started accelerating, And, now with a total world population of over six billion, the rate of growth is slowing while in some countries population numbers are starting to drop.

Ceaseless change, day-by-day moving on into the novel, the untrod world of the future, also characterizes the modern economy.

Beginning in Great Britain in the eighteenth century, industrialization spread to the United States, to Western Europe, to Japan, to Eastern Europe, and since World War II has been penetrating the rest of the world.

In the process of industrialization, massive structural shifts take place. In 1820, 80 percent of the American labor force was in agriculture.

Today it is under two percent. There is now a growing tourism industry to show curious visitors what a farm is like!

Britain's leadership in industrialization was built on coal, iron and steel and textiles. In 1920, there were 1,250,000 miners; at the end of World War II, 700,000; by 2000, coal-mining in Britain was no longer a significant economic occupation. The story is similar in iron and steel and textiles. Everywhere in the high income countries, the fraction of the labor force in manufacturing is decreasing.

Corporations that do not keep up with change, die. From the beginning of the rubber tire industry in the United States, Akron, Ohio, was its center. Akron firms dominated the world tire industry during most of the twentieth century. But, in 1982, the last tire was made in Akron.

Walras,[7] the founder of general equilibrium theory and a pioneer in the mathematization of economics, built on an analogy between the functioning of a system of interdependent markets and the equilibrium of the system of celestial bodies in classic mechanics. Consequently, he theorized that maximizing by consumers and producers under certain conditions would result in a general equilibrium of the economy where amounts produced and demanded in every commodity and factor market would be equalized.

Economic theorists have followed in Walras' footsteps— though in recent years they have been reluctant to follow his acknowledgment of inspiration from Newtonian mechanics.

In Newtonian mechanics, equilibrium was believed to be a description of the actual universe; in economics, general equilibrium is rather a Platonic ideal that the real world might achieve if messy real world forces and human beings did not intervene. An economy is a complex *adaptive* system—evolving from learning or adapting to experience. A solar system or a galaxy evolves but does not learn. Applying the physical equilibrium model to the economy is, consequently, a category mistake.

The general equilibrium model, as Blaug says, has no empirical content and the theory *...would seem to lack any bridge by which to cross over from the world of theory to the world of facts.* [1980,191] In short, the general equilibrium theory, mathematically derived from a small number of basic axioms, is really more mathematics than a science whose truth is tested against the world of reality.

A general equilibrium model is not necessary to convince economists and laymen that competition and free markets are effective economic

---

[7] Walras was fearless in constructing his theory: Does economics as a physico-mathematical science require a measure of utility which escapes us? *Eh bien! This difficulty is not insurmountable. Let us suppose that this measure exists and we shall be able to give an exact and mathematical account...*of the influence of utility on prices, etc. [1896, 97, quoted and translated in Georgescu-Roegen 1971, 40] This may be the inspiration of the joke about the engineer, chemist and economist, lost in the woods, possessing only a can of food with no way of opening it, with the economist proposing as a solution: "Let's assume we have a can-opener".

methods to secure a better use of resources. Economic history and knowledge of the results of economic policy demonstrate this. The reason that a general equilibrium model for a capitalist economy is pointless and irrelevant is that it leaves out the very essence of the market economy—relentless never-ending change.

The classical economists were concerned with the economics of a stationary state towards which the economy was believed to be evolving, modern economists concentrate on the economics of an economy in equilibrium, ignoring the fact that the real economy is at best in transition to an equilibrium which may or may not exist and at which the economy never arrives.

Economic theory still mimics seventeenth century Newtonian mechanistic cosmos—with economic theorists, intellectual slaves to long-defunct and superseded natural scientists.

Amartya Sen has pointed out that equilibrium reasoning is logically deficient: equilibrium may not exist; if it does exist it may not be unique; if it exists and is unique, it may not be stable; if it exists and is unique and stable, it may be inefficient in the sense of not achieving Pareto-optimality. Finally, the fact that competition exists does not imply the existence, uniqueness, stability, and efficiency of a general equilibrium. [cited in Streeten 1997, 50]

The Austrian school of economics correctly believes that no equilibrium position is achieved: in terms of the "equilibrium" concept, all prices are disequilibrium prices. In the market process, information is discovered, adjustments made, and resources are shifted to try to keep up with changing conditions. Unless there is an omniscient auctioneer who controls the market and establishes the point of equilibrium, transactions must take place at "non-equilibrium prices". [Kirzner 1997; Rosen 1997] The market process results in *outcomes*, not in equilibria.

While an equilibrium is a position-of-rest or the final coherent state of balance, the economy is never static and both it and the society in which it exists are constantly moving on. An economy is not a rationally organized, objective system but rather a dynamic process that is constantly in motion and constantly changing with millions of participants acting on knowledge, most of which is becoming out of date.

The essence of an equilibrium model is stability: any disturbances that move the economy or an industry away from equilibrium must have negative feedbacks or must be over-matched by equilibrating forces or causes that restore the equilibrium. With negative feedbacks, small effects die away (as in diminishing returns and falling marginal utility) so equilibrium is reestablished.

In reality, change usually drives the economy farther away. Veblen and Myrdal, outside of the accepted economics canon, noted that some economic processes have positive feedback with effects reinforcing each other. Thus this results in a cumulative impact on an economy driving it farther and farther away from any initial assumed equilibrium.

The concept of equilibrium does not recognize the economic consequences of growing knowledge and increasing returns. The two are related to one another since a large part of the increase in knowledge comes from learning by doing or is inspired by the need to overcome problems that arise in the course of production. This is clearly manifest in industries, such as the high tech sector, with increasing returns. Here, it is obvious that the movement is away from any notional equilibrium.

It may cost immense sums to produce a new product. The new 777 Boeing took eight years of design and research and cost $8 billion to produce a prototype. After the product is developed, average cost falls rapidly. [Arthur 1993] The producer that aggressively exploits its increasing returns can gain a great advantage over its competitors. In the economy, just as in nature, speed in making change is essential to survival.

Keynes commented that it was Hume who began the economist's practice of stressing the importance of the equilibrium position rather than the ever-shifting transition to it. However, Keynes pointed out Hume did not overlook the fact that it is in this transition that we actually live. [1936, fn, 343] But, Keynes did not fully grasp that the basic motor of a market economy is evolutionary change. That is, the economy is *not* in transition to a fixed, definitive equilibrium position anymore than biological evolution is transition towards some ideal creature.

In a more religious period in history, people believed this life was a time of trials and tribulation in preparation for the next world where existence would be heavenly perfect. The same idea of perfection as a goal was accepted by many believers in the theory of evolution: that evolution governs the path that leads ever upward, that survivors must be fittest in some transcendental sense. And, in economics, the same state of mind leads market-idealists to believe that the economy is already in the optimum state of equilibrium, or is groping for such a state, or would achieve equilibrium if not for wicked or ignorant human interference.

Evolution and change in the economy are processes driven from behind rather than pulled ever closer towards a fixed goal. At any moment in time, one may be able to say, all things being equal and with no unforeseen changes, such-and-such will be the *outcome*. It is misleading to call this projected outcome, "equilibrium". This implies that if this outcome does come about, the forces involved will maintain it, or if it moves away, there are forces to restore it. And, the implication is that attaining equilibrium is desirable.

Unfortunately, neither in evolution as Darwin observed, nor in the economy is it guaranteed that the optimum.will result. It is perfectly possible that some species, fittest by all measures, may have been destroyed simply because they happened to be in the wrong place at the wrong time. The species now occupying the former niche of the extinct species may simply have been more lucky at the decisive time.

If economics must have a natural science metaphor it should rather come from biology than seventeenth century physics. In the course of his life, Marshall became increasingly convinced that biology was more closely related to economics than Newtonian Mechanics was. He observed that human societies like biological nature are constantly evolving. Since neither the precise direction nor speed of the change can be precisely predicted, the "laws" of economics are no more than statements of trends or tendencies. [See Kamarck 1983, 21-2; Kaldor 1985, 58]

The biological metaphor, while helpful, is not perfect for the economy. The agents in the economy are conscious players on their own account, not merely acted on by the environment. The economy is a complex, constantly changing, *adaptive* system in which each agent—individual, firm, industry, nation—is constantly acting and reacting to what the other agents are doing. As an opportunity is grasped and exploited by one agent this may open up opportunities for others as competitors, as partners, as parasites, or as predators. In the final analysis, the equilibrium optic obscures the real economy.

Heisenberg's uncertainty principle describes a fundamental property of the world. As Hawking points out, this means that we cannot have a scientific theory or model of the world that is completely deterministic. [1988] Richard Feynman, one of the most brilliant physicists of our generation, put it this way,

> ...physics has given up on the problem of trying to predict exactly what will happen in a definite circumstance. Yes! Physics *has* given up. *We do not know how to predict what would happen in a given circumstance*, and we believe now that it is impossible, that the only thing that can be predicted is the probability of different events. (Italics in original) [1995,135)]

There is much theoretical work going on which does not fit into the accepted canon—the work at the Santa Fe Institute on complexity, non-linear dynamics, evolutionary game theory, inductive rationality. Almost all of the models developed are multiple equilibria, creating the problem of how equilibrium selection will be decided—through institutions or public policy.[8] Note that even in this pioneering work, instead of reporting that the models result in multiple *outcomes* (avoiding the implication that these are desirable or likely to persist) for which some criteria for choice will have to be developed, the equilibrium mind-set still rules.

Growth

Economic theory has had problems in accounting for economic growth. A realistic appreciation of the process is crippled by the equilibrium mind-set. Economics cannot neglect history. The present is influenced by the

---

[8] David Colander alerted me to this.

past. There were divergent roads and the present was not inevitable. There were many possible worlds, to understand the one we have, we have to know how it evolved.

The evolution of formal economic thought on growth has gone roughly as follows. In the early standard model, it was simply an increase in the aggregate quantities of labor, capital, and in the use of land, which resulted in increased total output (recognizing, however, the existence of diminishing returns to inputs). This model was improved by recognizing that there was more to the story: there was growth in productivity (beyond that from specialization) from growth in capital per worker and spillover from exogenous innovation in the rest of the economy. In recent years, theorists have taken the innovation process into the model, making it endogenous, through assuming productivity growth from investment in human capital and in research and development. [Taylor 2000, 90-1] All this undoubtedly helps to explain the growth that occurs but it leaves out what drives the process in competitive free market economies.

Adam Smith observed that with growth of the market it became possible to specialize and this led to increases in productivity. With the lowering of costs, markets could be further extended, and more specialization became possible. With specialization, the division of complex tasks into simpler ones leads to the development of machinery, further cost reductions and further growth in the size of the market. In this process, specialized firms become possible and come into existence. With the growth of specialized labor and the stimulus that comes from interchange of knowledge and experience, there arises a concentration of activities in a particular locality and even a particular country. This is the phenomenon illustrated today by Silicon Valley.

The advantage of a capitalist competitive market system is that in its essence it is driven to change, while a central planning system, like a secure monopoly, tends to become static. Capitalism is, as Schumpeter observed, *...by nature a form or method of economic change and not only never is but never can be stationary.* [1942, 42] It is this characteristic of capitalism that the Soviet and Eastern European socialist countries lacked which resulted in their lagging behind in spite of the tremendous sacrifices they imposed on their peoples.

Adam Smith, in what was almost an offhand comment, which has largely been overlooked, showed that he perceived that it was competition that is the *deus ex machina* of growth in a competitive market economy.

> The increase of demand,...though in the beginning it may sometimes raise the price of goods, never fails to lower it in the long run. It encourages production, and thereby increases the competition of the producers, who, in order to undersell one another, have recourse to new divisions of labour and new improvements of art, which might never otherwise have been thought of. [1937, 706]

Schumpeter came to the same conclusion: the force that powers the system's incessant transformation in a competitive market, is that profits come from change.[9] [1912, 128-156]

In the modern corporate economy in competitive industries, intensive effort is devoted to organizing and engineering change. Tens of thousands work in the research laboratories. There is now even a special source of capital—venture capital (over $50 billion disbursed in the United States in 2000)—that specializes in finding and financing new innovative entrepreneurs.

The result for the economy is exactly what the CEO of Johnson & Johnson describes as his company's top priority:

Continuous, non-stop, endless, relentless innovation... [Larsen 2000, 3]

---

[9] "Because the analysis is macroeconomic, it cannot easily take account of the market forces and fierce competition among firms for priority in new products and processes. Yet these, arguably, are among the key determinants of the magnitude of the resources the economy devotes to innovation and are at the heart of the explanation of the historically unmatched production and growth performance of free-enterprise economies."[Baumol 2000, 13]

3   The Corporation

With every influx of light comes new danger...There is a crack in everything God has made. It would seem there is always...this vindictive circumstance stealing in unawares ...this back-stroke, this kick of the gun,....—Ralph Waldo Emerson.

With the dismantling of the command-economies of the Soviet Union and eastern Europe, the general belief is that market forces now control economies throughout the globe. This, however, overlooks the fact that in the high income countries most economic decisions in production and distribution are taken within organizations. Multinationals like Daimler Chrysler, Exxon Mobil, General Motors, Royal Dutch Shell, Toyota, Unilever, are larger than many national economies. Organizations determine people's status and income, produce most commodities and services, and create almost all wealth. Most workers work within and for organizations. Even in farming, the sector of the classical individual economic independence, American poultry farmers, hog farmers, vegetable growers, are usually bound by contracts to secure their inputs from and dispose of their outputs to corporations. This system of embracing control is now being extended to corn and soybean farmers. In the United States, even most of the saving and investment takes place within corporations. That is, all this economic activity is within *command-economies*.

(This should not be taken to mean that organizations are run only by commands. Anyone who has been in charge of an organization, even in the military, knows that it is essential to motivate your subordinates to willingly cooperate in trying to achieve the purposes of the organization. If your subordinates act only according to command, you wind up with a collection of *Good Soldier Schweiks*. That is, people who obey the letter of a command but wittingly or unwittingly sabotage the intent.)

People in the Middle Ages in Western Europe and Japan lived in a *feudal* system, today people in the high-income countries live in a *corporate* system.

While the market may coordinate economic activity among firms, the major part of economic activity is coordinated through firms, nonprofits, or government. Herbert Simon has made this important point vividly: Suppose a Martian were to survey the earth with a telescope that revealed social structures, with the boundaries of firms shown in green and market transactions in red, he would report the earth's economy as mainly consisting of large green areas with a web of red lines running between them. [1991,27]

In the transition in Eastern Europe and the former Soviet Union, governments had no choice but to wrestle with fundamental organizational questions; how to: structure the newly privatized firms, provide strong management, provide access to capital, and adequately monitor the firm performance.

The internal structure of firms and the relationship of managers (and of corporate control) to their firms are crucial, governing elements in the functioning of modern economies.

Corporate decisions substitute internal bureaucratic processes for markets. American corporations usually pay out less than half of their earnings in dividends. They, thus, take the power to make investment decisions from the market—from their shareholders who might choose to make different allocations of their earnings. And, even the external markets in which corporations operate are not necessarily independent since *corporations may shape the markets within which they operate.* (Minolta, Fuji, Canon, Nikon and Kodak, the principal global producers of cameras and film, rather than accepting that they had to live in the market such as it was, worked together for five years,1991-6, in creating a new market through inventing a new camera and film technology. Corporations and markets evolve together in the growth of the economy.

Moreover, relations among firms are often governed by long-term contracts where power, custom, habit, or other nonmarket influences matter. In recent years, many American corporations have swung to the Japanese practice of establishing close long-term relationships with a few suppliers rather than using the market to procure their needs.

The way the corporate-economy works is at least as important as the way the market works.

> Even if the Arrow-Debreu model accurately depicted how market economies behave—that is, the relations between and among households and firms—it would provide insight into only a fraction of all economic activity. [Stiglitz 1991, 15]

The conclusion is vital for economics: the corporation is central in the economy of modern high-income nations. How efficiently the resources— people and capital—of the corporation are administered is key to the effectiveness of the economy.

There are critical questions that economics has to answer:

Does the corporation represent something new or does it fit comfortably into the neoclassical paradigm?

Why has the corporation superseded the market?

Neoclassical theory tries to explain how price guides the allocation of resources. Does this fully explain the allocation of resources by corporate managements?

Does the corporation use its resources optimally?

And, finally, if the corporation is more efficient than the market why hasn't a single corporation taken over the whole economy?

The Corporation—Theory and Reality

Historically, the concept of the corporation was well-established in English law as early as the fourteenth century. A corporate charter was granted by the throne for public purposes. Boroughs, guilds, ecclesiastical bodies were the principal recipients of corporate powers. Over the next two centuries, the legal rights of corporations were made clear: to hold property, to sue and be sued, and to have a life beyond the lives of its members. In the sixteenth and seventeenth century, the throne found it useful to create business corporations, mobilizing private funds through the joint stock device for public ends: the development of trade, colonization, privateering, etc. It was clearly evident that in their origin, corporations like the Bank of England, the East India Company, the Massachusetts Bay Colony, the railroads, had quasi-governmental powers and obligations. Ultimately, both in Britain and the United States, the government passed general incorporation acts which made the corporate form accessible to any competent business. [Chayes 1959, 32-37]

Modern corporations receive the privilege of corporate powers from the state and have a corresponding obligation to the general welfare.[1] Shareholders provide the finance necessary to outfit the corporation with its material assets. True, but modern corporations are dependent on the state for their creation and privileges and for the legal and physical infrastructure that make it possible for them to function. They are in some ill-defined sense autonomous social enterprises, that is, more than just economic organizations. The human capital embodied in the company-related skill and experience of its employees is increasingly more important in the modern high-tech corporation than its physical capital.

The supremacy of the modern corporation has posed challenges to economic theory that never existed before or were so insignificant they could be disregarded. The valiant attempts of conventional economics to stretch the old concepts over the new reality make much of accepted economic theory irrelevant.[2] Conventional theory tries to finesse the existence of the corporation in various ways:

- All firms can be regarded essentially as if they were owner-operated entities acting like individual entrepreneurs.
- Nothing has changed, relationships within the corporation are the same as in the market.

---

[1] According to the U. S. Supreme Court, *...the corporation is a creature of the State. It is presumed to be incorporated for the benefit of the public.* Hale v. Henkel, 201 U. S. 43, 74 (1906) quoted in Hessen 1980, 1]

[2] This subjects the discipline to cruel remarks such as those in the classic novel, *A Suitable Boy*, by Vikram Seth (who was himself trained as an economist): A son, with a degree in economics, is asked by his father to take over the management of the wealthy family's investments, *But, Baba*—protested Dipankaar, blinking in distress, *economics is the worst possible qualification for running anything. It's the most useless, impractical subject in the world.* [454]

- The corporation is only a bundle of assets belonging to shareholders.
- The corporation is nothing but a "black-box", it uses resources to produce goods, with the transformation controlled by known technology and prices.
- The corporation represents nothing more than a production function determined by technology and driven by profit.

Each of these approaches fail to grasp the full significance of the corporation. The theory is felt to be so deficient that business schools, Harvard for example, do not include basic microeconomics in their curriculum. Consulting firms *...reject economics as being fundamental to understanding business and advising clients.* [Lazear 2000, 116, 117]

To regard the corporation as being equivalent to an individual entrepreneur is to miss the most important changes that the corporation brought into the economy. The corporation is much more than a bundle of assets belonging to shareholders. The corporation is a legal fiction allowing ownership to be separated from management. Private individuals are empowered by the state to create and own an institution that limits the liability of the owners. The modern corporation, in addition to being endowed with the same rights as natural persons "to own and owe and to sue and be sued", has three important extraordinary powers.

1. The right to life without limit of time.
2. The right to own other corporations or be owned by them. (A corporation can create offspring without limit, generate siblings as needed, even experience death and reincarnation.)
3. The ability easily to acquire different nationalities for its offspring and siblings. [Vernon 1971, 4, 5, 206]

Enterprises in the industrial revolution required large amounts of capital and the rapidity of change in this new economy brought with it huge risks. The corporation made possible the mobilization of capital from many individuals and its limited liability removed the danger that a failure would wipe out a person's assets beyond those invested in the company. One significant consequence of this is

> ...the corporation...removed the most important limitation on the growth and ultimate size of the business firm when it destroyed the connection between the extent and nature of a firm's operations and the personal financial position of the owners. So long as owners were personally liable for the actions of their agents as well as for the finance of their firms, there was in general a sharp limit to the risk attendant upon extensive financial commitments, in particular in illiquid industrial assets, that owners would be willing to assume, as well as a close limit on the delegation of authority in management that could safely be permitted. [Penrose 1980, 6]

The state deals directly with its legal creation distinctly from the corporate owners: taxing, laying down the ground rules, and regulating it. The law treats the corporation as an artificial person and the corporation is truly an organism separate from its legal owners. Ownership, control, and management are separate functions—they can reside in the same person or group of persons. In the modern corporation they are usually separated.

The very size of the modern corporation creates problems, *per se.* It was possible to accept that a small owner-managed firm within a swarm of similar competitors did not need to be monitored for its effects on the community. Marquand's novel, *Sincerely Willis Wade,* makes vivid the tragedy—repeated hundreds of times in old industrial regions—when a mill passes from the control of a local owner-family, rooted in the town, to a distant corporate bureaucracy. Today, a corporate giant employing tens or hundreds of thousands of people may dominate the life of communities, regions and, at times, a nation. Even the United States government has had on occasion to bow to the power of a corporation: In World War II, Ford's Willow Run rolled out thousands of warplanes for the Allies. To ensure the Ford Corporation's commitment to the war effort, the U. S. government was forced to release Henry Ford's grandson from military service.

Macaulay reminds us of the traditional "English doctrine that all power is a trust for the public good." [1833, 296] The brute fact is that the impact on society of the concentration of large amounts of capital and a large number of people in a single organization makes it necessary to take into account more interests than just those of the stockholders and management. Some CEOs are conscious that power brings with it some degree of responsibility to the community and other stakeholders. Irvine O. Hockaday Jr., CEO of Hallmark, has expressed this point, strongly:

> ...the more a person or an institution aggregates power—in the form of human resources and financial assets—the higher the level of responsibility to use those assets wisely, with sensitivity and with a view beyond the bottom line. Corporations, with their vast human and financial resources, have greater potential—and therefore greater obligations—than most segments of society. [March 30, 1995, at Columbia University]

Ensuring that corporate management acts in the interest of the owners arose as a major problem with the modern corporation. In conventional theory, the significance of the separation between owners and management is assumed away by agency theory: corporate management is an agent, employed by the owners through the board of directors which the shareholders elect. As an agent, the management is assumed to act only in the best interests of the principals. Consequently, the corporation can be regarded as being equivalent to an owner-run firm.

Reality and practice are quite different. One striking example of how much conventional theory differs from reality is in the relationship of mutual fund management to investors in the fund. As a mere agent it would be inconceivable that it would be able to sell to third parties the right to manage, without the express consent of the savers who have money in the fund. In fact, the managements of mutual funds are set up as separate companies and are able to sell the right to manage the money the investors have entrusted to them. While investors are not serfs, their inertia makes it possible for the managers to sell them at a price usually around 2 to 5 percent of the total assets held in the fund. [Kuntz 1985]

The separation of corporate management from ownership brings a new factor into the economic process. The management acquires enormous power compared to the legal owners: it controls information; it has discretionary power; it normally recruits and selects its own replacements. The shareholder often has only a hazy grasp of where his "property" is and what it does. With this new player in the game, it is inevitable that the possibility arise of his having interests and motives that differ substantially or are even adverse to those of the legal owners. (See next chapter for discussion of this problem.)

The second conventional economics approach is to refuse to accept the reality of the existence of the fact that the corporation is an institution, a hierarchy, a command-organization. The theory, dissolving the firm into market-type contractual relations, argues:

> The firm has no power of fiat, no authority, no disciplinary action any different in the slightest degree from ordinary market contracting between any two people.
>
> The relationship of each team member to the *owner* of the firm...is simply a 'quid pro quo' contract. Each makes a purchase and sale. The employee 'orders' the...[employer] to pay him money in the same sense that the employer directs the...[employee] to perform certain acts. [Emphasis in original][Alchian and Demsetz 1972, 783]

These remarks reveal a disconnect from reality. It is ludicrous to believe that a middle manager, say, has the same kind of relationship to her CEO as she has to a salesman when buying an auto. The CEO determines what she is paid and, hence, her standard of living; he can structure her work so that she may move up the ladder or be shunted into a dead-end. The CEO can dismiss her (or she may quit) and lose her specific organizational capital. She incurs the cost of change, the possibility of months of unemployment, and the real danger that she may never get paid as much again. Her life-style, livelihood, the neighborhood in which she lives, her friendships, may all have been built around her job, occupation and job-location. The relationship to someone who holds that power of dismissal over her is not the same as her relationship to a car salesman. If the middle manager has a dispute over her contract to buy a car, there is a body of law she can appeal to and have an outside court adjudicate. In a disagreement, her boss decides—by fiat and she may have ensured that her days in the corporation are numbered.

As Coase perceived, the essence of a firm is that activities are co-ordinated, not by the market and by price, but by commands, discussion, bargaining within a bureaucratic structure. Internal forces, only partly governed by contract, replace the market mechanism. [Coase 1937]

Finally, the approach which has the firm defined by the production-function[3] is also deficient. This makes technology the major determinant of the size and character of the firm. Technology may help determine whether a productive process has to be under a unitary control or can be coordinated through the market. But any experience with corporate life teaches that there is much more in play than technology alone.

The median corporation of the top 187 in the Fortune 500 list produced 22 different kinds of products in 1965. [Vernon 1971, 285] General Electric today produces locomotives and dishwashers, owns airplanes leased to airlines, insures municipal bond issues, sells health insurance for pets in Britain, and even cleans restrooms in Florida airports! This is only a tiny fraction of the spectrum of its activities. What possible technology determinant dictates that all these should be under GE's roof?

There is a even greater weakness in the neoclassical approach. A decision has to be made, *what* product should the firm produce? Successful products are subject to a life-cycle: initiation, exponential growth, slowdown, and decline. [Vernon 1971, 70] Not all are successful. Even if the firm has developed an outstanding product, there is a problem of timing. If the firm beats its competitors in marketing a desirable product, it can count on scale economies and being ahead on the learning and experience curve to sell its product—if necessary, at a decreasing price since its costs will be declining as it moves down the curve.

The Boston Consulting Group, which advises corporations across the globe, apparently feels that "first to market" is the only sensible strategy to follow: a firm should never enter a market where a competent rival is established. A well-managed company which captures a larger market share than other firms will be able to push out the other firms because of its superior location on the falling cost curve. [Earl 1984, 136-140]

Social Preconditions

On my missions for the World Bank to many developing countries, I often found that one of the major problems was the absence of trust. Business owners were afraid to grow beyond the span of family control. They were afraid to entrust responsibility to outsiders.

Another, almost reverse problem, was that successful businesses were dragged down by the extended family and other social obligations of the owner. In societies based on extended families, an individual

---

[3] That is Q=f(L,K,t,etc) where Q is output; L, Labor; K, capital; t, technology; and etc, other inputs.

has deep ties with and feels an obligation to a large number of people. For survival value in a difficult environment, it would be hard to conceive of a better arrangement. But for economic development the extended family system has drawbacks.

A "big man" in the family is expected to be generous in helping with school fees, doctors' bills, "bride-price" or dowries. He is expected to pay for weddings and funerals, extend hospitality to all relatives and hire them. Family crises tend to prevent accumulation of capital or to drain away savings. A successful civil servant or company employee may be unable to withstand the pressure to contribute to the family and still live in the style expected by his milieu. Hence, the temptation to accept bribes or to "borrow" from public or company funds. As the expatriate bank manager in Africa remarked to me—revealing his own cultural biases as well illuminating African ones—*It is very difficult for the African to learn to put his duty to his employer above his duty to his family.*

Even in the United States, family expectations can be a problem. When the first John D. Rockefeller was asked the secret of business success, he replied, *Never let your wife know how much money you are making.* His wife was still doing her own laundry when he was already a millionaire many times over. [Kamarck 1971, 64-6]

Mark Granovetter has argued that the success of the overseas Chinese in Southeast Asia stems from the fact that their particular social structure and position makes it possible for them to overcome the conflicting problems of trust and family demands. Their close-knit community has a high level of trust. Capital is pooled, credit given, and authority delegated without fear. The social structure makes malfeasance difficult to conceal and largely inconceivable for anyone to engage in. On the other hand, the overseas Chinese are a small minority and within it the kinship groups are so sharply defined that the number of relatives with claims on a successful business is small. [Granovetter 1990, 102-3]

The Contribution from Organization

In recent years, the "New Institutional Economics" (NIE), an interdisciplinary combination of economics, organization theory and the law, has created a more realistic theory of the corporation than that in neoclassical economics.[4] NIE presents many valuable insights and clearly helps towards the understanding of the corporation. [Miller 1993] As the New Institutional Economics correctly maintains, firms and markets are alternative ways of managing the same transactions.

---

[4] See Holmström and Roberts, "The Boundaries of the Firm Revisited" (1998), Bolton and Scharfstein, "Corporate Finance, the Theory of the Firm, and Organizations" [1998], and Gibbons, "Incentives in Organizations" [1998] for a more extended review of the current state of theory on the Firm.

> Whether a firm makes or buys—that is, produces for its needs or procures a
> good or service from an outside supplier—turns largely on the transaction
> costs of managing the transaction in the firm, as compared with mediating
> the transaction through the market. Which transactions go where depends on
> the attributes of transaction, on the one hand, and the costs and competence
> of alternative modes of governance, on the other. [Williamson 1996, 25)

Focusing on property rights also helps. Doing transactions outside
the firm may cause problems if it is difficult or impossible to write contracts
that will cover future contingencies that cannot be fully foreseen or fully described. In such cases, where one of the parties has had to commit resources
into specific assets, it would be vulnerable if the other party found it oppor-
tune to take advantage of changed circumstances. Such transactions then are
more suited to be taken into the firm.

> The theory takes ownership of non-human assets as the defining characteris-
> tic of firms: a firm is exactly a set of assets under common ownership. ...
> control over assets gives the owner bargaining power when unforeseen or
> uncovered contingencies force parties to negotiate how their relationship
> should be continued. [Holmström & Roberts 1998, 77]

While both the transactions and the property-rights approaches have
contributed towards a much more realistic theory of the firm than standard
theory, there is still more to the story. There are the critical factors of organizational innovation and investment in managerial systems and, there is almost always a personal factor involved.

The corporation is a bureaucracy and in every bureaucracy, corporate
or public, people, up and down the line, who have some power from being in
charge of an organization have some scope for pursuing a personal agenda.
They may opt for enhancing their power by increasing the size of their organization, even at the expense of the interests of the corporation, or on the
contrary choose to have an easier life by neglecting to take advantage of new
opportunities for the corporation.

On the plus side, the contribution made by organization and management is more than merely the lowering of transaction costs. An effective organization makes a productive contribution *per se*. This finding is often hard
to accept by people who have been trained to think as reductionists, i.e. that
you can understand the whole completely if you understand its parts and the
nature of their sum. Or, in economic terms that an economy is understood by
understanding the economic actions of individuals.

Perhaps the easiest way to persuade skeptics of the added contribution made through organization itself is through concrete examples. We are
made of the very same atoms that exist in inanimate matter. What is the difference between living and non-living matter? *Organization*—not a difference in the substance of matter itself—appears to be the only significant
difference between living and non-living entities. When in the course of
evolution, multi-celled organisms appeared, again it is organization that dif-

ferentiates them from their unicelled ancestors.

The principle that is being applied here is the natural scientist's analytical approach of hierarchical levels. Reality comes in levels. At each higher level, there is brought together or "chunked" in a new unit a number of things that at the lower, more detailed level are seen as separate. For each new higher hierarchical level we need additional explanatory theories, which neither deny nor contradict the explanations appropriate for lower levels. To understand the properties of water we need to know something more than the properties of hydrogen and oxygen. *Every chemical compound has some properties that do not exist in its constituents.* The important Boyle's Law on the behavior of gases relates pressure, volume, and temperature of a gas. It is meaningless at the level of a molecule. Similarly, an integrated irrigation system has to be analyzed as a unit; analysis at the level of the individual farmer is useful but inadequate.

The contribution that can come from organization *per se* is clearly seen in the military: A small well-trained unit can easily whip a large, ill-disciplined mass. The successful European imperialistic conquests of the nineteenth century owe as much to the superior disciplined tactics of the handful of soldiers employed as to their superior weapons.

The modern corporation, too, is more efficient than a market of autonomous individuals. An effective firm is more than the sum of its individual workers. People work together applying their specialized experience on common tasks. This cooperation results in preserving and creating new knowledge, giving the firm an advantage over the market. Gain also comes from the division and specialization of intellectual labor. Groups of people and individuals are enabled to work together in a coordinated cooperative team. Imagine trying to design and build a Boeing 777 by passing every single bit of work through a market. Not only would the transaction costs be enormous, the task would be impossible.

Naturalists report that an ant, termite, or bee colony behaves with a higher level of intelligence than an ant, termite or bee by itself possesses. There appears to be something of the same possed by human beings.

The gain from organization is similar to the benefits of a good seminar—it provides stimulation and creativity through exchange of knowledge. Creativity arises when people work well together. The result is a capability beyond that of any individual— just as a network of PCs may outperform a mainframe. In government and in the World Bank I was often impressed by the way a group of knowledgeable people working on a common problem would find a clearly optimal solution that could not have been conceived without the joint endeavor.

> A creative problem-solving team on the verge of an answer is a stimulating thing to behold and be part of. ...if the group is working right, not in a selfish or egocentric way... Like ants...or, ...an ensemble of actors, the group bands together to find the one most logical and productive answer. At moments like this—moments of break-through—every member of

the group feels a pride in the emerging solution and an exhilaration that can be described only as being off the ground. The group, ...has stood on a frontier, however modest, of human skill or execution, and has raised, so to speak, the flage at Iwo Jima. [Sissman 1997]

Most people like to feel part of a team or organization and acquire a loyalty to it that seems *wholly disproportionate to the material rewards they receive from the organization.* [Schwartz 1998, 43]

Except in grossly inefficient companies, the total contribution that emerges from corporate cooperation is greater than the sum of the parts. There results in truth what that overworked word *synergy* describes.

Large corporations rarely die. In recent years, when they go out of existence it is usually because they have been absorbed into even larger giant entities. "...by 1975, only 3 of the 99 industrials on the Berle and Means list of 200 largest companies in 1919-30 had been liquidated; only 1 had failed to grow; 28 had exited by merger; and of the 57 survivors, 55 were still among the 200 largest, while the other 12 were still on the Fortune 500 list." [Herman 1981, 68-69][5]

To refuse to recognize the contribution that *organizations* make to the *organizational economy* in which we live is, in the words of the old cliché, to refuse to recognize the role of the Prince of Denmark in *Hamlet.*

Key Role of Management

Economics now recognizes that improvements in production technology are vital for economic growth. At least as equally important is progress in the ways of organizing and managing large-scale enterprises and of coping with complex and changing material technologies. The revolutionary technological changes of the last two and a half centuries are intertwined with the evolution of the business firm and the invention of the business corporation.

Managers are decisive in firm and economy outcomes. How managers are recruited, trained, selected, monitored, and disciplined is highly important to how productive the economy is. The strategic and organizational decisions made by managements shape or determine the fate of the firm as well as how the national economy is molded and how it performs.

At the beginnings of industrialization, individual entrepreneurs, working directly in the productive process, through their own hands-on experience and trial-and-error were driven to make improvements in the process and product.

[5] A study of survival among the world's largest 100 industrial corporations, found that 23 percent of 1995's U.S. giants, 66 percent of Germany's and 75 percent of Britain's had also been in the list of the 1912 top 100 world firms. The 1995 American list is dominated by new giants in new industries such as Coca-Cola, Boeing, Hewlett-Packard, Cisco System. [Hannah 1998, 64]

The new technologies of production of the nineteenth century were highly capital-intensive. The railroads and the telegraph in the first half of the Nineteenth Century expanded the size of the potential market. This called forth a wave of innovation in industry (the Second Industrial Revolution) to respond to the new market opportunities. Large-scale operations were needed to take full advantage of the innovations that were creating new industries and transforming old ones. The key industries—iron and steel, copper, aluminum, chemicals, oil, tobacco, etc—had large economies of scale and scope. To fully exploit these it was imperative to mobilize and manage the large amounts of capital for the new capital-intensive manufacturing and for the new systems for marketing and distribution of the products that poured forth. It was the organization using knowledge, skill, experience, and teamwork that turned the potentials into actuality. [Chandler 1992]

Chandler has demonstrated that the economic growth in Britain, the United States, and Germany was dependent on how the managers built their business organizations and mobilized the investment to exploit new technological innovations and the economies of scale and scope that these made possible. [1977, 1990; Teece 1993]

At the approach of the twentieth century, the advent of the science-based industries of chemistry and electricity posed new challenges. To cope successfully, additional organizational and management innovations were required. The corporations that forged ahead in creating the new forms of management, in securing the large amounts of capital required, and in making the necessary investments in production and distribution became the leading corporations in the United States, Britain and Germany from the 1880s to the 1940s.

In Germany and Britain, the organizational capabilities determined the dynamics of the economies. The German economy forged ahead of the British. The British opted to continue the older forms of family-dominated and personally- or family-managed business enterprise while the Germans, like the Americans, developed professional managers. The new German technical universities trained men for industry. There was no "cult of the amateur" in Germany.

In the United States, the corporations came under the control of what Chandler calls *competitive managerial capitalism* by 1914. To meet the need for trained professional managers, American universities created business training schools with the help of endowments by wealthy businessmen. It was the management-controlled firms with their organizational capabilities that led and were responsible for economic growth in the United States.

As the scale of operations grew larger with the growth in the size of market and the capital requirements of the new technology, successful firms institutionalized the process of innovation.

General Electric is one of the world's most successful corporations. It attained the world record corporate market capitalization of $560 billion in September 2000. John F. Welch, Jr., the CEO, described how GE's preeminence was achieved.

Here's how we went about it.

Our dream, and our plan, well over a decade ago, was simple. We set out to shape a global enterprise that preserved the classic big-company advantages—while eliminating the classic big-company drawbacks. What we wanted to build was a hybrid, an enterprise with the reach and resources of a big company—the body of a big company—but the thirst to learn, the compulsion to share and the bias for action—the soul—of a small company. The foundation for our future was to be involved in only those businesses that were, or could become, either number one or number two in their global markets. The rest were to be fixed, sold or closed.

We cleared out stifling bureaucracy, along with the strategic planning apparatus, corporate staff empires, rituals, endless studies and briefings, all the classic machinery that makes big-company operations smooth and predictable—but often glacially slow.

As the big-company body was developing, we turned from changing its hardware to the infinitely more difficult task of changing its software—toward creating, in GE, the spirit and soul of a small company. Most successful small companies possess three defining cultural traits: self-confidence, simplicity and speed. We wanted them. We went after them. [1996, 1-5]

Note from this description: a) the importance of the management factor and b) the importance of how an organization is structured and motivated—neither of which is taken account of in conventional economic theory.

Optimization?

While the modern corporate-economy in the high income countries has proved itself superior to a pure market economy, it does not follow that it necessarily operates at optimum efficiency or that it makes an optimal contribution to society.

The usual assumption in economics, of course, is that market pressures force private business organizations to operate at optimal efficiency. It is assumed that the managers are motivated and motivate the rest of the organization so that the corporation is striving, or is forced, to maximize profits. If profits *are* maximized, then, costs must be minimized for any given output and the organization is operating at maximum efficiency.

Corporations do not automatically accept the guidance of the market in making their decisions. Someone has to decide whether a product should be developed or modified, the timing of any action, and the market in which it is to be introduced, etc. The price of a product, while influenced by market considerations, is set through an administrative process. It is affected by corporate policy on market-share, inventory, competitive positioning, long-term strategy and short-term tactics—and by the personal ability and standing of the corporate officers involved. Very few corporations pay out all their profits to shareholders, so they have to allocate investment of retained earnings. Decisions have to be *made* and are determinant.

There is a very important difference between economic decisions flowing out of the impersonal market and the decisions taken in an organization. People in an organization, especially those with some responsibility, have some leeway and can exercise some discretion. The economic forces of the market may penetrate and pervade the organization but people in the corporation still have to make the decisions. This means that there is a problem of securing the necessary information and filtering it through human beings. And, probably even more important, there is the opportunity for a whole spectrum of human emotions and motives to come into play. It is this enlarged role for a range of interrelationships which is one of the elements that makes a corporate economy different from the classical conventional economy driven by the market.

Adam Smith over two centuries ago detected a fundamental inefficiency in joint stock companies.

> The directors of such companies, however, being the managers rather of other people's money than of their own, it cannot well be expected that they should watch over it with the same anxious vigilance with which the partners in a private copartnery frequently watch over their own. Like the stewards of a rich man, they are apt to consider attention to small matters as not for their master's honour, and very easily give themselves a dispensation from having it. Negligence and profusion, therefore, must always prevail, more or less, in the management of the affairs of such a company. [700]

The lesser care of a manager for the corporation's money than for his own, which Adam Smith spotted, still operates. Lawyers know, for instance, that if they bring suit for a corporation-caused injury it is preferable *not* to identify the particular manager responsible and try to collect from him. If they sue an officer in his own name he will fight like a tiger. But when he settling on behalf of the corporation, he will be more forthcoming; the money is the corporation's, not his. [Stone, 1976, 59] It is surprising that those economists who are most protective of the assumption that individuals always maximize their self-interest, appear to be inclined to exempt managers from this motive.

The so-called 'Alchian thesis" or the "Alchian-Friedman Argument" is widely accepted in neoclassical economics. This is the contention that firms must be rational profit-maximizers since only such firms survive the processes of natural selection through competition. Any firm that does not rationally act to maximize profits will fail in the struggle against firms that do.

Although Armen Alchian is widely tagged with this thesis; he strongly rejected it.[6] It was Milton Friedman's version that is orthodoxy.

> Let the apparent immediate determinant of business behavior be anything at all—habitual reaction, random chance or whatnot. Whenever this determinant happens to lead to behavior consistent with rational and informed maximization of returns, the business will prosper...; whenever it does not, the business will tend to lose resources and can be kept in existence only by the addition of resources from outside. The process of 'natural selection' thus helps to validate the hypothesis [of profit-maximization behavior]. [Friedman 1984. 223]

Alchian, in contrast, correctly argued that firms basically could not take profit-maximization as a goal because of uncertainty, "Where foresight is uncertain, 'profit-maximization' is *meaningless* as a guide to specific action. (emphasis in the original)[1950, 211] What matters is positive profits. Those firms that realize positive profits, survive; those that have losses, disappear. All a firm has to do, is to be better than its competitors, even if all concerned are inefficient, not in competition with "some hypothetically perfect competitors".[7]

> ... the greater the uncertainties of the world, the greater is the possibility that profits would go to venturesome and lucky rather then to logical, careful, fact-gathering individuals. [213]

Alchian demolished the contention that surviving firms will learn by trial and error to maximize profits. For this to work, a firm must be able to identify an action as a successful trial to be repeated or as an error to be avoided. Over a period of time, there has to be a continual ascent toward some *optimum optimorum* without intervening descents. A past successful trial may prevent the firm from trying an even more successful strategy. In any case, the changing environment destroys most of the basis for comparison. These changes may even result in making some other firm more profitable. And, of course, in circumstances of increasing returns, a firm that once secures a temporary advantage may not be overtaken for years.

M. A. Adelman, graphically describes corporate management as *...struggling through a viscous fluid of inertia and misunderstanding toward that boundary, which does not even have the grace to stay put. Information about the boundary comes often as a kick in the slats; sales are being lost, profits dwindling...*[1972, 494]

---

[6] Kay (1995) conclusively proves this.

[7] Alchian's point here can be illustrated by a story: Two hikers in a desolate, treeless valley in the Rockies suddenly discover a ferocious grizzly bear a few yards away charging toward them. One hiker drops his pack preparing to run. His companion says, "It's hopeless. You can't outrun a grizzly." The hiker replies, "I don't have to; I just have to outrun you."

We have assumed that a firm in striving to produce profits tries to produce more efficiently. But a corporation may also secure profits by exploiting power. It may exert power over its suppliers (cutting what it pays), over its buyers (DeBeers offers a buyer a single assortment of uncut diamonds at a non-negotiable price and no choice), over its labor force (increasing intensity of work or holding wages down), over government (getting favorable tax legislation, "corporate welfare", favorable treatment in provision of infrastructure). All these are instances regularly reported in the business press of actions that corporations often take as a way of improving their "bottom line".

Power and efficiency are not exclusive strategies. Both may be simultaneously pursued. [Pitelis 1998]

Internal Agendas[8]

Corporate divisions and other units often have their own internal agendas that may supersede the drive to maximum efficiency. [Leibenstein 1982]. Economists now acknowledge that *rent-seeking* or parasitism exists in government; it exists within corporations as well.

Chunking, bringing units together into a higher hierarchical organization is not costless. There is a loss in determinism. In some physical systems, the constituents are sufficiently reliable and can be sufficiently predicted that the system itself is virtually deterministic. (A brick wall, for example.) But this is not true of humans or of groups of humans. Consequently, as we move to higher levels of organizations of human beings (from the one-person firm, to the division, to the corporation, to the economy), the system loses at each level some element of determinism and predictability.

In state-owned industries and in large private corporations, bureaucratic rivalry often drives corporate decisions—playing a similar role to that of profits in small-scale capitalist enterprise. The bigger my division, my section, or my company—the more important I am.

People down the line in the corporation are on salary and do not benefit directly from maximization of profits. A few corporations are aware of this and do include some element of profit-sharing in employee compensation; others try to finesse the problem by attempting to instill a corporate culture of achievement. This may help—everyone likes to be on a winning team—but not for long when the result is, as recently in the United States, that greater produc-tivity leads only to downsizing and layoffs.

Dilbert by Scott Adams, a comic strip on corporate life is highly popular with people who work in corporations. The strip graphically portrays the argument in this section.

---

[8] In Williamson's terms, individuals and units may engage in "sub-goal maximization" and "opportunism".

As an employee I may try to make my job more interesting through innovation—it may contribute to profits or just to costs. Corporate policy dictates that I travel economy-class. Okay, I follow the rules obediently but I pick the airline, and the route—if I can get away with it—to maximize my frequent-flier miles, even though this may cost more.

Airlines sell "coach tickets" that provide an automatic upgrade to first or business class but which cost more than "coach tickets" that don't. Senior executives take this option to appear to be roughing it. The expense account thus conforms to policy but the travel expenses are higher.

Security is important so as an employee, I try hard, using every tactic possible including personal politicking, to protect my turf.

In short, employees have their own sense of perceived interests. Prominent among employee motives is the usual bureaucratic jockeying for power, position and prestige. Individuals, divisions, sections, branches, and subsidiaries have their own specific objectives to pursue and these do not necessarily coincide with the objectives of the corporation. At some point, all these internal frictions culminate in so reducing the overall efficiency that further growth may even threaten corporate existence.

Corporate management is usually left quite free to follow its own goals whether these are the interests of the corporation as a whole, empire-building to satisfy the ego of the CEO, paying unconscionably high incomes to top executives, arranging an easy unstressed life for managers, or providing enjoyable prerequisites for management and the board.(But in the 1990s, as we discuss in the next chapter, in the United States, some corporate managements had a rude awakening.)

Richard G. Darman, a top Reagan administration official, in 1986 described corporate managements as a "*corpocracy*"with its tendency to be like a bloated, risk-averse, inefficient and unimaginative government bureaucracy. T. Boone Pickens, a noted corporate raider, agreed that most top corporate managers think like bureaucrats rather than like entrepreneurs.

Not all managements desire to maximize profits. Some opt for an easy life, others want only to maintain market share. Others are quite content to do better this year than last. [Kamarck 1983, 91-4; Galbraith 1974]

It would be a miracle under these circumstances if every CEO were the best person for his job and if he performed at his personal best for the benefit of the corporation. Even if he is under pressure, as long as he does better than his alternative, he may still survive and prosper. While in the long run a disasterously-run corporation may go to the wall, in the oligopolistic environment in which much of the economy exists this may take a long time. As Herman described the situation in 1981,

> ...extremes of oligopoly can be found among large corporations in a given country—witness the dynamism of the computer and semiconductor businesses in the United States, on the one hand, and the lethargy of the automobile–steel–rubber tire businesses, on the other.

By the end of the last century, the auto industry had been shaken up by Japanese competition; the rubber tire companies had mostly succumbed to foreign takeovers, and the steel industry was dominated by newcomers. These industries had been relatively well-protected against import competition and their live-and-let-live cocooning had fostered comfortable cushioned lives for managers for a couple of generations.

American businesses largely self-finance their growth through ploughing back their internal savings. In the 1990s, the Standard & Poor's 500 paid out only 40 percent of their earnings in dividends. (Some earnings were used for stock buybacks, thus boosting stock prices and giving investors capital gains instead. Overall, at least 50 percent of earnings were available for investment in the corporation.)

A main function of corporate headquarters is the allocation of capital among the various divisions of the company. How efficient are these internal capital markets? One argument is that corporate internal capital markets are more effective than external capital markets because headquarters is better informed and can ensure that its funds are used optimally, whereas outside investors are poorly informed and cannot monitor effectively how funds are used. However, empirical research suggests that internal capital markets are not all that efficient. [Bolton and Scharstein 1998, 109] In investing in their own company, managers acquire more power, more prestige, and the opportunity for paying themselves higher incomes for running a bigger corporation. Most of the conglomerates built in the 1960s performed badly in the 1970s. In the 1980s, the favorable results of many takeovers came from the dismantling of the earlier conglomerates. The economist record on conglomerates is a good example of how economists can go wrong in automatically assuming that everything that happens in a market must be justifiable.

> Ever since the conglomerate merger wave of the 1960s, economists have tried to understand the efficiency properties of conglomerates. In the late 1960s, this meant marshaling arguments for the superiority of all the conglomerates being created. For the last 15 to 20 years, this meant trying to understand why the conglomerates have been largely dismantled and why highly diversified firms seem to sell at a market value discount. Recent work by NBER researchers suggests that one of the main problems with conglomerates is the very same factor cited as a strength in the 1960s: they create internal capital markets and bypass the discipline of the external capital market. [Vishny 1998, 3]

The investments that do flow through the capital markets are also distorted. Lenders minimize risk and uncertainty, by lending to a firm that has a large pool of internal saving—repayment is more assured even if the particular project being financed does not pan out. [Thurow 1983, 145-150]

Conclusions

Corporations do not grow infinitely large. As sketched above, it is the accumulated frictions of human beings working together that explains the puzzle why all economic life does not fall under the sway of one universal corporation.

While innovations in management techniques have made possible enormous corporations employing hundreds of thousands of workers, eventually they run into problems of control. The top echelon has the herculean task of trying to get its organization to work towards the goals it sets. It is difficult to manage a large number of people who have to be sorted into hierarchies of separate units and sub-units for purposes of control. Inevitably, all this introduces degrees of freedom into the system that make possible the accretion of self-serving practices throughout the organization.

If growth in size brings growth in market power the profit advantages from the latter may more than offset diseconomies from large size, This allows the corporation to grow beyond its most efficient size until at some indeterminate point, even the advantages of market power fade or political forces or managerial prudence step in to call a halt.

The successful existence and growth of the corporate economy shows that this way of organizing production, distribution and marketing has proven superior to the pure market. Superior, yes, but, as we have seen, this does not mean that the corporate economy necessarily results in an optimal utilization of resources in the economy.

The New Institutional Economics has made a break-through contribution in demonstrating that the corporate organization of economic life cannot be understood without the help of other disciplines. The main theme of this chapter has been that for a realistic explanatory economics, NIE's findings need to be supplemented by the broader view of human nature and ways of understanding that are argued for throughout this book. NIE leaves out the productive contribution that organization *per se* makes beyond economizing on transaction costs. Together, these explain why firms can be more efficient than markets. More efficient but not necessarily optimum.

It is fundamental to embrace the fact that the modern dynamic free-enterprise private-property system is, in its central core, *managed*—not market—*capitalism*— influenced by market forces but with an important set of its own nonmarket dynamics.

Mainstream economics has been unable to integrate institutional analysis into the building of general equilibrium models.[9] It has tried rather to finesse the problem by trying to assume that it did not really exist as a separate matter. For an effective economics, it is crucial to add the study of the corporation to the scope of the discipline and to recognize that much can be valuable that does not fit into the old standard tool box.

---

[9] I owe this point to Francis Bator.

4 Corporate Governance

They meet once a month, gaze at the financial window dressing (never at the operating figures by which managers run the business), listen to the chief and his team talk superficially about the state of the operation, ask a couple of dutiful questions, make token suggestions (courteously recorded and subsequently ignored) and adjourn until next month. [1970, 49]—Robert Townsend describing a typical board of directors of his day.

The corporation suffers from the Original Sin of organizations. As formulated in Robert Michel's Iron Law of Oligarchy, the leadership of an organization desires to hold on to office. It tries to entrench its hold by controlling information, manipulating rewards and punishments, mobilizing resources to ward off attacks, and it tries to pursue its own interests even if at the expense of the organization it leads. [1962, 365; Williamson 1996, 205]

While initially around the beginning of the twentieth century, large US corporations were mostly under owner or finance control, the inexorable trend was towards management-control. By the mid-1970s, Herman found that management controlled 83 percent of the number and 85 percent of the total assets of the 200 largest nonfinancial corporations and 78 percent of the number and 80 percent of the total assets of the 100 largest industrial corporations. [1981, 66]

One of the most important problems of the economy is how to motivate managements to run their corporations most efficiently in the interest of the general economy. Society depends on them for the creation of wealth.

Prior to the modern corporation, the owner-manager usually invested in and managed his own enterprise or kept a close eye on the person he had chosen to manage his assets. For most of the nineteenth century in Britain and the United States, capital came from family, friends, and neighbors. Growth was financed from retained profits with the dominant motive one of long-term survival. [Kindleberger 1984,192-93]

The position today in the United States and Britain is quite different. (In Japan and Germany, the story again is different.) The dominant enterprises not only separate ownership from management and control, but are sensitive to capital markets that are driven by short-term expectations.

The division between ownership, control, and management affects the dynamics of the economy. Elements of indeterminacy come into play. With information imperfect, costly, and controlled by management, managers have considerable discretion and power. Objective economic forces alone no longer suffice to explain behavior.

Usually, it is assumed that in most modern corporations with widely-held share-ownership, ownership is separate but management and control are in the same hands, but this is not always true. When share-ownership is widely dispersed, an intermediary institution may have the power to exercise effective control over the management.

The Role of Individuals and Institutions

The total value of stockmarket capitalization at the beginning of the twenty-first century was around 150 percent of GDP in Britain, Switzerland, and the United States; around 100 percent in France and Japan; and around 50 percent in Germany and Italy.

In the United States, individuals, historically, have owned most of the shares in corporations. As late as 1970, individuals still directly owned as much as 80 percent of total shares. The position is very different now. Since 1997, individual ownership of stock shares in the United States has dropped to below 50 percent of the total. Over half of the shares of the corporations listed on the stock exchanges are now held by institutions: pension funds, mutual funds, insurance companies, nonprofits, trusts. While an individual's shareholding is ordinarily a minuscule fraction of one percent of the shares of a company, some institutions are large enough investors in a corporation that their votes can be significant in electing corporate boards. The share of the U. S. equity market held by the 100 largest institutions was 37 percent in December 1996. [Gompers and Metrick 1999]

Direct individual ownership represents under a fifth of the total British shares. Most shares are held by institutional investors (pension funds, insurers and unit trusts).

The growth of institutional ownership in the United States and Britain means that, now, as in Germany and Japan, intermediaries separate the ultimate shareholder-owners still further from the management of their assets. The ultimate investors thus have to hope that the two successive links of agents to the corporate real assets do not pursue agendas that conflict with theirs.

Since public pension funds have to be risk-averse they are run by cautious officials. Fund mangers and insurers may not wish to antagonize corporate managements with whom they do or expect to do business. As a result, most institutional investors have remained passive and have not challenged corporate managements. But this is changing as we discuss below.

Auditors are another means of exercising control over corporate managements. They are effective, in most cases, in ensuring reasonably honest corporate accounting and preventing outright fraud. But not always, as the frauds in the Maxwell and BCCI collapses demonstrated. Auditors are selected by the Board of Directors, often by a committee made up of outside directors. So far, so good. However, they are subject to "moral hazard", that is, in plain English, perverse incentives. If their report is unfavorable they may lose the client. Auditors are professionals and it is the ethics and the pride of the profession that has to be relied on to keep auditors doing their job responsibly.The incentive to tread lightly was reinforced in recent years as the auditing firms secured tax and consulting work from their clients. The American Securities and Exchange Commission found in 1999 that almost half of the partners of PricewaterhouseCoopers had violated the law and conflict-of-interest rules of the profession. Business Week editorialized that this is... *but the latest evidence of the erosion of independent auditing.* [February 7, 2000, 138] The SEC then announced that it was proposing to ban auditing firms from offering non-audit services to their clients.

The possibility that auditors would protect shareholders from abuse by corporate managers is remote. And, most important: the major economic interest of securing optimum effective management of corporate resources is not in auditors' terms of reference.

In the United States and to a lesser degree in elsewhere, the private pension funds of corporate employees are invested in stocks of corporations other than their own. Of the total of some seven trillion dollars in American pension funds in 2000, well over a trillion was in funds in which labor unions have some voice. As a result, employees have become owners of a large fraction of corporate capital.

In a few corporations such as United Airlines, Avis, Weirton Steel, when the company fell on hard times the workers saved their jobs by taking over the company. The dichotomy between owners and managers in these cases was eliminated. The line between profits and wages was blurred. Peter Drucker, an outstanding management guru, has gone so far as to call the ownership of corporate capital by workers, the beginning of "post-capitalist society".

For this to prove true there are still many problems to be solved. The rank-and-file workers in Avis were still almost as much isolated from major management decisions as their counterparts in Hertz and eventually sold their stock. Employee-owners succeeded in making Weirton Steel profitable but when five years later in 1989 the company was in need of new capital investment, a stock issue diluted the worker control below 50 percent. How the worker stake in United Airlines will play out in the long run is still to be seen.

Worker ownership is making management heed the interests of the workers and other stakeholders: beginning in 2000, bonus pay for the top 625 United mangers will depend on employee satisfaction, customer satisfaction, and on-time performance—all these to be measured by outside surveys and government statistics. The unions plan to extend this to Northwest and Transworld, where they also own shares.

One continuing success of employee-ownership has been United Parcel Service of America, Inc. (UPS). It has revenues of around $30 billion, owns 149,000 vehicles and 500 airplanes, and employs over 300,000 people. Of these, under half—managers, some other employees, and retirees—are allowed to own stock. The non-owning employees look to the Teamsters Union for protection of their interests. In 1999, to secure more capital to finance its expansion in markets around the world, UPS sold, for the first time, around $3 billion of stock to outside investors. However, by selling stock whose shares have only one vote apiece while the internal shareholders' shares have 10 votes apiece, the employee-shareholders keep 99 percent voting control.

Power of Corporate Managements

How far, and in what ways, can the shareholders, ensure that the corporate manager acts only in the interests of the corporation and not in his own at the expense of the firm?

American managements have been unique in being complete masters in their corporations. While usually the independence of management from shareholder control is also largely true of British companies, British managements have been restrained to some extent by the old-boy customs and ties of the City of London.

In the United States and Great Britain, in many corporations, all or a majority of the directors are officers or employees of the corporation. In these companies, there is not even any pretense that the managements are being chosen by the nominal owners of the corporation.

In most corporations, the CEO chairs the Board, makes the agenda and controls the meeting—a dissident director has no firm base for leadership. Pierre A. Rinfret, a Wall Street veteran, who served on more than 15 boards of directors, has stated publicly that the so-called "independent director" is a rubber stamp and a patsy for management and that directors totally and completely fail in their fiduciary capacity as representatives of the stockholders. [1993]

In those corporations where directors are not members of management, the management usually hand-picks the outside "independent directors". Friendships, connections such as CEOs serving on one another's boards link directors and management. Some directors provide services or commodities to the corporation on whose board they serve. The pay for serving on a board is frequently relatively quite high—an academic can easily double or triple his income from a few directorships—so a director may think twice before being "uncooperative". Many corporations provide pensions for retired outside directors. (B.F. Goodrich's is typical: $26,000 a year for life after the director has served on the board for 10 years and reached 55.

Paying consulting retainers to directors in addition to board fees is another effective way of ensuring allegiance to management. At W.R. Grace & Company, the chairman maintained his position with the help of director-supporters who held lucrative consulting contracts with the company. In addition to the regular director's annual retainer and meeting-attendance fee and expenses, in 1994, one director received $610,000 plus an option on 40,000 common shares; another, $420,000; a third, $310,000 plus $24,000 for car services; and a fourth, $200,000 plus $69,000 for car services. Institutional stockholders finally removed the entrenched chairman in 1995 after it became public that on top of a $1 million-a-year pension, the company had spent $189,000 on him for nursing care, $191,000 for security guards, and $250,000 for the use of a New York apartment. The corporation had also engaged in some sizable unauthorized financial transactions with the chairman's son.

CEOs sweeten their relationships with directors by providing favors such as making company planes available for personal or family purposes, letting a director use the corporate apartment for visits, inviting directors on cruises and theater parties, etc.

James Robinson, CEO of American Express kept his directors cooperative while the company reeled from public embarrassments.

> Despite the clamor of journalists and Wall Street analysts, the quiescent American Express board long showed no signs of impatience, packed as it was with Robinson's pals (Ross Johnson, ...Drew Lewis), loyal luminaries whose firms received sizable fees (Henry Kissinger, Vernon Jordan), and others, who rarely opened their mouths at meetings (Ambassador Anne Armstrong, diva Beverly Sills Greenough). [Burrough 1993, 195]

Even when there are no financial inducements, a director gets affected by social influences—he doesn't want to appear to be the odd man out, to upset the CEO by asking disturbing questions, to violate the pleasant social atmosphere of the meeting. If there are developments that worry a director, to go into them would mean prolonging the meeting and wrecking dinner plans or holding up his colleagues who have a plane to catch, etc. People become familiar with one another and start to think alike. They acquire loyalty to the corporation as it is and become defensive to criticism and calls for change. After serving on a Board for a period of time, the directors begin to share goals with the CEO and identify with him.

One inducement to better performance by a manager is the threat of a corporate raider. This potential threat, is a blunt instrument. It is like the threat of revolution to a government. A government has to be extremely bad, unresponsive to its people, and weak before revolution becomes a practical choice.

A corporate management worried by a proxy battle can threaten investment advisers, banks and security houses with loss of business if they do not support the incumbents. The expense of a proxy battle is borne by the shareholders pushing for a change. This can cost millions of dollars, while management has the corporate treasury to support its slate. A single individual usually holds only a minute fraction of a public corporation's shares. Even if she, by herself, could influence the management to perform better, the gains would be shared by all the shareholders while all the costs of the monitoring would be borne by her. As a result, dissatisfied shareholders usually bow to the free-rider imperative and do the *Wall Street walk* —sell their shares.

Corporate managers have the choice between allocating their effort toward increasing profits of the corporation or increasing their own income at the expense of the shareholders. The vitality of the economy depends on how these choices are made. What governs here is not so much the Market as the culture and economic, legal and political institutions of the country. A vice-president of the United Auto Workers, after visiting Germany reported,

> It is amazing to me that in Europe the corporations appear to feel that they have a moral obligation to their employees, but also to their community where they are located. These are things that just seem to come naturally in the European culture,... [Ryback 1998,83]

Corporate managers have many opportunities for "rent-seeking", that is, to use their power for their own advantage. The business press reports examples almost every day—some so outrageous that the *Wall Street Journal* characterizes them as "lessons in social-ism".

> ...the formula that has suited Time Warner's brass since the company's 1989 birth: rewarding mediocre performance with stupendous sums extracted from shareholders, who are 'taxed' to provide a safety net for pinstriped panhandlers. [Lowenstein October 5, 1995]

The pay-packets of corporate managers appear to be a market anomaly. It is hard to believe that the incomes of many CEOs of major firms are determined by pure market forces. Certainly it would be difficult to be convinced that as a class American managements have always been greatly superior to the Japanese. In the 1980s. the results from competition were rather that in the case of many companies the opposite was true. In 1980, at the start of the successful Japanese large-scale incursion into American industry and markets, Japanese top executives earned only a little more than one sixth the compensation of American top managements. [Kaplan 1992]

The discrepancy between American and German CEO incomes was highlighted in the DaimlerBenz take-over of Chrysler in 1998. Daimler's CEO's pay in 1997 had been $1.9 million; Chryslers's, $16 million.

The after-tax real wage of the average American worker fell 13 percent in the twenty years, 1970-90, while the average CEO's earnings increased over 300 percent. [Crystal 1991, 27] The rate of increase in CEO earnings continued in the 1990s to greatly exceed that in earnings of workers. By 1995, the survey done for the Wall Street Journal found that the earnings gap had stretched "into a vast chasm": the heads of about 30 major companies received 212 times higher compensation than the pay of the average American employee. (In his day, J. P. Morgan had restricted the pay of the heads of the companies he controlled to no more than 20 times that of the workers.) The chasm yawned wider: by 1998, the average CEO was paid 419 times the pay of a factory worker [Lublin 1996, R1] [*The Wall Street Journal*/William M. Mercer 1995 CEO Compensation Survey, 1996, R15; *Business Week*, "Special Report", April 29, 1998, 65; "Executive Pay", April 19, 1999: 72-90.]

Share options, which became particularly common in the United States in the 1990s, but which are also used in Britain, and France, are defended with the argument that they align the interests of top management with those of the shareholders. This is partly, but not entirely true. Options are often granted at a price below the market quote and when the market dips, boards reprice the options at still lower prices. Options, moreover, provide an incentive for managers to incur debt to secure funds to buy back shares and so boost the market price—even though it may not be in the corporate interest to increase its default risk.

Company reports often emphasize that compensation is set by outside directors. But, these are often CEOs themselves and have an interest in establishing a generous level of compensation. Research studies on the subject conclude that higher CEO compensation is not necessarily associated with better performance by the firm. [Tevlin 1996] This is reinforced by the practice of corporations rewarding failed top executives with generous parting settlements: Jill Barad, $50 million with a $1.2 million annual pension from Mattel; Stephen Hilbert, $49 million although his policy put the continued existence of Conseco in question; Michael Ovitz, $39 million after 14 months at Walt Disney; John R. Walter, $26 million after seven months at AT&T.

Another blatant abuse is exploiting "perks": taking income in the form of kind (corporate apartments, vacation resorts, autos, use of corporate planes for personal purposes, theater parties, expense account entertainment of all kinds). The perks do not show up as earned income of the managers but are buried in the accounts as costs. Managers may milk the corporation through getting the corporation to buy goods and services from other corporations that are secretly owned by the managers; or by getting "kickbacks" ("money under the table") or other benefits from suppliers for steering business their way.

A fashionable way during the 1980s for managers to profit from theirposition vis-a-vis the shareholders was to take the corporation into private ownership by the managers through a leveraged buyout (LBO). The managers and members of the board of directors have superior knowledge of the real worth of the company. Their actions and the publicity they issue provide the possibility of inducing stockholders to put a lower valuation on the corporation than the true market value. Taking the corporation private makes sense only if there is a considerable discrepancy between these two valuations.

In an LBO, managers buy the company's equity from the public shareholders using money borrowed by the company itself. This loads the company with a massive debt. However, the interest on the debt can be written off against taxes—thus the government provides a subsidy for this asset-shuffling. Once the LBO is accomplished, costs are slashed to service and pay off the debt. To do this may mean cutting research and whatever else is not immediately necessary. Then, after a few years when the corporation shows higher profits, stock is sold to the public again, often allowing the executives concerned to pocket immense profits.

This is not a mere theoretical possibility. A leading business magazine, reported that institutional investors thought the 1985 sale to management of Bibb Co., a Georgia textile manufacturer, was an instance of "...a management acting in its own self-interest." One such investor, Robert Fritz, a vice president of Cleveland's Central National Bank, which owned 4,000 shares commented: "I think they are trying to steal the company and take it private before somebody else buys it..." [Willoughby 1985]

In the 1980s, leveraged buyouts shot up from a total of under $1 billion in 1980 to a peak of more than $60 billion in 1988 to fall again to less than $4 billion in 1990. A study found that many transactions, particularly in the last years of the buyout frenzy, were overpriced or/and recklessly structured. In the these latter years, managers and the other interested parties increasingly took money out of the buyout right away, instead of keeping a stake in the future success of the companies. [Stein 1991, A12]

In the United Kingdom, in the late 1960s, there was an outburst of mergers. The management decisions to merge "...seemed to be taken with very little forethought and analysis and in quite a hurry." Research on the later results of the mergers, concluded that most were not a success: profits of merged firms tended to be lower than could have been expected from the records of the constituent firms. [Slater 1980, xxi]

In the United States, there have been five merger "waves" in modern times: 1890s,1920s,1960s,1980s, and 1990s. In the decade of the 1980s the total value of U.S. assets changing hands in the mergers, acquisitions, and leveraged management buyouts was just under $2 trillion. More than 55,000 firms were affected. At the height of that wave, in 1988 alone, mergers affected 10 percent of total stockmarket capitalization and seven percent of GDP. One hundred forty-three of the firms included in the 1980 list of the Fortune 500 were acquired by 1989. That is, around a quarter of the corporate assets of major firms was involved in the 1980s gigantic shake-up.

In the 1990s, the wave of mergers began mounting again year by year: from $100 billion in capitalization in 1991 to an awesome $1.9 trillion in 1999. The contagion also spread to Europe reaching a total of $1.5 trillion the same year. One reason for a concentration of mergers at particular times is unusually favorable stock prices. In a bull market, managements can raise money easily or have cash on hand.

Most mergers fail.

> A stream of studies have shown that corporate mergers have even higher failure rates than the liaisons of Hollywood stars. One report by KPMG, a consultancy, concluded that over half of them had destroyed shareholder value, and a further third had made no discernible difference. [*The Economist* July 22, 2000, 19]

The exciting game of acquiring corporations absorbed many managers during the 1980s. Studies have shown that shareholders in the *acquired* corporations profited, walking away with amounts greater than the market value of their stocks before the takeovers. Shareholders in an *acquiring* corporation lost There are no conclusive studies of the extent of the diversion of managerial, legal and financial talent into financial dealing and wheeling. And, corporations were enticed to promote executives who were good at financial manipulation rather than those who were good at the main business of the company. There are several indications that this warping of the managerial elite of the economy was important in the United States. Business news in Japan in the 1980s was full of reports of new product developments, new market initiatives, new export drives. In the United States, the news was of corporate raiders, mergers, acquisition battles.

Acquiring other companies requires managers to spend large amounts of time, energy, and money in the acquisition and in trying to fit the two companies together into an integral whole. Melding two companies together is a difficult task. Today, one of the greatest problems is to get two computer systems meshed into one. And then there are all the cultural problems of reconciling the different formal procedures, rules and ways of doing things. Every organization has its own peculiar informal ways ("how things are done"). It takes time for the new company employees to discover the correct new dispensation.

Buying a company often means taking on debt, whose service then absorbs resources that could be better used elsewhere.

Governments have found it necessary to intervene to protect shareholders (the nominal owners) from managements (the nominal employees) by obligating corporations to make their financial information public and banning insiders from profiting from information not available to shareholders. The SEC in the United States is a living proof of the bankruptcy of the concept that corporate managements are merely the efficient agents of their shareholder-principals. Many other countries have done little to recognize this problem. In France, firms have few if any independent outside directors, lack audit and pay committees, are often bound together in cross-holdings, bosses sit on one another's boards, and there is no disclosure of managers' compensation.

There is evidence that the buyouts of the latter half of the 1980s in the United States were motivated by the generous treatment that managers arranged for themselves and the lucrative fees of the investment bankers arranging the deals. [Coffee 1988; Shleifer & Vishny 1990; *The Economist* September 10, 1994, 87-8; Kaplan and Stein 1993]

A study on the motives for corporate takeovers was presented to the 1995 annual meeting of the American Academy of Management covering the 106 publicly-traded American companies of $100 million and over that were involved in acquisitions during the highly active year of 1989 and and the quiet year of 1992. The most important motive appeared to be managerial ego—managers want to build a bigger empire for themselves, creating value is secondary. A CEO may even prefer the joy of hunting and acquiring companies to the humdrum routine of managing a company. [*The Economist* August 15, 1995, 52-3]

Charles Bluhdorn is an interesting example. After making a fortune in commodities, in 1956 he bought Michigan Bumper, merged another acquisition, Beard & Stone Electric Company, into it and called the new company, Gulf & Western. This was fun. Without any clear rationale he bought New Jersey Zinc, Desilu Productions, Merson Musical Products, Consolidated Cigar Corporation, Quebec Iron & Titanium Corporation, Madison Square Garden, Furniture City Plating Company, Bonney Forge & Foundry, Rocket Jet Engineering, Collyer Insulated Wire Company, and Paramount Pictures. He then discovered that making movies was even more fun and, he turned out to have a knack for it. Paramount produced hit after hit. He died in 1983 and his conglomerate was then dismantled. [Korda 1996]

Comparison of U.S., U.K., German, and Japanese Systems

After a hundred years of corporate capitalism, there is still no conclusive solution how best to secure optimal corporate governance.

In the United Kingdom and the United States, banks do not get involved in corporate governance. They do not need to monitor enterprises closely because their loans are usually backed by collateral or security, including the physical assets of the company.

In the United States, the political antagonism to financial power which kept the country from creating a central bank until 1913 and preserved a highly decentralized banking system also kept banks from playing a strong corporate governance role.

The Glass-Steagal Act enacted in the thirties (and repealed in 1999) explicitly prohibited banks from holding equity. Bank-holding companies were forbidden to own more than five percent of any unaffiliated, non-subsidiary, nonbank firm without Federal Reserve Board approval, and their holdings must be passive. For similar reasons, property and casualty insurance companies were prohibited from owning a noninsurer while life insurance companies can only hold up to two percent of assets in a single firm's equity and not more than 20 percent in equities overall.

The 1940 Investment Act, in order to ensure diversification of investments, restricted the proportion of a firm's equity that a mutual fund could hold to ten percent.

Under ERISA (Employment Retirement Income Securities Act of 1974), corporate pension funds are required to diversify. These pension funds, which became important after World War II, in any case were careful to avoid getting involved in corporate governance matters. Since each corporation's fund is controlled by its corporate management, it keeps out of other managers' businesses and they reciprocate.[1] No such inhibition is present in public pension funds and, as described below, some have begun to take an active role.

In the United Kingdom, the banking system is made up of a few large banks and neither they nor the insurance companies are forbidden to meddle in corporate governance. But by custom, tradition, and old-boy relationships, the financial institutions refrain just as in the United States.

The situation is quite different in Germany and Japan which have bank control-oriented models; that is, monitoring of corporate managements by banks.

In German firms, in contrast to the United States, ownership is heavily concentrated. The five largest shareholders on the average own close to 50 percent of a firm's equity. Many firms are still run by the owner. There are still comparatively few public firms. In large firms, shares are mostly held by banks, life insurance companies and other financial institutions, and nonfinancial corporations. In these firms, individuals hold less than a fifth of the total.

---

[1] For an authoritative and detailed description and r eview of legal and regulatory constraints on corporate control in the United States, Germany and Japan, see Prowse (1996).

The German banks are key. They are the biggest source of external finance which is provided mostly in short term loans that are rolled over constantly. This, of course, keeps the company on a short tether. The three large universal banks, Commerz, Deutsche, and Dresdner, hold shares in the corporations they are the bankers for and also vote the proxies of the individuals who leave their shares at their bank.[2] [Prowse 1997, 9]

Large German corporations have two boards: an executive board of managers and a non-executive supervisory board. The latter has, by law, half of its members elected by the workers and the other half elected by the shareholders. The chair is elected by the shareholders and has the casting vote. The chair is often a banker.

The early 1990s recession revealed that German managements could make as bad investments as Americans and could be as slow in reacting to new situations. Part of the problem is that the supervisory board meets no more than four times a year and is highly influenced by the management board. The German system of corporate governance is, therefore, no guarantee against bad economic decisions. But, then, no system can ever be. It also does not appear to be completely immune to exploitation of companies by their managers even though it does seem to avoid some of the outrageous practices that occur in the United States.

In some European countries, voting by shareholders is strongly discouraged by the system: in France, shareholders have to give a power of attorney authorizing their custodians to vote; in Belgium, Italy, the Netherlands, Sweden, and Spain, shareholders can only cast their votes if they are actually present at the annual meeting. Many companies issue bearer shares so the corporation may not know who its stockholders are. [*The Economist*, "Shareholder voting, Voiceless masses", October 31, 1998, 74, 79]

In Japan, institutions predominate as share owners. Individuals hold directly less than a fifth of equity. The center bank of a group (keiretsu) and its network of corporations are linked together by cross-holdings of shares. (See discussion in Chapter 14) Banks and insurance companies alone own around a third of all shares. Corporations own just under a third. Companies typically own shares in other companies belonging to the same keiretsu. With each company owning stock in the others, a controlling or majority of shares in each company is held by the keiretsu. A main bank is one of the members of the keiretsu and it has representatives on the boards of the other members.

The corporate board per se generally exercises little control over the management. It is usually made up of long-time corporate employees put on the board as a reward for loyal service. At annual meetings, ordinary stockholders have often been kept in line by the

---

[2] Since the mid-1980s, security markets have become more developed and the influence of the German universal banks has declined somewhat. [Vishny 1998, 4]

sokaiya (racketeers). In return for a financial payment, the sokaiya guarantee that no one ask awkward questions at stockholders' meetings.

The relationship with the main bank is an incentive for effective corporate management. The main bank may intervene if a management performs so badly that it jeopardizes the bank's loans. In such cases, the top executives' pay is cut and they may even lose their jobs. Research appears to find that this ownership arrangement does result in better management. [Aoki and Kim 1995; Prowse 1997; Lichtenberg & Pushner 1992]

Recently, as Japanese companies have reduced their reliance on bank loans, relying more on equity and retained earnings, the power of the main banks has diminished. The Keiszi Doyukai, an association of corporate executives, has begun to advocate that at least 10 percent of boards should be outside directors. One institutional investor, Nomura Asset Management, has announced that it may begin to vote its shares against unsatisfactory managements. The sokaiya are also beginning to lose some of their effectiveness. Ryuichi Koike, a leading member, was sentenced to nine months prison in April 1999.

No one of these systems—American, British, German, Japanese—is completely satisfactory. Corporate managers have the opportunity, to greater or less degree, to secure returns for themselves beyond those economically justifiable by their contribution. Corporate managers who prefer the easy life or who are poor performers, in most instances, may continue to run their corporations with impunity. Under such circumstances, the corporate managers can be considered as living as leeches on their companies.

There is of course no measure how much shareholders lose by managements siphoning off earnings or, from the national economic perspective, how much GDP is lost through indifferent or inefficient managers.

Market for Corporate Control

Can there be an efficient market for corporate control—as an asset that is separate from the value of the assets of the corporation per se? It is too easy and too tempting to assume that there must be a market for corporate control, and that, being a market, it must therefore lead to optimum results. This certainly cannot be true in all cases. And, it certainly was not true in Continental Airlines. On January 25, 1998, the Board of Directors chose a takeover offer from Northwest Airlines instead of one from Delta. *The New York Times'* report read as follows:

> The following is a multiple-choice test.
> In considering a takeover offer, whose interest should the directors treat as more important?

A. The public shareholders.
B. The controlling shareholder, who sits on the board.
C. The employees.
D. The management.
E. All of the above except A.

When the directors of Continental Airlines met on Sunday to review two offers, it appears their answer was E. The other groups are doing just fine. Only the public shareholders got nothing out of the deal the board accepted. [Under the Delta offer, all shareholders would have been treated equally. —AMK]

    The biggest winner of all is the controlling shareholder, Air Partners, the group led by David Bonderman that took Continental out of bankruptcy in 1993 and is now cashing out. Its investment was about $66 million. Its profit, including money previously received, surpasses $700 million. [Norris 1998, D1]

    In early capitalism when shareholders in a corporation were few and intimately involved in the corporation, a change in management presumably took place when the owners of the corporation decided as a matter of business to do so or sold out to new owners. Even today in small firms that are dependent on private placement and private equity sources, the investors will typically control the company's access to further capital and will often insist on board representation and voting rights. Only when corporations have thousands or millions of shareholders, none of whom has more than a tiny percentage of the total stock, and managements consequently are largely free of direct control by the shareholders, do corporate raiders come into existence. As a result of the separation of the control of a corporation from share-ownership, the power to control management becomes a separate valuable asset.

    Ineffective use of corporate assets in the new conglomerates and elsewhere was sufficiently prevalent in the 1980s, to call forth "corporate raiders" to try to profit from this opportunity. "Corporate raiders" (individuals or groups who seek to profit by seizing control of a corporation), were an important economic and financial force in the United States in the 1980s and to a lesser extent in the first half of the 1990s. Since 1980, more than 10 percent of the corporations listed in that year's Fortune 500 have been captured in a hostile takeover or changed hands as the result of a hostile takeover bid. Until very recently, such hostile threats have been almost nonexistent in Japan and Germany. [Prowse 1997, 9] This is no longer true in Germany: in early 2000, Mannesmann was the subject of an open successful hostile takeover by the British firm, Vodafone AirTouch.

    The results of successful corporate raiders are not necessarily optimum for the economy. Raiders are not usually interested in *manag-*

ing the corporations they take over; what they want is *control* over the management and the assets of the corporations.

The most prevalent justification advanced by the raiders is that their proposed new management will make a better economic use of the corporate assets than the existing management. Much of any extra value resulting from a takeover comes from the tax gains created through the substitution of debt for equity.There appears to be some substance in many instances to the negative side of this argument: that the existing management may not be getting the most economic use out of the resources of the corporation. This does not necessarily mean that the raider's management will actually do better. Buyers, like Campeau and Lorenzo, were able to take over major companies and then ran them into the ground. (See Appendix A)

The most famous or notorious raiders have shown that they are interested in securing control for the opportunities for gain from financial transactions. They may dismantle the corporation, sell off parts of it, and after exploiting all the opportunities, sell the remainder to move on after other prey.

Some raiders establish such a fearsome reputation that the managements of targeted companies try to buy them off. They use corporate assets to pay a premium price to the raider for the shares he accumulated. This has acquired the genteel name of *greenmail*. When a corporation directly buys back a block of stock from a *greenmailer* at a price above market, it is simply predation. The corporation is clearly worth less and may have been drastically weakened by the bleeding. There has been no offsetting contribution to the economy or society. The nation is no richer; the producers are poorer. Greenmail is just as much a forced levy on the company as the extortions of the Robber Knights of the Dark Ages on passing merchants.

In the *Time-Warner* merger in 1991, the *Time* management paid a group of banks $5 million to persuade them to refrain from helping anyone else who might wish to attempt a hostile takeover. Shareholders' money was thus used to bribe banks to keep from financing what might have been a more lucrative tender offer for their shares. [Dunne 1992, 54]

There has been little definitive economic research on corporate raiders. But a fairly clear picture emerges from the examples reported in the financial press. *The Wall Street Journal*, which editorially supports corporate takeovers as being part of Schumpeter's "creative destruction" also reports on how the corporate raiders operate. From these it is evident that many would fit better into Schumpeter's category of "social waste". (See Appendix A for a summary account of the operations of the raiders.)

In the five-year period, 1985–90, companies taken in hostile takeovers, were valued at more than $140 billion. Following on the RJR Nabisco takeover, the junk-bond market collapsed for about five years.

One cause was the spectacular bankruptcy of Robert Campeau's takeover empire of department stores. The second was the collapse of Drexel Burnham Lambert—the major junk bond investment bank as the result of the conviction and imprisonment of its leading partner Michael Milken, in November 1990. With Milken gone and the crash of the S & Ls, which had been a principal market for such bonds, the raiders were deprived of much of the finance that had made their activities possible. The jail sentences for several main players, the drying up of finance for others, discouraged the use of this blunt instrument in the early 1990s.

At the same time, many corporate managements succeeded in getting provisions into their charters to erect barriers against raiders: such as staggering the terms of directors, issuing stock to particular stockholders with multiple voting rights, etc.

While the raiders may have had a beneficial effect in stimulating corporate managements to be more effective, it also made managements more ruthless in trying to save themselves. Loyalty to workers, communities, consumers is set aside. Recognition of responsibility for externalities impinging on others is softness that cannot be afforded. Managements attempt to act as "lean and mean" as they claim to be.

While corporate raiders and forced takeovers are a crude solution to the problem of mismanaged corporations they are not an effective means to eliminating corporate abuses, or sheer inefficiency of the "corpocracy" in many corporations.

In those cases where a corporate raider succeeds in taking over the corporation and dismantles it, the private return to the raider is perceived by him to be greater than from keeping the corporation intact. In some cases spinning off parts of the old corporation will result in higher efficiency. There is no doubt that some existing corporations have been shaped more by the ego-trips or empire-building ambitions of top management than by business or economic considerations. On the other hand, decisions on the fate of corporations that are influenced more by the hope for profit from financial manipulations than from running productive plants are likely to harm rather than help the GDP. Furthermore, the raider does not take into account the social costs of his decisions. These can be enormous. When a plant is closed a community may be devastated and the capital invested in the creation of well-running and cooperative communities, wasted. The skills and the experience of workers, managers, technicians may be rendered valueless.

Corporate Governance Reforms

A better solution to corporate mismanagement is corporate governance reform. The large institutional shareholders, particularly pension funds, in the past usually followed the policy of voting with management. It was not until relatively recently that some of the funds realized that shuffling shares around in their portfolio was no help. They held such a large proportion of the shares of some corporations that bailing out was no longer a feasible option. They had to improve the way the company is run.

The U.S.1993 tax act, also, forces institutional investors to become less passive. Under the act, American stockholders have to vote upon the performance-pay plans of any company that pays annual compensation over $1 million to its CEO or to any of its four top policy-makers. In order to receive a tax deduction for such pay, a company must obtain approval of objectively verifiable criteria for executive compensation from a majority of its shareholders as well as a compensation committee of independent directors.

Fidelity, a manager of just under one trillion dollars in investment funds in January 2000, votes at the annual meetings of nearly 3,000 publicly traded companies. While it usually votes to support the company's management, it has started to take a more active role. It withholds votes or votes against proposals that are likely to hurt the value of its stockholdings. In 1993, it began writing to company chairmen to protest when it held a significant number of a company's shares and disagreed with policy. It has voted against a management position. [*Fidelity Focus*, Fall 1993, 24] It was also involved in ousting Kodak's CEO.

The California Public Employees' Retirement System, CalPERS, which is the largest public pension fund in the country and holds over $110 billion in assets, took the lead beginning in the 1980s to try to improve corporate management. From the 1500 corporations in its portfolio, CalPERS each year identifies the companies that are among the poorest long-term relative performers in stock price compared to their industry peers. CalPERS then meets with each company's independent directors to discuss performance and shareholder value. For example, in meeting with Stride Rite on January 24, 1996, CalPERS proposed that directors should take their fees in stock rather than in cash, and questioned the role of one board member who collected consulting fees from the company while acting as a director. If the company does not take measures to improve, CalPERS may file shareholder proposals or vote against the management slate of directors. In 1997, CalPERS issued a set of basic requirements for the structure of corporate boards.

CalPERS and the State of Wisconsin Investment Board have gone into the courts with shareholder suits. The securities laws were amended in 1995 to allow institutional investors to lead in such suits and CalPERS and the Wisconsin Board took advantage of this almost immediately.

Teachers Insurance & Annuity Association–College Retirement Equity Fund (TIAA-CREF), the world's largest pension fund (around $300 billion in assets in 2000), joined by the AFL-CIO pension plans, has become the most influential actor in improving corporate governance. Beginning in 1995, TIAA-CREF began to employ former CEOs as well as a staff of governance experts to work on improving the boards in companies in which it invests. The fund monitors governance practices at these companies and any that fall short get letters, often a visit from its staff. If this does not work, the fund files shareholder resolutions and uses its voting power. It has had some success: Heinz replaced insiders by a majority of independent directors; Disney now holds annual elections to its board, added two independent directors, and let a "poison pill"expire. (A "poison pill" is an arrangement protecting the corporation from a hostile takeover bid.) Seven other corporations removed their poison pills; and the fund has won other governance concessions from dozens of companies that it targeted. [Byrne 1999, 75-79]

With the new activism by the pension funds, *Business Week* depicted the changed environment for corporate boards.

> In the clubby, cozy world that typified the corporate boardroom, CEOs packed their boards with trusted friends and colleagues who rarely challenged the chieftain's policies—or prerogatives. meanwhile, few paid much attention to how well directors performed the job they're paid to do: looking out for shareholders.
>
> Today, however, all that has changed. Fueled by pressures from such activist investors as TIAA-CREF, the world's largest pension fund, and California Public Employees' Retirement System (CalPERS), stronger governance practices are going mainstream. In boardrooms across Corporate America, directors are struggling to redefine the rules under which they should—and shouldn't—operate. Just as important, many are taking a hard look at how responsibility for a company's performance should be split with the CEO. [December 8, 1997, 90]

In the United States, the pressure on managements from the institutional holders to improve the returns for shareholders has had significant results. By the end of 1993, two dozen CEOs of major corporations were forced to leave because of their dismal performance. The list of corporations affected included such giants as General Motors and IBM, American Express and Westinghouse, as well as smaller companies like Digital Equipment Corp. Apple Computer and Carl Karcher Enterprises Inc. The founder of Carl Karcher was ousted by his board even though it was primarily composed of longtime friends.

The W. R. Grace corporate board was cozily comfortable with its management. In March 1995, TIAA-CREF forced the company to get rid of the chairman and half the directors and to impose a mandatory retirement age of 70.

The Scott Paper Co., once one of the 100 largest American corporations, had gone downhill a long way when Albert J. Dunlap ("Chainsaw Al") became the new CEO. He cut director compensation from around $50,000 a year to 1,000 shares of common stock a year. He cut most of the public relations, real estate and lobbying staffs, closed the Washington office, fired 11,000 workers (a third of the labor force), and sold the company's comfortable headquarters in Philadelphia. Total return on the shares tripled. [Ferguson 1994, A19] Dunlap then sold the company for $9.4 billion to Kimberly-Clark in December 1995, pocketing $100 million for himself in the transaction. (In his next job, at Sunbeam Corporation, he cut 12,000 jobs, closed profitable plants, bullied the other officers, and ran up huge losses. The board of directors fired him in June 1998.)

One-fifth of the CEOs of the Fortune 100 companies were replaced in 1997. The median tenure of the CEOs in office, by 1998 was falling to four years. [Ackerman 1998, E4] In 1995, 60 percent of corporations gave pensions to directors, by the end of 1997, only some 15 percent still did. [*Business Week* December 8, 1997, 104]

To help towards improving governance, *Business Week* began in 1996 to publish an annual survey of the best and worst boards of Corporate America. This was based on the judgment of many of Wall Street's biggest investors, prominent governance experts and an analysis of the structure and rules under which each board operates. In 1999, Disney, First Union, Archer Daniels Midland, Bankamerica, Dun & Bradstreet, Sears, were leading American corporations that were included in the list of worst boards.

General Motors was also on the list in spite of some early reforms. The board of General Motors, after dethroning the CEO in 1993 had introduced some re-forms which were copied in other corporations. The non-executive directors began to elect a lead-director to chair meetings restricted to their own membership; they reviewed the CEO annually and took responsibility for planning for his successor. Finally, the whole board, not the CEO, started choosing and nominating new board members. However, by 1996, when the new CEO chosen in the coup had dug in successfully, the older habits began to reassert themselves. The outside directors stopped having meetings restricted to their membership and no longer chose a fellow director to lead them.

Among the best boards in 1999, General Electric, Johnson & Johnson, Campbell Soup, Compaq, led in a list that included many of the most successful corporations of the day, such as Intel, Texas Instruments, Home Depot, IBM, Merck, Dell, Apple Computer, Wal-Mart, Hewlett Packard, Ford. Even American Express was now on the best-board list. [January 24, 2000, 144, 146]

The criteria for judgment were how well a board carried out its primary responsibility to scrutinize rigorously the company's strategic plans, to evaluate managers against high performance standards, and to control the process in which the CEO was chosen. Board members were expected to show freedom from ties to the CEO or the company (not doing any consulting or other work for the company), not be involved in interlocking directorates (CEOs serving on one another's boards) and they are expected to own significant amounts of stock in their company.

In addition to the pressure for improved governance, a number of industries have become exposed to fierce competition through globalization, deregulation, changes in legislation (American laws now allowing nation-wide banking), expansion of free trade areas, or the building of the European Union. The comfortable oligopolistic position of companies in American regional or national markets that had allowed them pricing power was mostly destroyed as the widening market meant encountering new competitors.

Impact on the Economy

In responding to institutional investor pressure and the cold winds of global competition, since 1992 American managements have almost completely transformed the corporate economy through mergers, takeovers, reengineering, restructuring, cost-cutting, and downsizing. There has been a major redeployment of assets in the economy. Thousands of plants have been closed. Production has been concentrated in other existing or new plants in the United States or abroad. Companies like GE milked funds out of stodgy "cash cows" and invested them in fast-growing enterprises. Whole layers of management hierarchy have been eliminated, 44 million jobs were abolished and 73 million new private sector jobs were created. Over half of the labor force in 1998 were in new jobs. [Zuckerman 1998, 19, 21]

Cold breezes have also begun to penetrate the comfortable world in which nonAmerican CEOs have lived. The pressure on corporate managements from institutional investors has spread to countries outside the United States. CalPERS has joined with local investors in Britain, France, Germany, and Japan in this effort. In 1998, in the Netherlands 15 Dutch pension funds holding the equivalent of over $40 billion in assets joined together to begin to investigate the corporate governance practices of all companies included in the Amsterdam market index. One of their initial actions was to protest Royal Philips Elec-tronics generous options distribution to managers. The CEO of Baan, a software company, was forced to quit. In Germany and Britain, pension funds and mutual funds have also begun to stir. [Business Week, November 30, 1998, 52- 4]

As Table 4.1 shows, beginning in 1994, the winds of creative destruction resulted in a sharp rise in the average return on American corporate assets.

Table 4.1 Return on Equity, 1972-1997
(Standard and Poor's 400 Industrial Firms)

Years	ROE*
1972-79 average	0.15
1980-89 average	0.15
1990	0.17
1991	0.11
1992	0.12
1993	0.15
1994	0.24
1995	0.24
1996	0.25
1997	0.26

*Based on beginning-of-year book-value.
(Source: Fruhan, Harvard Business School 1998, 46)

One consequence of the pressure on CEOs, however, has been to induce them to try to secure comfortable market-power through merger or acquisition. This appears to be one of the motives behind the merger wave of the late 1990s. (A similar motivation had induced John D. Rockefeller to create his Standard Oil Trust. He scorned the "academic enthusiasts" and "sentimentalists" who believed in the beneficent effects of competition. He believed instead in the "... idea of cooperation against competition".) [Chernow 1998, 68, 70]

As a *Business Week* editorial frankly explained:

> *Consolidation trumps competition.* A great merger wave is washing over industry after industry, from banking and finance to pharmaceuticals and autos. Until now, overcapacity defined the world economy, generating intense corporate competition and unleashing deflationary forces keeping prices stable or falling. This may be ending as consolidation begins to dominate, curbing competition and ending downward pressure on prices. [emphasis in original, May 18, 1998, 210]

In American banking, the number of banks decreased by 30 percent from 1988 to 2000. A study by the Federal Reserve Bank of Boston found that in the markets that become more concentrated banks pay lower deposit-interest rates. [Simons & Stavins 1998, 25]

A June 1, 1998 ad by Marriott, the leading food and facilities management services provider to corporations, health care institutions, higher education and school system in the United States and Canada, read as follows: "When you're looking for the most outstanding solutions to your outsourcing needs, there are only *two companies* to consider... *and they've just become one.* Sodexho Marriott services." [Emphasis in the original]

By 2000, three firms (Goodyear-Sumitomo, Bridgestone, and Michelin) had secured control of 60 percent of the world's tire market.

Eighty percent of the world market in autos and trucks was concentrated in six firms.

> GM (controlling Isuzu, Saab, Suburu, Suzuki, and alliance with Fiat Motors. GM acquired 20 percent of the shares of Fiat Auto in 2000 and may be allowed to buy the rest of the firm between 2003 and 2008; Fiat received in return 5.1 percent of GM's common shares, making it the largest single shareholder in GM)
>
> Ford (controlling Aston-Martin, Jaguar, Land Rover, Mazda, Volvo autos)
>
> VW (controlling Audi, Seat, Skoda)
>
> Toyota (controlling Daihatsu and has a joint factory withGM and also cooperates with it on a range of engines)
>
> Renault-Nissan (controlling Samsung Motor),
>
> DaimlerChrysler (controlling Mitsubishi Motors, 10 percent stake in Hyundai)

The remaining two significant auto firms have three to five percent market shares and may be swallowed within a few years. Peugeot Citroën already cooperates with Renault on big engines and with Ford on diesel engines. Honda cooperates with GM on engines.

If the mergers and consolidations result in the construction of global oligopolistic markets, a high ROE (Return on Equity) will be attainable through the exploitation of a company's market power. The cold winds of relentless pressure for efficiency will die down. And, the new global oligopolists like their American predecessors (US Steel, General Motors, International Harvester} may be able to relax again into a bureaucratic comfortable life-style for managers and staff.

Economics and Corporate Governance

The high importance of corporate governance for the functioning of the economy is becoming more generally recognized by policy makers. A Working Group of the Bank for International Settlements in 1998 on *Strengthening the International Financial Architecture* recommended that action should be taken to strengthen corporate governance in financial institutions and non-financial corporations. [Bank of International Settlements 1998, 2.2]

> The OECD governments declared in 1999 that:
>
> Increasingly, the OECD and its Member governments have recognised the synergy between macroeconomic and structural policies. One key element

in improving economic efficiency is corporate governance, which involves a set of relationships between a company's management, its board, its shareholders and other stakeholders. *[OECD Principles of Corporate Governance*, 1999, 1]

How well corporate managements do their jobs has is one of the key determinants in how well the economy functions. It is Pollyannish to believe that existing institutional and legal arrangements guarantee that the operations of corporations result, as assumed in axiom-based economic theory, in optimal results. Except for the conscience of corporate management and the varying value of good public relations, there is no inducement for corporations to pay serious consideration to interests of the community when they conflict with maximum profitability. Employee stakeholders have also no inherent rights—how they fare depend on the importance of their unique skills and the degree and strength of their unionization.

Improved responsiveness of corporate managers to the financial interests of their shareholders is consistent with the view that the sole duty of the management of a corporation is to the legal owners, the shareholders. While corporations have obligations to their shareholders, it does not necessarily follow that they should be run for the sole benefit of their shareholders. The workers, the community, suppliers, customers, all have a stake that is at risk in the corporation.

In modern high-tech industry, the specialized skills of the knowledge-workers are the critical elements in the success of a firm. Earlier in the century, in the mass production industries, the physical investment in plant and machines, paid for by investors, was key while workers possessed few skills easily learned. Today, the investment in specialized skills that workers learn for the specific needs of the firm pays off in increased wages and security in the job over time—if the firm or some raider does not downsize them or shut down their plant. A community also may have a large investment at stake if it has had to provide a considerable infrastructure to support a plant. All this is fairly obvious.

If a corporation is run solely in the interests of its shareholders, the external costs that a corporation may impose on a community, on its workers, and its consumers and suppliers will not enter into its decisions. Whenever this is true, the corporation's costs, and its returns do not reflect the true economic consequences of its operations and, as a result, the operation of the economy falls below the economic optimum. While American corporations made themselves more competitive and more profitable for their shareholders through the creative destruction gale of the 1990s that swept over the American economy, an immense uncompensated cost was inflicted on the millions of workers who lost their jobs and the communities that lost their industrial plants.

The state is the only institution that has the power to act on behalf of the community to ensure that both individuals and corporations act responsibly in the interests of the society as a whole. The *OECD Principles of Corporate Governance*, declared that

> ...governments have an important responsibility for shaping an effective regulatory framework that provides for sufficient flexibility to allow markets to function effectively and to response to expectations of shareholders and other stakeholders. [2, 3]

In Japan and Western Europe, the state and the culture influence corporations to take some account of the interests of labor and community stakeholders. In Japan, companies may even put the interests of their workers ahead of the interests of their shareholders. And, Japanese corporations accept the paramount position of the national interest.

The American state does not impose any responsibility on corporations to compensate communities or workers for losses from restructuring of corporations. But some feeling of obligation to the community exists in the United States, too. Courts have upheld management decisions to give money to charity, education and the arts for the benefit of the community even though these gifts were not related to share-value. Corporations are among the biggest donors to universities. The SEC lays down rules designed to secure adequate information to protect investors. There are anti-trust laws and environmental protection laws. Utilities may be subject to regulation. The National Labor Relations Act was intended to protect workers in organizing to represent their interests to management. Banks are closely supervised. Massachusetts insurance companies require state approval of any proposed move out of state. The government imposes various mandates for corporate action.

The experiments in worker-ownership put the interests of workers on center stage. Massachusetts and a few other states authorize places on the corporate boards to be filled by worker representatives. In practice, however, this has been a dead letter. CalPERS, the large California pension fund, which takes an active role in trying to secure better corporate governance, has announced that it supports companies that achieve good economic performance without sacrificing the company's work force.

Beginning in 1997, the labor movement in the United States began to experiment in using their influence in the retirement funds in which they have a voice or control to bring pressure on managements in the corporations in which the funds are invested. Around 14 percent of all the corporate shares in the United States are held in this way.

In some countries, banks are looked to as the means to keep managers up to the mark. (And this may evolve in the United States also, with new legislation breaking down the barriers between banking and security-dealings.) The development of professional ethics to govern the actions of the institutional investors and corporate managers—policed by a professional body as well as the government might also help. Share-holding institutions ("money manager capitalism") represent a large number of people and if they take this responsibility seriously, they may come closer to being a rough proxy for the general good. However, since they inevitably have to weigh the interests of shareholders more heavily than those of other stakeholders, they will still fall short of the representing the complete interests of the participants in the economy.

In the final analysis, one can only conclude that while the ideal of corporate managers performing in the optimal interests of the economy could be more closely approached through various reforms it will never be possible to arrive there. However, this is important for the efficiency of the economy and, consequently, corporate governance is an essential subject for economists.

5 Services

The less...we trouble ourselves with scholastic inquiries as to whether a certain consideration comes within the scope of economics the better. If the matter is important let us take account of it as far as we can.
—Alfred Marshall.

The progress of plumbers is painfully slow—
It makes me unbearably nervous.
They say it's a service economy, so
How come I can't get any service? —-Marty Fridson.

The United States and the other high-income OECD members are now "services economies". Most of the GDP—more than two-thirds— is now produced in services and most employment—as high as four-fifths—is in services. This is also true of consumption—three-fifths of household spending is now on services. The United States, the United Kingdom and Canada were the first services economies and have been such for more than half a century. (The same is now true of the European Union and Japan. American wholesale and retail services alone produce a greater proportion of GDP than manufacturing does and provide over forty percent more employment.

Around a third of all services produced and consumed in the United States are sold to government—federal, state, and local. Even while professing a philosophy of shrinking government, in the twelve years of Republican rule, 1980-92, the number of workers employed by American governments continued to grow and by the end of the period had surpassed the total number of workers in manufacturing.

International trade in services has been growing more rapidly than trade in merchandise in the recent years. Trade in services is now around one-fifth of total trade.

Even in the output of material goods a large part of the labor force is producing services rather than producing material goods. Both in Britain and in the United States the proportion of service-occupation workers in the total employed in manufacturing is around a third. In short, in the real world the *economic good* of economic theory is now much more likely to be a service than a material commodity.

A bias against services has existed in economics from the beginning. Adam Smith ruled that menial servants, the sovereign with his officers of justice and war, churchmen, lawyers, physicians, men of letters, musicians, opera-singers, actors, etc., are all *unproductive laborers.* [314-5] While modern economics is not so condemnatory, too little attention has been paid to understanding the real significance of services and their implications for economics and policy. Services are a different category. A service economy is fundamentally different from a material-goods dominated economy. Some service characteristics may be similar to those of material goods but they differ in measurement, markets, and price behavior. (The special characteristics of the *professions*—the category to which economists belong—are covered in Chapter 8.)

How services are defined and classified is not consistent in the different national accounting systems nor consistent in practice among countries using the same system.

Essentially, services are products that are consumed at the time and place of purchase. But, "services" is a loose concept: precise lines are difficult to draw between categories and categories tend to overlap. Natural gas, for example, is classified as a service. This is a good illustration of the difficulty. Natural gas is a consumer good, an intermediate good as a fuel for industry, and is used as a raw material in some chemical industries. It is not a material good and is not tangible in the usual sense. Yet, natural gas occupies space, its quantity can be measured by instruments, it is sold by volume, and, unlike most services, it can be stored.

There are many systems of analytical classification of services:

1. how a service relates to the production of material goods;
2. its degree of dependence on the use of fixed capital;
3. the kind of demand it satisfies, i.e. consumer, producer, government;
4. by economic categories, i.e. service functions, service occupations, service industries, service products.

Services differ in their relationship to material goods. One large set is directly dependent on and complementary to material goods. These help: to produce material goods, to finance, insure or account for them, to distribute them to consumers, to maintain them for the buyer, or to dispose of worn out or unwanted goods. Some in this category depend on fixed capital and directly help produce or distribute material goods but are not usually an integral part of the goods-producing enterprises. These include transport, communications, electric power, gas and water.

These are sometimes not classified as "services" but as "Intermediate" between the "Secondary" and "Tertiary" sectors. This category is so involved with public purpose that there is a substantial body of good theory and applied economics in each case. In 2000, employment in transportation and public utilities was 5 percent of total U.S. nonagricultural employment. Of course, these services are also directly consumed by consumers as well as by the material-goods producing enterprises. These industries are therefore producers of both intermediate as well as final products.

All other services do not make great use of fixed capital. General government, finance, insurance, real estate, wholesale and retail trade, and miscellaneous services—all may use some capital good but their main source of value-added is the human contribution. These services employ a growing proportion of the American labor force. Employment in these services grew from 40 percent of total civilian employment in 1929 to 75 percent in 2000.

"Miscellaneous services", the largest category in the group (28 percent of total U. S. civilian employment in 2000), is composed of many different activities. The largest is health services (hospitals, nursing facilities, doctors, dentists) which makes up over a quarter of this group. The second largest category of this group is business services (building maintenance, protective services, computer services, management consultants). The rest of this category included private education, hotels and other lodging, social services, personal services (barbershops, hair dressers, etc), legal services, amusement and recreations, etc.[1]

The increases in *employment* in services do not necessarily entail corresponding large increases in direct *consumption of services by consumers*. Most of the increase in services–employment has been in the services within manufacturing enterprises and in *producer services*, i. e., services which individuals, business firms, nonprofit organizations and governments provide and usually sell to producers rather than to the consumer. While medical services and education have grown apace, *personal purchase* of other services has grown more slowly.

Consumers have supplemented the *services economy* with a *self-service economy*. As is typical of our constantly evolving, mutating economy, household machines replace some services from outside the household. Much of this is voluntary: clothes-washers replace laundries; disposable diapers displace diaper services; personal autos displace public transport; the cinema is replaced by a rental video; records and cassettes substitute for concerts. The personal computer is replacing some outside legal, medical and other services. In Arizona, when a married couple agrees to

---

[1] The Material Product System (MP) of national accounts of the former centrally-planned countries essentially distinguished public utilities, communications and transport from all other services. It then drew an additional finer distinction within the first group between "productive services" and "nonproductive services". "Productive labor" was considered to be labor acting on nature to satisfy human needs, providing the community with material goods for means of production and consumer goods. Productive services were those directly connected with physical production and included the transport and communications services used in producing material goods and the utilities—gas, water, electricity—which are used in producing material goods. Any services which do not increase the total quantity of material goods were not regarded as "productive". Transport of passengers, communications not involved in production of material goods, utilities consumed by individuals not in the process of production were all "nonproductive" services. [United Nations 1971, 2-3]

The Courcier system of national accounts, used in many francophone countries, treats the value added in public administration, financial intermediaries, nonprofit institutions, and domestic services as transfers and excludes them from the calculation of gross domestic product. [Shelp 1981, 61]

separate, they can avoid lawyers and, instead, go to computer kiosks with interactive, multimedia instructions that connect them to a state-licensed software program. At a court, the judge reviews the documents produced by the computer, hears the case and grants the divorce, if justified. The computer also will help people to obtain and fill out forms for small claims and other common legal matters.

Lawyers themselves are increasingly relying on special computer programs to generate forms, to look up precedents, to inform them of the current statutory law. In medicine, too, modern technology is supplementing and supplanting human services. The cardiologist's computer tells him whether his patient's EKG is normal. A computer checks a patient's heart pace-maker by listening to it over the phone.

Business firms have been successfully imposing the provision of some unpaid services on us: fast-food restaurants have trained us to clear the table after we have eaten; we have to write our creditor's account number on our check when we pay bills: a utility may get us to read our own meter every other month; we collect the items we want and take them to the cashier in supermarkets and department stores; many items we buy come unassembled and we have to put them together. This "self-service economy" is part of the explanation of the paradox of why, though we are living in a "service economy", we find it hard to get any service.

Statistical Inadequacies

Even though services employment is now far more important, the effort expended on collecting adequate data on services has been far below that on material goods. Governments and international organizations have concentrated on collecting data on the production, trade, and consumption of material goods. The US government collected data on 10,000 categories of material goods classified into 420 different types of manufacturing industries. In the services sector there were only 130 different classifications. Many of these covered a wide diversity of activities under a single heading; "business services" includes everything from window washing to management consulting.

A new statistical system for the United States, Canada and Mexico was started in 1997, to be fully integrated with other national statistics by the earliest in 2004. This new North American Industry Classification System (NAICS) will replace the old Standard Industrial Classification (SIC) which originated in the 1930s. NAICS will collect more information on service activities and groups them into new sector classifications (Information; Professional, Scientific and Technical Services; Arts, Entertainment and Recreation; Health Care and Social Assistance). While historical statistics will not be available to link much of the new data to the past, the system will provide much needed information on the economy that we are living in.

The services industries pose many conceptual problems for the measurement of product and productivity. There are problems in measuring product and productivity in material goods production—mostly problems of how to measure quality changes and price changes [See Kamarck 1983, 42-44] Measurement in services has similar but less manageable problems. According to the Bureau of Labor Statistics (BLS) productivity on American railroads in one 15 year period rose by 4.7 percent a year; the Bureau of Economic Analysis in the Commerce Department estimated it as rising only 2.3 percent a year. In the airlines, the BLS figure for the period was 3.6 percent annual *gain*, the BEA reported a 0.2 percent *decline*. [Malabre 1992, A5] The Congressional Office of Technology Assessment (OTA) has shown that the statistics of international trade in services are far from accurate. For 1984, for example, the official figures reported $44 billion of export of services; the OTA study had it in the range of $69-91 billion. Imports of services were officially reported as $42 billion; the OTA estimate was $57-74 billion. [*The Economist* Sept. 20, 1986, 81]

In the services, in addition to the difficult measurement problems there is a lack of suitable concepts to apply. General government and nonprofit organizations do not sell their services so no proper measure of their output can be constructed. The practice instead is to estimate net output—the amount left over after deducting purchases—using the convention that net output moves like full-time equivalent employment. No return to capital and land and no depreciation are counted, and no indirect taxes are levied on the compensation of employees. The figures for labor earnings thus are taken to be the estimated contribution to national income, to net national product, and to gross national product. It is, consequently, *impossible* for productivity to increase. If a social security administration succeeds in reducing the size of the payroll needed to issue a given number of checks, output as measured for the national accounts has decreased and there is no change in productivity.

The productivity of a fire department or police force, for example, depends upon the degree of protection they provide against fire or crime losses. How can it be measured? Statisticians have been attempting to cope with this problem by developing physical output measures—such as the number of arrests by police, the number of students enrolled for schools—for a number of government and other services. While these measures are better than the simple quantity of labor input, they are obviously far from adequate. [Kendrick 1985; Hulten 1985]

In health services, one of the largest sectors in the economy, it is questionable whether output can be taken as equivalent to expenditures (amounting to $1.3 trillion in the United States in 2000). What is the value of a cure? While output is sold, the market is hardly free: consumers rely on the medical profession itself for information on the quality and quantity of the product to be purchased, there are restrictions on competition in the medical profession, and most health care in high income countries is paid for by third parties.

The productivity of some services sold to producers is also difficult or impossible to measure. The productivity of an engineering or management consultant should be measured by the contribution they make to the efficiency of the firm advised. Sometimes, a consultant is retained to take the blame for painful changes that the management has already decided on. Here, the contribution of the consultant comes in the form of reducing the adverse effects on the relationship between the management and the staff affected—the true impact on the output or costs of the firm is hard to assess. The measurement of productivity of educational services, such as those of an economics professor may be even more difficult. It is not simply the greater earning power of the student as the result of having imbibed economic wisdom. If the student becomes an important decision-maker in government or a corporation, the greater economic benefits to the economy that result from her better economic decisions surely should at least in part be attributed to the teacher.

Not only are the data scanty or inaccurate and the concepts needed inadequate or lacking, work on definition, classification, analysis and the impact on the workings of the economy has been insufficient.[2]

Some Growth Theories

Since the growth of services is one of the principal dynamic forces in the economies of the twentieth century, some understanding of the process is essential. A. G. B. Fisher and Colin Clark suggested that an economy progressed through stages of development. As economies develop from their initial agricultural stage, per capita product goes up. industry grows and replaces agriculture as the dominant economic activity. Then, services replace industry as the most important sector. This description appears to have been roughly authenticated by the history of employment in the European high-income countries. However, this model cannot be taken as a reliable indicator of the pattern of development of later industrializing nations.

Reality is more complex. Studies have shown that the stages of development pattern of growth does not always hold true. Kuznets' and OECD studies do show that the share of agriculture falls and that of industry initially rises with increasing per capita GDP. However, the behavior of services is inconsistent. The share of the services sector rises at first when per capita GDP of less developed countries start to grow but

---

[2] Robert J. Gordon, for example, discovered that there are two substantive causes, beyond the probable measurement difficulties and errors, of the apparent productivity slowdown in services. The electric utilities and airlines, for example, appear to be approaching a technological frontier beyond which productivity growth slows. And, in the United States, weak unions, a falling real minimum wage, and immigration combine to keep wages in some service industries (like food retailing, restaurants) low and this encourages over-hiring compared to other industrial countries. [1996]

then levels off when countries begin to reach lower middle-income levels (US 1968$ 200-290). Very small countries or city-states (Singapore, Hong Kong, Malta, Kuwait) that specialized early in their development on services may have services sectors employing more than half of the population while still comparatively poor. [Blades 1974,137-8]

The Clark-Fisher model (of successive shift of employment over time from primary to secondary to tertiary) also did not hold true for the United States and Canada. In the United States and Canada there was a significant shift from primary directly to services. [Kuznets 1971,147] Similarly in the newly industrializing nations that go directly to the latest technology in manufacturing, the decline in farm labor is not mostly absorbed in manufacturing but instead in services. The more rapid urbanization in industrializing nations today also leads to a more rapid growth of services than was true of the present-day high income countries when they were industrializing. [Singelmann 1978,113-6]

To understand modern economies, theory should be able to explain why the services have grown the way they have. The service industries are so complex and composed of so many different types of activities that no single theory can account for all. The forces affecting government services, social services, and professionals generally are discussed in other chapters in this book. There are several other hypotheses that help explain to growth in the services in the modern economy.

Victor Fuchs, an outstanding pioneer in services economics, has pointed out that part of the growth in services employment is not real but only a statistical phenomenon. When a manufacturer contracts out services (such as cleaning, legal advice, security, data processing, advertising), which were previously performed in-house, the services sector as statistically measured increases—a lawyer is still giving legal advice but he is now counted in the service sector rather than in manufacturing.

While the statistics are now more accurate after this change, what is measured has also undergone an important qualitative change. The service is now coming through an external market. The manufacturing enterprise no longer has organizational responsibility for the future or for the treatment of the people involved. It is highly likely that the outside service will be provided at lower cost to the enterprise and may be of higher quality in relation to the cost. A high-wage or high-salary enterprise tends to pay its lesser skilled workers more than they would usually earn elsewhere. If the company out-sources such jobs to an outside service, even if the contractor is not more efficient, the company can reduce its costs without injuring its standing with its own staff. Lower costs for the service may mean that the demand for the service will be higher or if the need is invariable and the outside service is more efficient that the resulting employment is lower.

A second cause for the relatively faster growth of services is that some services have a demand income elasticity greater than one. Consequently, as real income per capita grows, these services grow faster than the proportional increase in income. Thus, with the growth of national income, services absorb a larger proportion of income and provide more employment. This hypothesis clearly applies to many services that are "superior goods". With higher incomes people shift from buying more material goods, the demand for which may be satiated, to consuming new services, such as recreation, legal, and even health. While we may switch to throw-away products in response to a rise in relative prices of maintenance and repair services we cannot switch to throw-away bodies in response to higher health costs. People are living longer. Very old people need more medical attention than younger people. For all these reasons, employment in and the prices of health services have risen more rapidly compared to material goods than most other miscellaneous services. [Linder 1970]

These reasons, however, do not account for all the rise in prices of health services. Health markets in medical care and hospital care are not competitive markets. This is at least in part because of guild-like behavior by doctors and because of a whole array of other institutional factors which are subject to change. Because output is measured in these services by its cost to consumers, a rise in price translates into a rise in measured output.

Higher per capita incomes may result in higher spending on educational services by some people because it is regarded as an investment. Some kinds of education are believed to increase earnings potential of the individual or are necessary to pass the credentials barrier to higher income jobs. This partly explains the growth in education services as per capita incomes increase. In general, an educated work-force raises the productivity of the entire economy. On the other hand, education may be regarded as a consumption good, i.e. it enriches enjoyment of life or makes people better citizens and parents but does not directly result in higher monetary income. Being able to afford this type of expenditure obviously is related to the level of income and will be more prevalent in higher income countries.

Another reason for the growth of employment in the services sector is based on the belief in a slower growth of productivity in services compared to productivity in material goods production. On the assumption that productivity in services truly does grow less rapidly, Baumol has produced a simple, important, "cost-disease" model to illustrate the dynamics of the growth of the service sector in an economy. [1967,1985, 17-19, 301-17; Saunders & Klau 1985, 92-3]

In the Baumol model. the economy is regarded as consisting of two sectors, sector "A" (e.g. material goods) in which productivity is growing and the other, sector "B" (e.g. services), in which productivity is not growing. It is then assumed that wages in sector A grow in line with the increase in productivity, and wages in B grow in line with the wages in sector A. Then, unit labor costs will remain constant in Sector A over time (as higher wages are offset by higher productivity). Unit labor costs will rise in sector B—wages rise in step with Sector A but productivity does not. If the ratio of real outputs between the sectors remained constant as the economy grew, then more and more of the labor force would have to transfer from Sector A to Sector B. Sector A's share of the rising output would be produced with a decreasing share in the total number of workers. Sector B would have a constantly growing share of the labor force while its share of total real output remained the same. The statistics, therefore, would show a decrease in productivity in the total economy and a slowing down of the economy's rate of growth.

The name, "cost-disease" model, is not completely appropriate. A more accurate name would be the "unbalanced-sector-productivity" model (USP). There is nothing unhealthy about the fact that because of inherent characteristics, productivity in one sector of the economy grows at a different rate than in another.

Productivity in some services cannot grow at all or only slowly compared to material goods output: some personal services are valued precisely because an individual is devoting his time to you. This is true, for example, in consulting your lawyer, your doctor or financial adviser. Similarly, the quality of restaurants, crime prevention, teaching, and social services to the poor, needy and mentally ill—in all these instances—is related to the amount of labor time spent on these services. While symphonies and operas can be recorded and reproduced there is a strict limit to how many violinists or tenors can be dispensed with and still have an acceptable performance. Services such as repair and maintenance are difficult or impossible to standardize completely.

But while it is true that productivity in some services grows more slowly than in material goods production, it is doubtful that productivity in the services as a whole has stagnated as much as the statistics indicate. A substantial portion of the gap may be more a statistical phenomenon than a real one. BLS data, for example, showed no increase in retailer productivity while stores were introducing computerized equipment that moves check-out lines faster, updates inventory information constantly, synchronizes supplier deliveries with actual needs, etc. The spread of computers, modems, office copiers, fax machines throughout the different services must have increased productivity in quality or quantity—otherwise the investment in these machines would not have been made. Revised BLS figures now take better account of these developments.

These hypotheses do not exhaust the list of broad forces affecting growth in services. The growth of population resulting in greater density of settlement, change in institutions and modern advances in technology often provide new opportunities for new services to arise. For example, the new widespread use of credit cards and the ability to use them in ordering merchandise by mail or phone led to a flowering of catalog firms offering a large variety of products. New firms are now selling over the internet. Many firms in new service industries are small, sometimes consisting only of the proprietor. They also typically use little capital per worker. This means that entry into most of these industries is relatively easy. And, consequently, these industries can rapidly respond to or pioneer in any change in tastes or new demands that can be met by such small enterprises. Many of these are also seen as a possible alternative to unemployment by workers who have lost their old jobs permanently in manufacturing.

Changes in social habits and in the culture of high income countries create and change services. With the movement of women out of the home into the paid labor force, unpaid services that they rendered before in the family now have to be provided through the money-nexus and entered into the economic calculus. In the nineteenth century, formal education of children in industrialized countries was largely moved out of the home and into schools. Now, day-care of younger children, and practically all the former women's chores are available as paid-services.

After World War II, people in all the high income countries began to retire from the active working force by age 65 or before. Retirees generally consume more services (travel, entertainment, medical services) and fewer material goods than active workers. The popular elder hostels and other senior learning centers for retired people are good examples of education as a consumption good and of services created specifically to meet the needs of retirees.

Other changes in social habits from greater wealth also lead to greater consumption of services. As people work fewer hours they engage in more leisure activities and require more service personnel to repair their domestic toys (VCRs, computers, power lawn mowers) as well as to help in landscaping and the garden.[3] As the average standard of living in the high income countries ensures satisfaction of basic physiological needs, a growing number of people scorn continuing to pile up material goods and instead turn to searching for a more spiritual or less-stressful life style. Such people may enter a services activity, such as social work, the ministry or even become members of a cult that provides the bare basics.

Economic Implications

The implication often drawn from the shift from industry to services is that decline or disappearance of manufacturing industries does not matter. This

---

[3]When we lived in Southern California, every Tuesday afternoon, a gardener came to water, clip and plant; on Wednesday, a specialist cleaned the swimming pool, tested and improved the chemical composition of the water; on Thursday morning, a housecleaning team did the whole house. A private security service regularly patrolled the neighborhood. Our son was transported to and from school by the bus that came by the house every day. Restaurant menus were kept by the phone to order meals to be home-delivered from our restaurant of choice. Parties at home could be organized, catered and cleaned up by specialist firms. Even school reunions, tracking down the people to be invited, running the festivities; the organizing of family finances, paying bills, etc could be done by specialist services. If one of the family had adjustment problems there were a multitude of eager counselors outside the home willing to give advice for pay.

reaction is based on the analogy that the earlier shift from agriculture to industry in an economy usually meant moving to a higher level of income. Consequently, it is taken for granted that this is the inevitable "creative destruction" of economic development. We do not really know the extent to which the growth of services depends on and contributes to the continued existence and prosperity of the manufacturing industries. If the manufacturing industries were to vanish many service activities would vanish with them. An OECD study found that on the average in the OECD countries a quarter of the GNP produced in the services is directly linked to goods-production. [Cohen & Zysman, 59; Blades 1987]

The earlier shift should not be misunderstood. In the process of economic development, agricultural output does not decrease, rather it increases, but productivity increases even faster. This usually results at first in a relative and eventually an absolute decline in the numbers of workers directly employed. Around 1900, while output continued to increase, the absolute number of workers in American agriculture began to fall. Most of the present American "farm population", although residing on "farms", earn the bulk of their income from non-farming occupations. The farmers who do earn most of their income from agriculture now number only a few hundred thousand and their incomes are above the average of non-farmers. [Gardner 1992, 81-2]

The shrinkage in farm employment has meant depopulation of parts of the United States. As farmers left, the towns serving and dependent upon them have dwindled and died, stores, banks and schools closed, doctors, lawyers, ministers left. In the South as the cotton-picking and other machines displaced share-croppers, millions of uneducated people left and moved to the cities, creating ghettos and the inner-city problems of today. Similar depopulation occurred in parts of the American Mid-west during the 1980s as industrial workers were displaced by new more effective machinery, or plants were closed by import competition.

But outside of agriculture proper there are a number of industries and services that directly depend on the continued existence and output of agriculture. The food-processing industries get their raw material from farming and are usually so time- or transport-cost-dependent that they can only exist in close relationship to farming output. The agricultural research, extension, education, trucking, finance, accounting, and other services all depend directly on the existence of agriculture.

The rising productivity in agriculture was an important force in stimulating these activities. The growth of the food-processing industries and the inputs suppliers such as the agricultural machinery, fertilizer, pesticide industries all depended on the vitality of agriculture. Similarly, there are large sectors of services that depend on the continued existence and vitality of manufacturing industries.

Because prices of services rise more rapidly than goods, when output is measured in constant dollars rather than current dollars the relative growth of the service sector is considerably slower. Calculating in current dollars, the share of services in U. S. personal consumption expenditures rose from 54 percent in 1987 to 60 percent in 2000. In chained 1996 dollars, the share remained constant at 58 percent. This also means that the relative contribution of services to the *real* national product grows less rapidly than the growth in its share of total employment.

It is more difficult to control price inflation in the services than in material commodities. With 1982-84=100, the consumer price index for urban consumers in December 1999 was 146 for commodities but 191 for services.

In view of the complex character of the services sector, generalization about the causes of this price behavior is somewhat dangerous. The differing price behavior among services results from different causes and each particular service activity would need to be analyzed separately—as is done in those sections of this book on the public sector and the nonprofits.

Probably one general cause is at work in those cases where the services purchased are complementary to material goods. In these cases, the good and the complementary services may be bundled in the buyer's mind as meeting a single purpose. If a firm has a truck for transport, the total cost of transport includes the cost of the truck and the cost of maintenance, gas, oil, etc. If the price of the truck drops while the cost of maintenance increases, with an unchanged total cost of transport, the increase in cost of services may have no or minimal effect on the decisions of the firm.

If demand is cut for material goods, inventories may pile up putting pressure on the enterprise to hold prices down or even to cut them. Services normally cannot be stockpiled and are not sensitive to this kind of pressure. They are also in the main not open to competition from imports. It may be more difficult to switch a supplier of a service than when buying a loaf of bread, for example. There may be a personal factor involved as in seeing your doctor or there may be more personal trouble involved as in moving your bank or brokerage account.

Because many services are nonstandardized and have a personal relationship component they are particularly open to being accompanied by "tips" or bribes. The US postal service has a rule forbidding the acceptance of gifts by postmen but your mailman expects and usually gets a Xmas gift from you. Even the woman who delivers my newspaper expects and gets a Xmas gift.

In some of the miscellaneous services, their special price and wage behavior may be due to the special characteristics of their labor market. There are the services, for example, that for historical and cultural reasons were largely dependent on female labor. The growth of demand for these services appears to have resulted in a demand for female labor greater than the increase in new supply. The unemployment rate of adult females, customarily above adult males, fell below the male rate during this period. As a result, wages of non-managerial service workers grew faster than wages in manufacturing (which largely employs males). Since the wage-level in manufacturing was considerably above that in most services, it was possible for wages in services to increase more rapidly without attracting much labor from manufacturing. [Rappoport 1987]

Colleges and universities have imposed steep price rises for tuition and room and board. Here, the strong demand for college education, particularly at prestigious academic institutions allowed them to take advantage of collecting quasi-rents.

In services that are complementary or substitutes to material goods, as the productivity in goods output rises more rapidly than in services, the price of a good may fall relatively to the price of its associated services. To cope, the rising relative cost of maintenance services, for example, may be avoided by producing throw-away commodities or by accepting lower standards of quality in maintenance. This is another part of the answer to the modern lament: "If we are a service economy, why can't I get any service?"

One of the few principles that economics has developed which has great value and is not easily perceived from plain common sense is the theory of comparative advantage. While the theory is applicable to all goods; this is not true of all services. Personal services and many leisure services cannot be internationally traded so the theory cannot apply.

Services are not just different from material goods; they have a different impact on the economy. The impact of changes on output caused by changes in demand for material goods may be magnified by changes in inventory. This inventory-caused intensification of changes in demand is absent from changes in demand for services. Services sectors do not show inventory cycles. Services, however, are not fully immune to the cycle, being affected not only by consumer but by producer spending. They are becoming somewhat more cyclical because industrial companies have farmed out jobs to service companies.

One consequence of all this is that employment tends to be more stable in the services sector. The post-World War II recessions in the United States have affected the industrial goods producing sectors only. During these recessions, employment dropped in the industrial goods sectors but continued to grow in services, as shown in Table 5.1.

Table 5.1 Percent Changes in Employment by Sector

Recession	Industrial-goods	Services
1957-58	-10	+1
1960-61	-06	+1
1969-70	-07	+3
1973-75	-12	+3
1981-82	-11	+1
1990-91	-07	+3

The result is, also, that the growth of the service economy has contributed, to a moderation of all the major fluctuations in the business cycle. [*Economic Report of the President* 2000, 76]

While the high-income services economies have become more stable, the less developed countries now carry more of the burden of the business cycle. These countries have always suffered from the greater volatility of prices of primary commodities compared to industrial prices and, most of the African countries still remain producers of such commodities. The industrializing Asian countries are becoming producers of the high selling-volume industrial goods for the world. While this is a step up, they are now still affected by the inventory business cycle from which the high-income countries have partly escaped.

A services-dominated economy may require changes in emphasis or different public policies than a goods-producing economy does. To improve productivity in manufacturing, measures to encourage investment in new and improved machinery, for example, are high on the list. To improve productivity in services, investment in human capital is all-important. For better productivity in the service industries. general education has to be improved and illiteracy eliminated, child care made available, and the tax laws and unemployment insurance reworked with the provision of retraining programs to increase the mobility, adaptability and willingness to learn of workers.

6 The Public Sector

In the long-run every Government is the exact symbol of its People, with their wisdom and unwisdom;... Like People like Government.— Thomas Carlyle.

In today's economies the influence of the state is pervasive throughout. The immense growth in the size and influence of government during the twentieth century is the most important development in modern economies. Unfortunately, economic theory has little explanatory power to account for this growth. Most economic theory

> ...treats government as a maximizing entity. Similar to private households, the public household is construed as choosing among allocative and distributive outcomes so as to maximize some utility function. ...Governance resides in the confrontation between a well-ordered utility function and a list of options and prices. Given information about the government's utility function and the constraints it faces, conditions for optimal fiscal conduct can be derived. [Wagner 1997, 160]

Neoclassical economic theory, as characterized in this quotation, is woefully inadequate—no government "well-ordered utility function exists", for starters. As Herbert Stein pointed out, economic theory largely overlooks or does not cope well in analyzing the causes—much more complex than the working out of individual maximization—that govern the size and the dynamics of the public sector. [1989] Theory emphasizes the role of the state as an instrument to cope with market failure. It is much more than that: recourse is necessary to a broader set of knowledge, as I will try to show.

Economics does not have a good measure of the real output of the public sector. The national accounts take the output of public services as being equivalent to the cost of inputs. (See discussion in preceding chapter.) The government is the major player in the market economy—as a buyer, seller, transfer-agent, regulator and stabilizer. Around a quarter to over a half of Gross Domestic Expenditure passes through government accounts. The United States is thought of as being an industrial country—but, there are more people employed in government than in manufacturing.

Government services appear to be a "superior good" with the volume rising more rapidly as a county's GDP grows over time. One in four workers is employed by the state in France, one is six in Britain, and one in seven in Germany and the United States.

In the European Union more than half of all adults get part or all of their income through the government. This comes in the form of salaries for civil servants, pensions for the aged, unemployment benefits for people out of work, etc. This probably means that two-thirds to three-quarters of all families have someone whose principal source of income comes from the state. Over two-fifths of American adults get their principal income through a government. Consequently, more than half of all families must have a family member receiving money from the state. [Rose 1985]

What is responsible for this growth and the wide extent of state power? More than narrow economic forces are at work– the influence of culture, attitudes toward income redistribution and taxes, history, and much else.

This chapter will first take a quick historical look at how we arrived at today's large role of the state. Then, we will consider the various theories that attempt to explain it and arrive at our own more inclusive model. Finally, since the story is incomplete without it, there is a section on the indispensable bureaucracy which defines, promotes, and runs the state.[1]

Historical Background

The role of governments has grown steadily over the modern era. As Europe emerged from the Middle Ages, a money economy began to appear. Government took over defense and law and order from the feudal lords. The king—no longer able to meet expenses from the produce of his own land—now had to resort to taxation. And, in response the private sector tried to control the public purse which extorts money from it. So began the evolution of popular government and democracy. [Break 1980; Musgrave 1980]

By the eighteenth century, the Physiocrats and Adam Smith agreed that governments should principally restrict themselves to the enforcement of peace and of justice, to defense against foreign enemies, and the provision of essential public works (that private enterprise would not or could not provide or that were for special reasons unsuitable to be left to private enterprise).

The Physiocrats and Smith overlooked another role of the state that was already evident in embryo in a few countries. That is, the state as an independent creative force. In Prussia, the state created the nation and united Germany. And then, it created the educational structure that sparked Germany's successful economy. The French king with his bureaucracy

---

[1] This chapter is not concerned with the theories of public investment—how the government allocates investment among competing public projects. There is a large developed body of theories on these subjects. I have already expressed my views in *Economics and the Real World*, Chapter 9, "Welfare Economics and Cost–Benefit Analysis".

created France and initiated the beginnings of French industrial development. Following on the Glorious Revolution of 1688, changes in the English legal system (on freedom of commercial enterprise, limited liability, bills of exchange) laid the groundwork for, and made the industrial revolution possible. [Kaldor 1996, 18]

When the United States came into existence, the role of the federal government was so minimal that it is hard for a modern mind to grasp. Fifteen years after the U. S. constitution providing for a federal government was written, only 291 people, including the president and the Chief Justice, were located in Washington. Less than 10,000 people were on the federal payroll. Of these, most were in the armed services. Of the 2,875 non-uniformed personnel, 79 percent were in the revenue-producing departments. Of course, state governments were responsible then for much of the little that was expected from government. [Young 1966, 28, 31]

As late as 1870, in the major industrial economies (Britain, Germany, the United States, and France) public expenditures averaged only around eight percent of GDP. The United States was the lowest at around four percent and France, the highest at around 13 percent. [Tanzi & Schuknecht 1995]

When World War I began, little more was expected from most governments than providing defense, law and order, public works and a stable currency. The state had, however, taken on the indispensable task of establishing the rules and context of economic activity and enforcing the property and contract laws needed for the private enterprise market economy. The Russian transition has highlighted the vital importance and the disastrous consequences when government fails in carrying out this vital responsibility.

With World War I and the Great Depression, government expenditures began to pass the 20 percent mark. Public expenditures grew rapidly everywhere as the high-income OECD[2] countries in the post-World War II period constructed or expanded new welfare-states. The growth in transfers after 1960 was almost explosive. From 1960 to 1980, government spending as percentage of GDP grew from 28 percent to 41 percent in the ten most important high income countries. Around 1980, the rate of growth slowed—but continued into the 1990s. The United States lagged in public expenditure growth in the seventies, advanced more rapidly during the 1980s Reagan era but is still the straggler among high income countries. In the OECD nations, government expenditures averaged, at the beginning

---

[2] The OECD (Organization for Economic Cooperation and Development) is the organization of the mainly high-income industrialized countries. It was established in 1961 as the successor to the Western European countries' coordinating organization of the Marshall Plan. As of 2001, its 29 members included, in Europe: Austria, Belgium, the Czech Republic, Denmark, Finland, France, Germany, Greece, Hungary, Iceland, the Irish Republic, Italy, Luxembourg, the Netherlands, Norway, Poland, Portugal, *Spain, Sweden, Switzerland, Turkey, the United Kingdom, and outside of Europe: Australia, Canada, Japan, Mexico, New Zealand, South Korea, United States.

of this century around 44 percent of GDP; the U. S., 30, and Britain, 40.

As a welcome but unplanned consequence of the growth in the share of government, the economy has become more stable: recessions have become less frequent and less severe and business expansions have become substantially longer. [Cohen and Follette 2000, 35; Blanchard 2000, 71]

Much of our present understanding of what belongs in the public sector was learned through hard experience that the private sector could not be trusted with certain activities; they had to be run by the state. There are also other functions that only a government can consider undertaking– the private sector is ruled out because of the time-frame, the risk, the magnitude, and the lack of any monetary payoff.

In England, for example, the government promulgated after 1660 a considerable body of regulatory legislation. But, this did not initially entail a corresponding growth in government. What we would now regard as governmental functions were "farmed", that is, contracted to private enterprise. The privately-owned Bank of England managed the public debt; private printers did government printing; some taxes were collected by private tax-farmers.

Army officers supplied the uniforms and food for their units; naval officers and crews were paid in part or whole from prize-money from captured ships. Prisons were run by businessmen getting their profits from sale of food and privileges to the prisoners. Officials of the mint refined and assayed precious metals for private customers. Queen Elizabeth's ambassador to the Ottoman Empire was appointed, paid, and his embassy maintained by the joint-stock Levant Company.

The administration of justice was left to local unprofessional officials who worked without pay or found ways of remunerating themselves through perquisites or opportunities for profit, legitimate or illegitimate. The streets were patrolled by privately-hired parish watchmen—old men given this employment to keep them fed.

The market was relied on to enforce law and order; a modern police force was not established until 1829. Economic incentives were employed directly. Vagrants and beggars were collared by local farmers and run out of the parish to hold down the "poor rates" or were put to work as forced labor on the farms. Volunteer informers were rewarded for denouncing criminals. Thief-takers earned money by tracking down and delivering criminals to the courts for trial. A remnant of this historical practice still exists in the United States—bounty-hunters pursue criminals who have fled after posting bond. [Hughes 1987, 26-7; Viner 1971, 51-52]

The most successful entrepreneur in this market attempt to control crime was Jonathan Wild who ran a profitable conglomerate. He recruited and trained thieves; set up a rental service in burglar's tools; and had his own sloop to transport goods abroad when necessary. He kept personnel files on the thieves. He negotiated with the original owner for the return of stolen goods for a price.

Wild was also a thief-taker; uncooperative thieves were delivered to the courts. If a large enough reward was placed on the head of a particular thief, Wild would turn him in. He had a flock of professional witnesses available to meet the demand for any testimony desired.

Wild was highly regarded by the magistrates. He helped convict thousands of thieves and claimed to have sent over 70 to the gallows. He lived well and was respected as an arm of the law. It was only in 1725 after Parliament passed a law making it a crime to accept a reward for restoring goods without prosecuting the thief that he, too, was sent to the gallows. [Hughes 1987, 613-4]

Today, to the modern mind, the maintenance of law and order appears a government function. This remains true even though in the United States and Britain nowadays, expenditures on private security measures exceed those on public police forces. These expenditures are regarded as an imposition resulting from *government-failure*.

Over a hundred years ago, Adolph Wagner pointed out that development of an industrialized economy would result in rising public expenditures. The costs of public administration, law and order, and of the needed regulation of economic activity would increase. Also, cultural and welfare activities provided by the government would grow more rapidly than income as they tended to have a positive income elasticity of demand. Activities which earlier, people could perform for themselves move into the public sector.[3]

In the process of modernization, as the market and its accompanying individualism, penetrates deeply into society, social cohesion weakens. Neighborhoods, extended family and clan ties, local communities, and other forms of social belonging have declined in importance. Problems that no longer can be handled within families, churches or other social organizations are passed on to the government to solve. That is, government is called on to make up for *societal failure*.

The increased complexity of industrialized economies depends on adequate transport and communications. These are, in differing degree at different times, natural monopolies. Consequently, in most industrialized economies governments own or regulate roads, railways and airways, own or regulate the communication systems.

---

[3] Living in a rural area of my town, like people a century earlier, we get water from our own well, dispose of our own refuse and wastes and, with our five neighbors, maintain our own private road. In other parts of the town, the higher population density has made private wells unsafe and the town has had to provide a public water supply and is beginning to make plans for a sewerage system. In much of the town, private roads have also become impracticable. With more people and more autos, the town has had to take responsibility for most of the roads in town. When many people live on a road or use it as a through road, cooperative maintenance becomes impossible. The need to be able to exercise the right of eminent domain and the natural monopoly characteristics of services like water supply and roads make government involvement inevitable.

In the nineteen-thirties the United States and other industrialized economies began to accept the revolutionary idea that the government should have an active role in trying to manage the economy. The hardships of the Great Depression threatened political stability and laissez-faire doctrine went out the window. The refusal of the Weimar Republic to abandon financial orthodoxy opened the road to power for Hitler.

After World War II, it became widely accepted that the state had some responsibility for the economy. How far the state would intervene varied from country to country—farthest in countries like France, Germany, and Japan with traditions of activist government. In these countries, the state had a long history of promoting certain economic activities, including the founding and managing of key industrial enterprises.[4]

Macroeconomics, (focusing on the role of government in utilizing fiscal, monetary, income or other policies to influence the behavior of the entire economy), essentially began with Keynes during the Great Depression. Since about the 1980s, various theorists have attempted to produce a "scientific" macroeconomic theory based on the same assumptions as those in the conventional microeconomic theory. Frank Hahn and Robert Solow have completely demolished this attempt in a masterly analysis. In sum, the theory is *...squarely based on perfect foresight, infinite time optimization, and universal perfect competition. ..., this is the economics of Dr. Pangloss, and it bears little relation to the world.* [1997, 2]

As Francis Bator has pointed out, the standard old-fashioned open economy variant of the Cambridge Massachusetts Keynesian model remains enormously useful. In other words, *The genius of macroeconomics consists of felicitous oversimplication, which is traded off for concrete conclusions that are much harder if not impossible to obtain from less simplified models.* The very fact that macroeconomic models tend to be rough and do not pretend to aspire to unattainable rigor is a strength that make it possible *...to derive concrete (if frequently controversial) conclusions.* [Baumol 2000, 11]

Government affects the size of and composition of investment and saving through its tax system and borrowing. Its tax and trade policies and regulations affect what consumers buy. It is involved in the health care of its citizens. It enforces the rules that make a free enterprise-contracting economy possible. Through tax policy and regulations it allocates economic benefits and creates the framework for corporate policy. Government social security and welfare systems redistribute income.

---

[4] The active role that government played in the early stages of economic development in the United States is often forgotten. From 1790 to about 1842, *...state governments took the active lead in promoting economic development through infrastructure investment and legal innovation to promote corporations and banks. From the 1840s on, local governments ...took over most of the important infrastructure investment in education, highways, water systems, sewer systems, and public utilities.* [Wallis 2000, 62]

In the knowledge-based economies of the twenty-first century, education and research are the twin engines of growth. And, government is crucial in both. It is next to impossible for an organization conducting basic research to profit from being able to keep fundamental findings its own property. Consequently, corporate-funded R&D concentrates on applied research and product development. Only government (or a giant monopoly like the former AT&T) can make the long-term commitment to basic research. The same is true of education.

Government plays a central role in maintaining the continued assent of the sovereign masses with their democratic egalitarian political ethic to the inegalitarian distribution of incomes and wealth resulting from the operation of the economy.

A growing public opinion is pressuring governments to take a moral responsibility to protect the environment. There is also a strong movement for government to conserve biodiversity: no existing species of life on earth must be knowingly allowed to perish. [Wilson 1992, 342]

Among the other important policy matters that governments are struggling with, sometimes only half-consciously, are questions like: how far do government responsibilities stretch for size-of-population planning, energy conservation, management of natural resources?

All these are government concerns in countries across the world.

The Welfare State

As early as the British Poor Law Act of 1388, local communities were required to help paupers. The Catholic Church, however, carried most of the burden. The sixteenth century Protestant Reformation confiscated the lands of the church and left the poor and homeless stranded. The state had to step in directly. The government of Queen Elizabeth I in 1601 introduced compulsory taxation to support the poor. In each parish, an annual vestry meeting elected an overseer to administer the law under the supervision of the local justice of the peace. [Persky 1997, 180]

With the coming of industrialization and the growth of cities, in the nineteenth century the state in all industrialized countries began to take some responsibility for education and public health. Like many public sector activities that are unquestionably accepted today, when public education was first proposed it was strongly resisted. It was clearly "socialistic" that the government should tax *me* to educate *your children*. Even as late as 1907, the artist, Degas, could comment to a young Russian woman,

> You too, you are going to corrupt your people now, by education, mademoiselle. It's Jews and Protestants who do that, who destroy whole races with education. Obligatory instruction—it's an infamy. [Extract from Harry Graf Kessler's diary, in Fenton 1996, 53]

Industrialized economies require a high level of literacy and of general and technical knowledge among the population. Consequently, nations now usually accept that the provision of the so-called *merit goods*, education and training, at the common expense is necessary. Education of children is made compulsory whether parents wish it or not. Similarly, a minimum level of public health is also seen as needed and public expenditures to control or eradicate disease, to improve sanitation become a part of the public sector. Housing is still at the margin: Some modern states intervene so that a minimum level of housing is assured to all however low their income may be: the sight of homeless people roaming the streets or sleeping in doorways makes compassionate people wince as well as making cities more unpleasant places to live.

Beginning with Bismarck, the political and social necessity began to be recognized for providing some refuge for people suffering from the harshness of the market. In 1883, Bismarckian Germany inaugurated the first social security program, beginning with a sickness insurance scheme, followed the next year by a work-injury program. Other social insurance programs were introduced in rapid succession by Germany and then by other industrialized countries. To provide some mitigation for people suffering from the fall-out of the operations of a market economy, a citizen is insured at least partially against: unemployment, disability, medical expenses, impoverishment in youth and middle age, and poverty in old age.

The fastest growing part of the public sector since World War II has been in the redistribution of income. There has been a general consensus since the Physiocrats and Adam Smith, that the state has a responsibility for administering *commutative* justice, that is, justice in relations between pairs of individuals. The unfettered free enterprise system resulted in enormous contrasts between the great wealth of a few and the hunger, squalor, and insecurity of the poor. In reaction against this, the great growth after World War II in the role of the state has come in the field of *distributive* justice, that is, in the intervention of the state to change an existing pattern of distribution of wealth or/and income.

In addition to providing collective consumption goods (defense, public safety, public administration, economic services) the modern state has thus become a welfare state, weaving a safety net for the unlucky or handicapped, providing merit goods (education, health), and redistributing income to prevent such inequalities of wealth that would offend the values of the society or threaten its stability.

For most of the centuries of Christendom, a woman could escape her prescribed social role by embracing chastity and assuming a new religious identity. With the coming of industrialization, machine power largely eliminated the need for brute strength in work and thus weakened the major physical advantage of men over women as workers. Since World War II, the development of and widespread use of contraceptives and the legal acceptance of abortion gave women the historic possibility of deciding on the control of the timing, or avoidance of pregnancy. This multiplied their opportunities for economic independence by earning income outside the home.

The new economic position of women is a historic change that is not yet fully comprehended or played out in results. Women have taken advantage of their new freedom to enter into the labor force en masse. In the industrial economies, the majority of women are now active workers.

The freedom and instability of free market capitalism are as a result mirrored in family relations. Traditional extended and nuclear families have severely dwindled in number through divorce; cohabiting unmarried couples and children born out of wedlock have become socially acceptable; millions of children are raised in single-parent families.

In the high income countries, women have opted for economic freedom by reducing the number of their children. By 2000, the birth rate in most of these countries dropped below the reproduction rate and, if this continues, national populations in a few years will start falling—plummeting in Italy, Spain, etc. The Italian and Japanese governments have taken some measures to try to reverse this trend—with little success so far—but, as of 2000, most countries have shown little awareness of the problem and even less desire to confront the prospect.

Sweden has gone farthest in helping mothers raise children. Local governments provide subsidized child care for preschool children, finance parental leave and parental insurance, and child and housing allowances. From 1963 to 1993 when Swedish women moved into the labor force, the whole increase in total employment was of women hired for local government jobs. Sweden, in effect, hired women to work together to look after their children. It provides an economic security floor for the family and children while accepting and encouraging the economic independence of women. The Swedish birth rate has also dropped below the reproduction rate though not as far as in other countries.

This Swedish approach entailed collecting the highest GDP percentage of tax revenues in the world. In the early 1990s, economic articles were characterizing Sweden as a failed economy but the Swedes were able to handle their then balance of payments and fiscal problems. By 2000, the rate of growth of Sweden's GDP was higher than any of the major countries in the European Union, it had low inflation and low interest rates, its unemployment was around half that of the EU's average, and it had one of the highest budget surpluses.

In the United States, there have been various approaches: some firms provide infant care centers and after-school activities for children of their employees. There are also various cooperative groups of parents that help one another in looking after children. Some churches also are helpful. With the high tax aversion of Americans, it is doubtful that the state will be able to provide the child services needed. Just as in the provision of health, reliance will have to be on the corporation to look after the families of its employees, voluntarily or under coercion. This approach, as in the case of health care, leaves a high percentage of people outside the system.

The most that can be said at this time is that the agenda on this social problem is still open. With the inequality of family incomes and wealth in the market economy, needs of children are likely to be adversely correlated with the resources of their parents. Single parents who need child care help most are likely to be in the bottom quintiles of the income distribution.

As a result of the welfare responsibilities that the modern state has assumed, transfer payments, the redistribution of income (subsidies, social security benefits, socialized medicine, negative income tax, etc.) generally total more than half of all public spending.

The conventional economic rationale for the welfare state is the one of externalities. The argument is that there are externalities associated with some "goods", that cannot be captured by a private provider or the recipient. For example, in the case of health insurance, an individual would like his associates not to contract a contagious disease but cannot pay for their health insurance. There is also the externality in all the aspects of the welfare state that society does not want to deny help completely to those with desperate need, even if they cannot pay for it.

A vital contribution of economics *qua economics* is to try to ensure that as far as possible economic incentives be used rather than direct administrative Diktats to achieve the desired ends; and to analyze objectively and to make clear what the purely economic costs and benefits of the redistributive programs are.

The welfare state and modern capitalism are Siamese twins. In feudal times, people knew where they belonged, their position in society might be lowly but it was as secure as it had been for their parents and grandparents before them. Capitalism brought in constant change and insecurity. The capitalistic market economy allows enterprises to fire workers, to restructure, downsize or reengineer firms, to abandon towns, regions or even countries that depend on them. To make the resulting insecurities socially and politically tolerable, there has to be some provision to blunt the sharp edges. *A major justification of the welfare state is that unfettered capitalism could never survive politically or socially without it.*

Regulation, Mandates

Government regulation of private enterprises is important to correct, to control, or to avoid what would otherwise be regarded as undesirable results of the market. It is a means of trying to secure a level playing field, to prevent ends being achieved by the exercise of power rather than by productive efficiency. Ideally, it guides the private sector's use of resources towards public ends. However, private objectives sometimes are also served. Regulation tries to control and guide change in the society and economy. Government regulations may represent indirect grants.

Building standards, food and drug regulations, financial market regulations, auto emission controls, safety standards for airplanes, fair housing rules, anti-monopoly laws, weights and packaging rules, etc., are intended to provide economic benefits to the economy as a whole or to different groups of people. Some of the costs of these benefits are borne out of general government revenues, some are borne by the economic activities affected and some are borne by the recipients of the benefits. There is no direct relationship between the benefit received by a recipient and the cost paid as there is in an exchange transaction.

The importance of regulation in the economy is difficult to quantify or even to roughly appraise. The first comprehensive report on the benefits and costs of U.S. federal regulations was compiled by the Office of Management and Budget in 1997. This initial attempt estimated that (in 1996 dollars) the total annual benefits of environmental and other social regulations came to around $300 billion and total costs were about $200 billion. Total annual costs of economic regulation were estimated at around $71 billion with no estimate being made of benefits.[5] These figures are, of course, very rough.[6] To get accurate figures of the costs and benefits of a regulation would entail being able to compare the situation with the regulation to the situation as it would be without the regulation. This is very difficult if not impossible in some cases. For instance, the loosening of the regulation of the Savings and Loan Associations (S&Ls) during the Reagan Administration eventually will cost the U. S. Treasury from the resulting widespread fraud and unwise investments around $500 billion. Nobody could have predicted this result.

Regulation of the financial markets was developed to try to ensure that the allocation of capital through the markets was safeguarded against predation. It turns out that regulation of the capital markets is a sine qua non for the effective functioning of a capitalistic economy—when it falls short as in the S&Ls, in the Russian capital markets, or the Asian banking sector, disaster results. As *Business Week* commented, *A modicum of government oversight is needed to referee markets and make sure they play by the rules.* [December 22, 1997, 110][7]

Environmental regulations are used for social ends and to override private profit considerations that allow pollution. Companies that are active in waste disposal and cleanup of pollution cooperate with environmental organizations to build public support for a cleaner

---

[5] In the United States, the Environmental Protection Agency estimated in 1990 that private firms, governmental agencies at all levels, and individuals spent $130 billion annually (over 2 percent of GDP) to comply with federal environmental regulations. Annual compliance expenditures for all federal regulations were estimated to be around $400 billion (well over 6 percent of GDP).[Portney 1994, 12]

[6] See Hahn, Robert W. (1998) for an analytic overview of this subject and report.

[7] Or as *The Economist* commented: "History is liberally dotted with crises caused by liberalizing finance without improving supervision" [October 30, 1999, "Killing Glass-Steagall", 19].

environment. In this case, the profit-seeking motive is harnessed to help achieve specific social ends.

Where there are significant externalities, regulation (or other government intervention such as tax or subsidy policy) may be necessary to ensure that the private calculus of the enterprise does not impose significant costs on the public that are not taken account of by the enterprise. In this, as in the public utility case while the simple economics of the marketplace have to be supplemented with public action, economics is able to provide a technique of analysis that provides a rough guide to policy action.

Government regulation by setting the rules for a market may make a major contribution to productivity. In 2000, Europe was way ahead of the United States in advanced wireless voice and data communication. The European countries had set a standard Unified Global System for Mobile Communications (GSM) thus making possible a continent-wide digital network. A single cell phone works from Iceland to Vladivostok and the Internet can be accessed everywhere Among other advantages for European economies, this created a huge base for European companies, Nokia and Ericsson. "By contrast, says Vodafone CEO Christopher C. Gent, the laissez-faire U. S. created 'a mess of standards' by letting multiple systems battle it out." [*Business Week*, February 8, 1999, 70, 130].

Private economic calculus often can enter into the government regulation of an industry or profession. Individuals or enterprises in the regulated activity use political power to capture or influence the regulating agency. If an industry is able to capture the control of governmental power to write rules for its industry it may be able to use it to curb competition, restrict entry of new competitors, provide a soft secure life for its members. Certainly at least a part of the resistance of the American airlines to deregulation of their industry was due to this set of motives. And, the enormous changes in relative positions of firms and the influx of new firms in the industry that resulted justified the apprehension of some of the firms.

If the general consensus in a country that the sustainable limits on how much of GDP can go through the public accounts have been reached, and private sector on its own cannot respond to a need, another approach is likely to taken. This, I call, the "Diocletian solution": faced with a somewhat similar impasse, the later Roman Emperors like Diocletian resorted to achieving public ends by imposing obligations on private organizations to meet societal needs. In the United States with the aversion to government, the Diocletian solution is an attractive alternative that the government resorts to.

The U. S. uses corporations to perform what are essentially public services. In the nineteenth century, before the corporate age, soldiers were armed by government arsenals and warships were built in government shipyards. Today, the armed services depend on corporations for their military equipment. Private firms are official inspectors of aircraft, military research is contracted out, most public research funds go to private corporations and institutions. Corporations collect the pay-as-you-go income taxes and Social Security taxes from their employees, follow the rules on employee retirement funds and health insurance, avoid government-banned discriminatory behavior towards their employees, clean up polluted sites, and follow other environmental rules. Banks are required to consider the interests of the community in their activities and their record is closely monitored by the government and by community groups.

Present Position

Now, at the beginning of the twenty-first century, in *addition* to all the historic roles of the state, there is fairly general, but not unanimous, agreement that governments should be held responsible for:

- intervening to correct market and societal failures;
- ensuring the provision of "essential services";
- protecting the public health;
- alleviating poverty;
- stabilizing and stimulating growth in the economy.

There is no general agreement that the state should actively intervene in the economy to promote or to guide economic development. A number of countries (Australia, Japan, South Korea, Taiwan, Singapore, and almost all the most recent industrializing countries), however, do regard this as a central task of government.

In the United States, the consensus is barely that government management of the economy should include the use of monetary policy, and to a lesser extent possibly fiscal policy, to try to moderate the business cycle. This ignores the fact that U. S. government actions have had a decisive effect in shaping the economy—from fostering nineteenth century canal and railway building and the creation of the land grant colleges, to research support of the present-day high- and bio-tech sectors.

A looming major problem for all the high income countries is the aging of the population. The rising productivity of the economy should easily support a growing proportion of elderly in this century, particularly since this is largely offset by a diminishing proportion of children. The real problem is not economic but fiscal: retirees in most of the high-income countries are supported in most part or wholly by tax income transfers from the active population. Social security pensions in the OECD countries range from 12 to 25 percent of GDP. Increasing this cost substantially in most countries runs into actual or assumed limits on the amount of GDP that can pass through government accounts without impairing efficiency, straining public tolerance or undermining personal responsibility.

Theories of the Public Sector

Almost from the beginning of civilization there have been theories attempting to explain or justify why governments do what they do.

This brief historical summary and the variations in the character and content of the public sector in different countries suggests that the accidents of history and of culture have a considerable influence on the role and scope of government. Accepting these noneconomic influences as omnipresent, there are several classes of explanations for the extent and growth of the public sector.

In the private sector, individuals act to achieve their purposes and aspirations through the market or through voluntary organized cooperation—in the civil society. But some human purposes and aspirations require the use of collective coercion, that is, the action of government. While coercion is the bedrock sanction of government, it is less costly and more socially effective if citizens obey voluntarily. In Lenin's brutal phrase, the state is both hangman and priest. Coercion is intrinsically undesirable but there are other evils that are greater or there are goals so desirable that resort to the state appears justifiable.

The central question is: why has society resorted increasingly to the coercive/persuasive machinery of government for meeting its needs?

The usual economic explanation for the role of government is the need to deal with "failures" of the Market. While we are said to live in a "market economy" there are large areas of human activity where experience has shown reliance on markets would be unsatisfactory and the public sector is instead the instrument of choice.

This is true for "public goods", for example. In these cases relying on individual pursuit of rational self-interest does not lead to the most efficient allocation of scarce resources. A "public good" is a commodity or service which if supplied to one person is available to others at no extra cost. (In economic jargon, such goods are characterized by "non-excludability" and "non-rivalrous consumption".) Examples of public goods are national defense, environmental protection, street lighting. In the pure case, the public good has the characteristic that the producer cannot prevent anyone from consuming it. In this case, private markets cannot operate at all. In the opposite case of a "private good", with which most of economic theory is concerned, if it is consumed by one person it cannot be consumed by anyone else.

Even if it were possible, charging a price for a public good would not be efficient. This would discourage some consumption. But additional consumption does not impose any costs so there would be a net loss of welfare, satisfaction or utility. Consequently, public goods are usually provided through governments and paid for by taxation.

Such goods sometimes are provided through the free association of individuals assessing themselves to provide the good. The difficulty here, of course, is that an individual who pursues his own self-interest may attempt to free-ride and contribute less than his share. When the number of people is small, social pressure is usually effective in stopping free-riders.

Public goods are vitally important in modern economies. The very *existence* of a private well-functioning market sector depends on them. A legal system favorable to private property and enforcing contracts; a monetary system, reasonably stable and facilitating transactions; personal security, maintained through law and order; excellent communications, roads, railroad or airways with reliable telecommunications—all these public goods provide the needed base for a private free-market economy to function.

The discussion so far reveals a cultural bias. It assumes that public sector activities can only be justified to cope with the failures or vices of an unfettered private market system. It is scarcely too strong to state that the public sector is regarded an aberration from the unfortunately unrealizable pure market system that should absorb all activities of all human beings.

In the early 1990s in the former Communist-controlled countries, it was only after experience had shown unsatisfactory performance in the public sector that recourse was had to the market. The market, from this perspective, is a way of coping with failures of the public sector.

Two Systems—Government and Markets

Regarding government as a means of coping with market-failure and the mirror-opposite approach of regarding markets as a means of coping with government-failure are both flawed. Each mistakenly assumes that the whole of society and the economy should be organized on a single, unique basis. It is like lumping the genders together and classifying everybody as females and failed-females or as males and failed-males. It is similarly mistaken to lump government and markets into the same logical basket and to expect a single system of economic motivation, morality and ethics to apply to both.

In one of her illuminating books, Jane Jacobs argues that there are *two* legitimate systems of morals and values: one for government and one for the private economy. The ethics of public service differ from the private emphasis on the "bottom line". The ethos of public bureaucracy are loyalty, hierarchy, tradition and tenure. Business relies on underlying commercial norms such as honesty, industriousness, and efficiency while the dominant theme is insecurity, change, and "looking out for number one". [Jacobs 1992]

Although Jacobs sharply demarcates the two systems of ethics for government and business. the division is not always a sharp line. Corporations historically originated as governmental bodies and even though they are now dominantly private, a residue of the public ethical system still clings to them. Directors, for example, legally owe duties of "care" and "loyalty" to their corporations and to their shareholders. Corporate loyalty is also expected of employees, even if in specific cases, everyone knows it is mere hypocrisy.

When the difference between government and market is not under stood and institutions or people try to apply the values from one sphere in the other, the result is failure or disaster. Government-run businesses tend to "bog down in waste, inefficiency, and disappointed hopes". And, businessmen in government almost invariably fail or fall short of the ethical standards expected of government officials.

A major systemic difference between the private economy and the government is in the determinants affecting decisions of individuals and of governments *qua* governments. There is an obvious divergence between private risks and social risks and between the rates at which governments and at which mortals discount the future. *Time horizons* of individuals and of governments fundamentally differ.

Individuals themselves have varying spans of time in making the various decisions that affect their own personal futures. These relevant time-periods vary among cultures, among individuals, and even for individuals at different times in their lives. Very young children find it hard to postpone a gratification until tomorrow. It is conventional wisdom that American corporate managers focus on quarterly results rather than on long-time market share as Japanese executives are said to do. Successful feudal families and royal dynasties had a time-horizon over generations as they managed the marriages of successive heirs to build their estates or the size of their royal domain over a century or two. This is how the Hapsburgs built their vast empire. In modern times, a few banking families like the Rothschilds and the Warburgs appear to have been similarly far-sighted. Some wealthy individuals today try to manage their estates to protect the interests of their children, grandchildren and great-grandchildren. But for most of us trying to get through the day, week, or year is as far as we can stretch.

Unlike individuals, the interests of the state and the society have an infinite time-horizon (although a particular government may also be deeply concerned with the next election). Government leaders, civil servants, citizens, have to believe that the nation sees no end to its future. This is why there is no economic calculus in determining the effort required for national defense. Policy-makers can calculate the cost-effectiveness of various alternatives of expending resources but not the option of whether the nation shall live or survive.

National defense, furthermore, is a clear application of the paradigm of the existence of two-differently organized and motivated spheres of human action.. Some Renaissance Italian city states hired mercenary *condottieri* for their defense. A *condottiere* felt that money was not a sufficient reward for dying. Ferocious in appearance, they were super-cautious in combat. In one notorious day-long battle, the only casualty was a condottiere— who fell off his horse and smothered in his heavy armor in the summer heat. The risks often were less and the returns higher from plundering the city the condottiere was hired to protect: Sforza took Milan permanently for himself.

Although as late as the American Civil War, privateers were still used in naval warfare. the easy slide from privateer to pirate helped to convince most governments that it was wrong to rely on market incentives for the defense of the nation.[8]

Modern states devote a great deal of care to training their military leaders in special service academies in which the emphasis is on inculcating loyalty, integrity and honor and on weakening any inclination for rational calculating pecuniary self-interest. Indoctrination at the American Naval Academy at Annapolis, for example, is directed to convince midshipmen that they have become part of something greater than themselves, that they have an obligation to the nation: it is their duty to place the accomplishment of assigned tasks before the needs, considerations, or advancement of any other ideal, organization or individual. [Maruna 1994, 36]

Where, as in new nation-states of Africa, this indoctrination in public sector ethics is inadequate, market motives take over and the country is plagued by military coups and corrupt military rulers.

Unlike government enterprises in some countries that are profitable ventures, American government enterprises usually run at a loss and are subsidized with tax revenues. Whenever the government does happen to possess a profitable enterprise (e.g. Conrail—the railway the government organized from the debris of the failed private railroads of the northeast), it is immediately privatized. When private capital fails at running an activity that is politically or economically too important to be allowed to perish, e.g. Amtrak and urban mass transit, the loss-making company is dumped on to the public exchequer.

Economics does provide a useful technique, cost-benefit analysis, in evaluating different investment projects within the same sector, e.g. among irrigation projects. It is inadequate for evaluations across sectors. The externalities of a factory and of a school are so different and so difficult to weigh that a choice between them, if one has to be made, may in the last analysis fundamentally depend on value judgments. [See Kamarck 1983]

Unless the infinite time-horizon of the state is applied, there is no economic case for educating children. In terms of the usual time-calculus and the usual range of interest rates used, the present value of any investment that has a pay-off beyond ten years is minuscule. Nowadays, however, nearly everywhere, it is agreed that education of children has an

---

[8] In recent years, in the failed African states, mercenaries have come into their own again. Sierra Leone, Angola, Democratic Republic of Congo, have all used foreign mercenary soldiers in civil warfare. Mali uses mercenaries to train its army. In Sudan and Somalia, mercenaries were retained by government or private interests to guard key installations or operations.

enormous economic payoff for the country and the economy. The same is true of much basic research and government investment in infrastructure.

Somewhat similar logic applies in some environmental matters. The normal economic calculus cannot cope when no useful cost-estimate can be made of the loss of a resource like the ozone layer for which there is no substitute. Weighing future costs and benefits with any acceptable discount rate fails to provide a clear result when the decision today will affect countless generations in the indefinite future and the pecuniary-measurable costs and benefits may be swamped by unmeasurable non-pecuniary costs and benefits.

What price can you put on reserving dolphins? There is no market for "existence value"—the pleasure people get from the knowledge that rare species, beautiful natural environments exist, even if they do not expect personally to see or visit them.[9]

The point is clear: it is a mistake to regard the core of government activities as merely an offset to market-failure; government is a fundamentally different logical category.

Public Spirit, Public Service

As long ago as the *Iliad*, the hero Sarpedon described the duty of leaders to the community: *Because we are the privileged, we must fight in the front rank, and kill or be killed.* Cicero argued that political power promotes the realization of the highest human good since governing for the benefit of the ruled develops the exercise of the virtues of justice and wisdom. This implies that governments use whatever policy instruments they have available, including taxation, public expenditures, public enterprise, etc. towards achieving the end of optimal public welfare. Devoted public service was common in the Roman Republic and in the early Roman Empire as the correspondence of the younger Pliny, for example, testifies. It must have been an important motive for the mandarins for much of the thousands-year old Chinese Empire. And it is generally the rule in the high-income advanced democracies of today.

Translating the Ciceronian theory into modern economic jargon: in

---

[9] "Contingent valuation" is a method used in an attempt to cope with the absence of markets An appropriate sample of people are asked what they would be willing to pay for the continued existence of a benefit or what they would accept in compensation for its loss. The technique gets its name from the fact that the values secured from the respondents are contingent upon the simulated or imaginary market that they are presented with. When such surveys are well done, with economists drawing on skills of related social sciences such as survey research specialists, cognitive psychologists, etc., the experience has been that the results do provide significant information on the nature, depth and economic significance of the contingent values. [See Portney, Hanemann, and a dissenting view by Diamond & Hausman 1994]

making policy decisions and in administration, the government—a unitary entity—maximizes a welfare function in which the arguments are economic objectives such as price, economic stability, and/or growth. The government—assumed to be wise, impartial and objective—ascertains the national welfare function, identifies the tradeoffs, identifies the dependent variables, and subject to the known boundary conditions and constraints, finds the policy measures that will maximize the welfare. The theory of optimal taxation fits in this by determining the minimal social loss brought about by tax distortions given the exogenously determined tax collection.

One difficulty with this Ciceronian approach is that it is not computable when transmuted into modern neoclassical theory. As Kenneth Arrow has shown, a social welfare function based on individual preferences cannot be calculated.[10] Governments and the public can aspire to achieve optimal public welfare but there is no mathematical logic—if the basic axioms of neoclassical economics are accepted—that can identify precisely what it is and if it has been achieved. For judgments to be made as to what will contribute to improving the social welfare it is necessary to make inter-personal comparisons—which modern conventional economics rules out. The difficulty is that it is not possible to ascertain whether the *psychic benefits* experienced by one individual are greater or less than that of another.

Conventional economics does recognize that government action to improve social welfare might be justified in circumstances where "Pareto-improvements" can be made. The argument goes as follows: The market theoretically produces efficient outcomes (assuming that the standard of ethics has no problem with unequal distribution of incomes and assets), so any governmental action will make somebody worse off. However, in the real world, with externalities, imperfect information, incomplete markets—the economy will not be Pareto-efficient and there can be some intervention, a "Pareto-improvement", by which the government can make some people better off without making anyone worse off.[11]

There are very few actions that meet this strict standard; most government interventions will help some people and hurt some other people. Even if everyone, except a narrowly defined special interest, could be shown to benefit, the theory would not sanction that a change should be made unless some way were found to pay acceptable compensation to persons adversely affected.

---

[10] Arrow's social welfare function is a functional relation that specifies a social ordering *R* over all the social states for every set of individual preference orderings. It is subject to a set of criteria such as that it must have a universal domain (i.e. cover every possible combination of individual preferences), have independence of irrelevant alternatives (the social choice made from a group of alternatives depends only on those alternatives not on others which are not available and not relevant), apply the Pareto principle (if everybody prefers A to B then A is ranked above B), and there is non-dictatorship (no individual should have decisive say). [See Arrow 1951 and Sen 1995]

[11] See Greenwald and Stiglitz 1986, Stiglitz 1998 for fuller exposition of this.

As the final section of this chapter will discuss, there is a satisfactory way out of this dead-end and one which empirical economists and the great economists of the past have taken.

Economics conventionally tries to understand human phenomena by focusing on the behavior of the *individual as an autonomous unit*. In the other social sciences, historians, sociologists, political scientists, and anthropologists, all learn that you cannot systematically ignore all social formations larger than the nuclear family.

For an economy and society to function effectively, there must be a basic minimum of feeling of community to confer legitimacy and to maintain some minimum of trust among the participants. With the great complexity of economic life and the large population numbers in most industrialized states, the willingness of citizens to pay taxes is strongly influenced by the strength of their feeling of community. Compared to even 50 years ago the nature of services now provided by the US government, for example, is more remote for the average American than it used to be. The basic research on diseases and the social and physical sciences now financed by the federal government, the subsidies to the arts, are much less evident to the citizen than the few public works of dredging ports and controlling rivers that the government was largely occupied with in the 1920s. Since reminding people that they are members of a community is easiest through evoking nationalistic themes, spending more on defense even at the cost of higher taxes is, perhaps, the only way that taxation can be popular politics.

A people may have goals that only the government can attain. Aristotle went so far as to assert, ...*the state is by nature clearly prior to the family and to the individual, since the whole is of necessity prior to the part.* As the widespread phenomenon of nationalism testifies, there are human needs which membership in a national community fulfills. Human beings have or seek membership in collective identities. People in any collectivity normally look to the head of it for leadership or guidance. This is also usually true of citizens vis-a-vis their national government. A person seeking an executive political office is more electable if the voters believe that the candidate has leadership qualities. The presidents of the United States ranking high in history and esteem are the ones regarded as strong leaders who were successful in accomplishing national goals.

Neoclassical theory conceives of the state as a kind of instrument of the market—the state is acting properly when it fills in to do what the market fails at. The reverse is often true: the state may use the market as an instrument of state action in attaining its goals. When an agricultural nation is determined to industrialize, the government is often relied on to bring about the desired change. Asian countries, led by a Confucian ethic, expect their governments to lead in bringing about economic growth.

Meiji Japan is one notable example. Singapore and South Korea are more modern instances. The first Korean pioneering producers of fertilizers, petrochemicals and refined petroleum products were public enterprises. The first integrated steel mill, one of the most efficient in the world, was also government-owned. These enterprises, started in part because of the absence of any willing private investors, were expected to, and did, achieve international competitiveness quickly. The government also intervened to create, encourage, and mold private enterprises (like the *chaebol,* Daewoo, Hyundae, Samsung*)* to implement the government drive for industrialization. The dynamic selective intervention undertaken by government in Japan and Korea in their forced marches to development was a role that could not have been played by the market on its own. [Westphal 1990] Similarly, in Taiwan, to get growth the government encouraged a multitude of small firms using competitive market forces.

The economic history of the continental European countries also demonstrates that the modern economy is highly indebted to this kind of independent initiative by the government. Aside from Great Britain, the railway infrastructure, for example, on which industrialization was based in most countries during the nineteenth century was financed directly or subsidized by governments.

The government contribution to American economic development has also been huge. The Erie Canal built by New York in the 1820's connected the port of New York City with the Great Lakes and the Mid-West. This opened eastern and European markets to the farm exports of the Great Lakes regions, lowered food prices in Europe, helped induce the repeal of the Corn Laws in Great Britain, established New York City's commercial and financial dominance, fostered immigration to the Old Northwest, and promoted economic development of the whole region. The intercontinental railways were all subsidized by the federal government. The Morrill Act of 1862 provided land grants to found some 70 universities across the United States. The vast Interstate Highway System in the United States initiated by the Eisenhower administration had, like the earlier railroads, enormous economic results.

All of the present-day important American high technology industries were spawned, and nourished by government action. The military induced and encouraged the development of the modern jet aircraft and sustained a pool of specialized engineers and skilled workers that enabled the United States to nearly dominate the the world aircraft industry. The only significant competitor, Airbus, was created, organized and financed by European governments.

The first large digital computer was built under contract to the U. S. Army and most of the early engineering development of computing machines was done by firms with strong government connections. As late as 1954, the International Business Machines Corporation (IBM) was still debating internally whether to get out of the computer business altogether for lack of sufficient opportunities to make money. Perhaps only the Air Force's contract for its SAGE (Semi-automatic Ground Environment) air defense system kept IBM in, for during the 1950s, more than half of IBM's domestic computing revenues came from its SAGE contract and some work on B-52 bombers..

The Kennedy administration's commitment to the space race led, by a series of fairly direct steps, to the rise of the semiconductor industry. [Warsh, 1984, 182-183]

The present American lead in biotechnology is due to the National Institutes of Health which have spawned a whole new industry of profitable firms. The National Institutes employ 13,000 scientists and with their budget of around $18 billion in 2000 are world leaders in financing basic biomedical research.

As for the high tech industries, Newt Gingrich, the conservative Republican speaker of the House of Representatives, stated flatly:

> In the development of the high-tech world the role of government...has been vital. The modern entrepreneur of Silicon Valley is creating an entirely new economy based on the scientific advances of three generations of government-funded research and development. The Internet itself is an example of government-funded research providing a platform upon which entrepreneurial success has been build. [1999, A19]

Peter Lynch (the investment guru of Fidelity Investments, one of the largest pools of investment capital in the world) has noted that the driving force of the American economy is the heavy federal spending on basic medical and science research:

> By the end of the 1990s, America will have added 17 million new jobs while the European Union, with one third more population will have added none. We have the same savings rate, the same education levels and it's not that we're smarter; our advantage is that America makes the investment in basic science.[Hunt 1999, A13]

In all these instances, the government acts to achieve a public interest. The market is used as a *means* not an *end*. This is a major qualitative difference. When the market is employed as an instrument of government policy, pure market economic analysis overlooks the major factor at play.

Public Choice

St. Augustine proposed an alternative theory to that of Cicero. Governing is not for the benefit of the ruled; rather, stemming from Original Sin, people desire to have power over others, not to serve the others, but to feed their own pride and vanity. [Weithman 1989, 61]

The modern version of the Augustinian theory, which also harmonizes with the fundamental selfishness assumption of conventional economics, is represented by the theory of "Public Choice". This regards the public sector as being like a private market with competitive bidding for the citizen's vote—just as businesses compete for the consumer's dollar. Governments are part of the institutional complex through which individuals seek to satisfy their individual wants. [Frey 1982, 45-9; Buchanan 1986, 1987; Romer 1988; Sandmo 1990; Rowley 1993]

According to the Public Choice theory, government behavior is taken as consistent with and analyzed on substantially the same basis as behavior in the economy. The basic unit of analysis is the individual who is primarily and rationally interested in maximizing his own utility function, subject to any outside constraints such as his income, time, and existing institutions. The behavior of everybody in the economy and in politics is explained by the same model: a person is motivated by the same set of purposes in the market, in the voting booth, and in the government.

Governmental action is seen as the resultant of pressures from politically–powerful individuals, interest groups, and corporations—all trying to secure unearned and undeserved advantages outside of the market. (This suggests that government is part of the Predator and Parasite sector of the economy.)

As usual, one can find that Adam Smith was aware of this possibility. He restricted it, however, to what he regarded as the pernicious influence from *business people* on government:

> The interest of the dealers, ...in any particular branch of trade or manufactures, is always in some respects different from, and even opposite to, that of the public. The proposal of any new law or regulation of commerce which comes from this order, ought always to be listened to with great precaution, and ought never to be adopted till after having been long and carefully examined, not only with the most scrupulous, but with the most suspicious attention. It comes from an order of men, whose interest is never exactly the same with that of the public, who have generally an interest to deceive and even to oppress the public, and who accordingly have, upon many occasions, both deceived and oppressed it.. [250]

The Public Choice theorists are right, of course, that political and economic interest groups do attempt to influence government. The result often may be a policy that varies greatly from any material welfare optimum. In Buchanan's words, *Public choice theory explains and interprets politics as the interaction among constituents and agents seeking to advance or to express their own interests.* [1987 "Tax Reform...", 29] It assumes that all concerned are driven by selfish motives all the time; that everyone is motivated entirely by selfish self-interest. The voter has a demand for certain services and commodities produced by the public sector. Through voting behavior, joining interest groups or political parties he tries to maximize his utilities produced by government. The supply of public sector output is the result of the utility maximizing of the politicians, government servants and bureaucrats.

The theory refuses to consider that any one in government might be motivated by any ideal of public service or professional ethics. In Buchanan's cynical view,

> Political agents seek to maximize their rents, subject to the general legal constraints against corruption, and to the temporal and survival constraints imposed by the electoral and institution structure. [op. cit.33][12]

Certainly, Public Choice gives an accurate portrayal of government at some times and some places and to some degree. But it does not universally hold true.

King Charles I may have lost his head because he believed in a Public Choice theory. In the summer of 1647, the King had discussions with Cromwell and other Army leaders in an attempt to negotiate a settlement to the Civil War. The attempt failed because the King was unable to come to an understanding with the Puritan officers. He told his confidential servant that he found it hard to trust them since none of the officers had asked for anything for themselves! He could not conceive that they could be acting out of public spirit and trying to reach an agreement in what they believed to be in the country's interest. [Fraser, 241]

One can certainly cite instances where government officials appear to be motivated by their own economic gain. Here is the description of a fund-raiser for South Dakota Senator Pressler held in Boston, Massachusetts in December 1995. Senator Dole, the future 1996 Republican Presidential candidate, introduces Senator Pressler to the assembled contributors:

> "I want to say just one word about Senator Pressler. He's running for reelection in '96—he takes money," Dole says, punching home the word as the audience laughs. "He takes checks." They laugh again. "It's legal in South Dakota to take money out of Massachusetts. Well, let me tell you something about Senator Pressler," Dole adds,... "There are probably a lot of people here interested in the telecommunications bill—it's the best thing that we've done all year as far as the future's concerned in technology and jobs," says Dole." ...And the chairman of that committee," Dole explains, as around the room ears perk up, "and

---

[12] When pressed, Public Choice theorists may deny that they really accept this narrow view of the motivations of public servants and voters, arguing that the assumption of self-interest is only adopted for methodological convenience. This would be more convincing if, then, at some point in the exposition there were analyses of the results of bringing in more realistic assumptions of human behavior.

the one leading the effort right now on a day-to-day basis, has been Senator Larry Pressler from South Dakota. Larry, thank you very much," Dole concludes with a bang, the auctioneer's gavel coming down one last time—Senator Larry Pressler! Sold to the man with the whales on his tie. [Samuels 1996, 51]

Perhaps not incidentally, both Pressler and Dole were defeated in the November 1996 elections.

Governments such as Mobutu's in Zaire and Marcos' in the Philippines could be classified as kleptocracies. Nicaragua was run by Somoza as though it were a privately-owned plantation. Power rather than economic gain appeared to be the driving force for Saddam Hussein in Iraq and Assad in Syria. These two countries are police-states, controlled by terror with the main objective of maintaining the dictator in power.

The Public Choice school deserves credit for trying to broaden the dimensions of economics. It recognizes the impact of power and of interest groups in shaping and influencing the course of the economy. While the Public Choice theorists believe in the market they refuse to accept that the results of a market-economy are always best. And, they recognize that people may pursue their ends through predation.

But the Public Choice extreme is not always characteristic of governments and peoples and certainly not universally true of the democracies. Public Choice theory is worse than being merely wrong. In its application to democracies, it is a corrosive doctrine that undermines democracy and good government.

Where the theory falls short is in accepting conventional economics' narrow view of human nature, that is, that humans are only egotistic, rational maximizers. Whereas in reality, people are complex, multidimensional, driven by different motives in different times and places, and imperfectly rational. Voters, pressure groups, governmental authorities and civil servants may be motivated to make decisions to promote social or economic goals for the general welfare as they conceive it. In particular, professionals in government service, influenced by their professional ethics and professional pride (whether or not devoted to Public Good), often try to do the best job they can—engineers to build excellent roads, doctors to further public health, economists to make good economic policy decisions.[13] Even though Pepys enriched himself through corruption while in the service of the English monarchy, he had enough pride in his work to have created an effective support department for the Royal Navy.

Public Choice theory resembles the Marxist theory of the state. They differ in that Public Choice uses the individual as the unit and Marx used class. For Marx, the political struggles for possession of the power of

[13] Note that Joseph Stiglitz in reporting on his experience as a member of the Council of Economic Advisers concentrates on what was accomplished in securing improvements in policy. [1998]

the state were struggles over the control of the means of surplus appropriation. The state was a economic resource for the bourgeoisie or the nobility. Both the Marxist and Public Choice theories are based on the assumption that the economic selfish motive is dominant.

Both the Marxist and Public Choice theories are too simplistic. The modern democratic state is not the executive committee of a ruling class and people act in politics for sets of motives that are much more complex than the universal pure utility maximizing assumption of the Public Choice theory. An individual may have different motives, different norms, different patterns of behavior, in different social circumstances—at work, at home, in a social club, in church, driving an automobile in traffic. Voters are not always simply following their perceptions of their own selfish interest in making their decisions. Some genuinely do try to vote to promote wider social or national ends. Other voters are influenced by family traditions of party membership, their perceptions of the character of a candidate, the personal charm or charisma of a candidate, etc, as well as personal economic interest. The various influences in play often may induce a voter to vote against his clearly-perceived own economic interest.

Finally, one can get the full flavor of the narrow viewpoint of Public Choice theory through analogy: A similar "Academic Choice Theory" could claim to explain that professors of economics try to maximize their fortunes by developing theories to please wealthy people who want lower taxes, less governmental regulation of corporations. If successful in producing such desired theories, a professor is rewarded by getting a high-salary chair created for him, by having his salary subsidized by corporate contributions, by having a university center created and financed for him by corporations, by receiving generous honoraria for talks to business conferences, by selling high-priced subscriptions to his economic news letter, etc. There are examples that fit this description but it is clearly false to believe that such a theory describes the economics professoriat. In fact, for generations economists have repudiated just such a criticism. [Kinsley 1986]

Both Public Service and Public Choice theories claim the ability to explain everything in government on the basis of a fundamental assumption that human behavior in government is driven by only a single motive. They dramatically differ on the motive but agree that there is only one motive to be considered. Each excludes all behavior based on irrational factors such as individual and group loyalty, passions, hatred, prejudices, ethics, professional pride, morals, religion. Each can point to concrete examples but, these like the description of the elephant by the six blind men each touching different parts of the elephant, do not correctly depict the whole.

I learned over and over in working with governments around the globe that policies are driven by many purposes and affected by many different cross-currents. Selfless wisdom, the ideal of service, professional pride, economic self-interest—are only a few of the factors involved.

Nationalism, for example, often trumps economic self-interest. Before the flood-tide of African independence in the early 1960s, the British had established the Federation of Rhodesia and Nyasaland in Central Africa. The economic case for maintaining the federation was strong; the nationalistic feelings of independent Northern Rhodesia and independent Nyasaland were stronger and the federation was destroyed. In East Africa, the British had established a set of well-run, useful and economically-logical regional entities: a currency board, a university, an airline, a railway authority, etc. All were dismantled by the newly-independent countries and replaced by more costly, nationally-bounded organizations, operating far below optimum size. There was a similar evolution in West Africa.

Trieste is another classical case. The city prospered as the port for central Europe and by the First World War was second only to Marseilles in the Mediterranean. Its economic livelihood depended on its connection to the Austro-Hungarian empire. However, the people were mostly Italian and their nationalistic fervor after World War I led them to union with Italy. This cut the city off from its hinterland and destroyed its prosperity.

Bureaucracy

The fact that government (like corporations) must work through a bureaucracy influences how public resources are used. There are common features in all bureaucracies. The making of government policy is not a coherent, consistent process with the single objective of informed pursuit of the public interest. The permanent bureaucracies vary among countries in the degree that they are committed to a public service ethic.

At the end of the Middle Ages, as monarchs won their battles against the great feudal lords, their new bureaucracies laid the basis for economic progress and the building of national states. The *Beamtenstaat* separated the personal interest of the office-holder from the function and prerogative of office and made possible the making and pursuit of coherent policy. By administering a known corpus of law they provided a definition and stability of law and order that was indispensable for growth. All this was prerequisite for the success of the emerging commercial and industrial interests in transforming the feudal economy. [Landes 1970, 125-92]

Individuals, organizations, and corporations make demands for services on government. But, the government does not only simply react to outside demands. Bureaucrats *within* government, discover new needs for the government to meet. A conscientious bureaucrat feels his professional responsibility for some aspect of national life and initiates action to cope with an emerging problem or to exploit some national opportunity: Experience in World War II teaches battleships are obsolete and admirals become advocates of the aircraft carrier; British and American Treasury officials want to avoid the international financial blunders of the twenties and thirties which contributed to the Great Depression and World War II and create the International Monetary Fund and the World Bank. The computer, the semiconductor, biotechnology, the internet, were all initiatives of the bureaucracy.

In the United Kingdom and Germany, there are families where public service in the civil or military branches of government is a cherished family tradition. France, Britain, Japan, India, recruit their top civil servants from the brightest graduates of their elite schools. In these countries working in government is valued for its social prestige and the opportunity to serve the nation.

In the United States, intermittent attempts are made to inculcate a philosophy of public service in the civil service and to recruit able people to show their devotion to country through a career in government. The American cross-currents are exemplified in President Kennedy's call, "Ask not what your country can do for you, but what you can do for your country", and President Reagan's watchword, "Government is not the solution; government is the problem."

In a public bureaucracy there is usually no connection between the people who pay a bureaucrat's salary and what he does. His work is rarely identified as being for the benefit of a particular taxpayer and the taxes an individual pays are not tied to the activity of any particular bureaucrat. There is no supply-demand relationship in the usual market sense.

The bureaucracy is run by the heads of the different organizations in it. Their motivations are similar to those in a corporate bureaucracy. A chief, taking seriously the responsibility for his area of competence, may see unmet needs, a way to do more, serve more people, and so propose an expansion in his bureau's responsibilities or staff. He may simply wish to maximize his budget and the number of people reporting to him; this way he can get promoted with a higher salary or an increase in personal power and prestige. Unquestionably, these are important objectives for some, perhaps, most bureaucrats. If the bureau provides direct services to the public, the users of the services may exert pressure to get better or more services and so induce the bureau chief, in the desire to avoid trouble even if he wishes a quiet life, to seek a bigger budget. All bureau chiefs report to someone. The demands of the supervisor may influence the budget asked.

The pressure is not always in the direction of increasing the size of the budget and the size of the bureau. To get a higher budget may require special exertion or a confrontation with the supervisor or colleagues. A bigger budget will make the bureau more visible and may result in closer scrutiny by the Budget organization or legislature. It may make it a more desirable target for opposition politicians in the legislature or envious bureaucratic competitors. A bigger budget and more numerous subordinates may disturb or destroy the quiet life the bureau chief has been enjoying. In some governments, as in the British government at the time of Pepys, what may matter more than formal status are the potential opportunities to enrich oneself.

What does seem to be a universal law—whether the organization is devoted to public service or to individual official selfishness—is that a bureaucrat usually chooses between growth or stagnation. He does not consider the possibility of asking for a reduction or elimination of his organization or function. The internal dynamics of bureaucracy are weighted then in the direction of expansion. A major force containing this pressure is the public unwillingness to pay higher taxes.

The controversy among theorists in the thirties on the viability of socialism centered on technical questions like the possibility of using marginal cost pricing in a socialist state for the allocation of resources. Generally, a reasonably optimistic conclusion was reached. However, one fatal defect of the Soviet and eastern European socialist economies was the bureaucracy. It was rigid, conformist, slow in response, ponderous, unimaginative. Soviet enterprises concentrated on making life as comfortable as they could for their managers and their workers: providing housing, raising food and building vacation resorts for their people; while hoarding inventories of materials and equipment and downplaying their capacities to the central plan authorities.

The Soviet economy was able to function largely through the utilization of unofficial, largely illegal, *tolkachs* ("pushers", or "expediters").[14] A *tolkach* was someone outside the bureaucracy who acted as a free-lance. If an enterprise needed a particular machine part, requisitioning it up through its ministry, across to the right ministry and then down to the machine factory might take forever. The *tolkach* found the plant that made such parts and figured out how it was to be obtained—perhaps through finding and supplying the plant with some needed cement.

Even in the democracies, no single theory, "Public Choice" or "Public Service" can explain the forces that drive decisions. There are many motives: the ethos of "Public Service", professional pride, the desire to promote the national interest, however interpreted—to unify the nation, to spread the national culture, etc.—and group and self-interest. There are also contending groups at work. Among these are bureaucrats contending for power, position, and trying to build greater empires or secure greater salaries or titles for the people concerned. And, of course, the other interest groups involved, in greater or lesser degree are the parliamentary parties or groups, regional interests, firms, industries, labor organizations, etc. The policies that emerge are a product of the conflicts, relative positions of strength, compromises, rhetoric, skills at manipulating public relations.

---

[14] Tolkachs emerge when one is confronted with a massive bureaucracy. In the Marshall Plan Mission in rome, a valuable employee in my U. S. Treasury office was a Neapolitan whose main job was to expedite matters through the Italian bureaucracy. He knew who decided what, would carry a paper from office to office getting the necessary approvals along the way. As the rest of the Mission caught on to secret of the effectiveness of the Treasury office, they borrowed our expediter whenever they had to get a quick reaction from the Italian government.

Public Service and Public Choice are theories of the two extremes of the spectrum of human behavior from disinterested benevolent to selfish, self-centered. Each can be right some of the time or in some place or other, neither is correct always and everywhere.

Final Word

The public sector will continue to be the most important in the economy. Since the economy exists to serve the society, not the society to serve the economy, the state must be effective in acting as the instrument that society uses for this purpose. A successful economy needs a robust and effective system of justice, and an efficient, honest and equitable public administration. Markets depend on the state to define and protect property rights and enforce contracts. Some essential property rights such as patents and copyrights are even *creations* of the state. Government is normally not an evil intruder but the essential actor on which the very existence of private property rights depends.

To preserve acceptance of a liberal free-market economy and democratic politics, government and the institutions of civil society must encourage competition, promote equality of opportunity, and guarantee the rule of law. For the survival of democracy and a market economy, there has to be some overriding, guiding principle of common good and public interest to mitigate the otherwise uncontrollable excesses of a profit-driven economy.

The top limit on the rate of growth of total public expenditures is set more by social rather than economic considerations. It is set by taxpayer perception of what is a tolerable level of taxation. The judgment of what is tolerable is not based on an economic calculus but gets determined by custom—the great basic force of inertia. Consequently, normally, government expenditures can grow only modestly, perhaps in line with growth in the GNP. During large scale upheavals—war, major depressions—the social constraint is broken and from that point on, taxpayers have a new and higher perception of what is a tolerable level of taxation. [Peacock and Wiseman 1961; Saunders & Klau 1985, 92]

In a free-enterprise society, the existing pattern of distribution of wealth; of individual knowledge, capacities and skills; and of family and other social relationships, affects the price-structure and the income-structure. The income-structure of today affects the income-structure of tomorrow. Since all individuals do not start with the same set of opportunities, some having inherited wealth, family connections, and favorable education, it cannot be argued that market outcomes are necessarily ethically optimum and, consequently, that state interference with income distribution cannot be justified.

Modern conventional economic theory can provide little guidance to the fundamental decisions on the shaping of the redistribution carried out by the state through taxation, regulation or grants. The accepted theory maintains that one *cannot* make meaningful interpersonal comparisons: One cannot add utilities and therefore one cannot say whether A is better off than B even though A's income may be greater. Present-day theory focuses on the *satisfaction* of the preferences of an individual. With the same income, the choices that John Jones makes may give him much more satisfaction than the choices that Mary Brown makes give to her. Note the contradiction that the theory gets itself into here. The whole theory of value is based on the assumption that everyone's psychology is the same. Yet when the theory is confronted with the real world wealth-problem of comparing the welfare of different people, it throws up its hands and abandons the field. [Blaug 1980, 80]

To be useful, economics has to give up the futile attempt to erect theory on the psychological emotions of individuals and move back into the material, empirical world. The concept that matters is not *psychological welfare* but *material welfare*. The focus has to be on the *how* and the *what* rather than the *why* of individual psychology. *Material* welfare can enter into economic calculus. Economics used to be the science of material welfare and thus could employ an empiricist methodology. Interpersonal comparisons can be made in material welfare and economics thus becomes meaningful and useful in making policy.

When one shifts to this more solid basis for economics, then, it is possible to compare how well off one person is to another. These comparisons may be rough and not precisely calculable but as a practical matter can be the basis of policy. The political world and its down-to-earth empirical economic advisers operate on the practical assumption that it is possible to ascertain in some rough measure whether government action can help or hurt particular groups. It is in fact impossible to make sense out of many major trends in government policy without perceiving who is going to be hurt and who is going to be helped. And, only by being able to weight the material benefits and the material costs is it possible to have any idea whether on net the nation as a whole is better or worse off.

This does not mean that government action necessarily will be directed to promote the material welfare of the nation or of any particular part of it. But whereas conventional economic theory regards the problem as insoluble; looking at the matter from the perspective of *material welfare* means that, given the will, it is possible to arrive at least a rough guide to action that will promote the material welfare of the nation. Note that the national accounts—GDP—measure output not psychological welfare. Governing motivated by Public Spirit is not therefore an impossibility.

As the economy and society changes, new perceived needs arise. They may be met through the market, voluntary association or the state—depending upon the specific demand, public perception, the dominant culture and the ethics of public service, chance, and history.

In the Palazzo Pubblico of Siena, dating from 1338-9, there are frescoes by Ambrogio Lorenzetti in the hall of the Council of Nine, the chief magistrates of the city-republic. One fresco depicts "Good Government": herdsmen with their animals, farmers and fishermen working, people dancing, and prosperous gardens and houses. On another wall is *mal governo*: ruined buildings, villages on fire, quarrels, trades neglected. The moral is clear: when governance is animated by Public Service, the governed benefit; if driven by Public Choice, ruin results.

As the Sienese knew, over six centuries ago, there is no one single determining theory that decides how a country shall be governed. The state has *choices* in what it tries to accomplish and how it does its work. The public sector in modern states has evolved in all its complexity in response to the social and economic needs of society as these emerged and changed with population flux and economic, social and technological developments. To understand, there has to be a realistic appreciation of the complex character of human motivation. No simplistic reliance on a theory of a single-valued assumption of the character of human nature is sufficient.

7   Civil Society

To do things which the state should not do... to do things the state is most unlikely to do... to pioneer ahead of the state and make experiments. —William Beveridge.

Over seventy percent of the members of the American Economics Association work for educational, research, international agency and other nonprofit institutions. Nonprofit institutions in significant respects do not fit the normal characteristics of the market sector of the economy.

Private nonprofit institutions fall outside the market and outside of the public sector. They are sometimes called the *Third Sector, the Social Sector,* or the *Civil Society.* This realm is so important that totalitarian regimes made it a priority to extend party control over it. Employment in this sector averages around five percent of total employment in most countries; varying from around four percent of total employment in Japan to over 12 percent in the Netherlands.

The civil society provides goods and services outside of government and yet it is not driven by profit-seeking incentives. Unlike government, a nonprofit has no power of compulsory taxation but must raise its funds on a voluntary basis. Unlike profitmaking organizations, it has no owners. Nonprofit organizations do not seek to generate monetary profits for the benefit or their owners or officers. They operate successfully outside the market. Their survival and multiplication strongly testify that they represent the optimal method of providing their particular spectrum of goods and services.

As economists we tend to see only the market and the government as the two choices confronting us. Our unconscious bias is that production of goods and services through profitmaking enterprises is normal, universal and eternal. When some activity is found to exist that does not fit, the reaction is to ask the question, "Why does this anomaly exist?" In fact, historically, the question could be asked the other way round with as much or more justification. The nonprofits have as much right to be considered the norm as the profitmaking enterprises do.The dominance of profitmaking enterprises is a development that has occurred only in the last two centuries. Nonprofits have as long a history in the post-feudal world and some religious associations go back to the Roman Empire.

In Italy, Monte dei Paschi di Siena, founded in 1472, is the world's oldest bank. It, like the Banca di Sicilia and the Banco di Napoli, was founded as a philanthropic foundation with pre-capitalist roots. In Germany, Bertelsmann, the global media titan, Robert Bosch, a large international engineering and electrical-equipment company, Carl Zeiss, an optical firm, and Fresenius, a medical equipment producer, are all controlled by foundations.

There is no reason to assume that organizing a nonprofit is any more extraordinary or abnormal than organizing a profit-seeking enterprise. Civil society includes most of the important institutions in our lives. It includes family (though some economists would include this in the market). Besides the family, the almost million and a half organizations in the United States that make up the civil society are varied, numerous, diverse, heterogeneous. They include churches, universities, museums, ethnic groups, social clubs, social movements, professional associations, unions, neighborhood organizations, international institutions, etc.

Day by day, everyone is normally immersed in some part of this civil society—the hospital that has treated us, the church or temple we go to, the charities we contribute to or that we do volunteer work for, the political party we support, the head-start program or day-care center down the street, the college or school we went to, the museums we visit, the Boy Scouts or Girl Scouts/Guides our children are members of. The list is endless.[1]

In the last century, there has been an extraordinary flowering of nonprofit organizations within countries and internationally. Nonprofit institutions have grown in importance since World War II. Nonprofits organized for religious, charitable, scientific, literary, and educational purposes (which do not engage in legislative lobbying and so can receive tax-deductible contributions) number well over 800,000. There are over half a million other nonprofits. Some of these are like the first category but do engage in lobbying. Others are business groups, labor unions, and social clubs. All organizations in this second category cannot receive tax-exempt gifts but like the first class are exempt from paying income tax themselves. In the United States, nonprofit institutions account for around ten percent of the Gross Domestic Product as currently measured. They employ around 10 million people (more than the total of federal and state government employees and more than the number of workers in the construction, transportation or textile industries.). The unpaid volunteers, who mostly make a part-time contribution, may total as much as 100 million people. Very few Americans are not involved in one way or another in helping the nonprofits function. Economic journals, for example, list

---

[1] When I left the international society of the World Bank and moved into an all–American environment I was impressed by the multiplicity of the nonprofit institutions that I encountered and became involved in. It was not unexpected that I might become a member of the board of trustees of a nonprofit such as a college or the community symphony. But it turned out that this led naturally into also becoming a member of an association of trustees of colleges and of an association of trustees of symphonies. It appears to be true that no matter what activity or interest you may have as an American there is some nonprofit institution that has been organized by like-minded people to make this activity possible or more effective. Or, if by some chance, you have an interest and it requires some organization to help pursue it and such organization does not yet exist, you get immediately involved in trying to organize one.

names of the hundreds of individuals who have helped the editors carry out their own usually unpaid tasks. On a parochial note: a quarter of the graduates of the Harvard Kennedy School of Government go into nonprofit management positions. The School in 1997 finally recognized the importance of the sector and established a special Hauser Center for Nonprofit Institutions to do research on and provide training for the sector.

Nonprofit organizations are especially important in the American health care sector: almost a third of U.S. health spending (i.e. around $200 billion) goes to nonprofits. Nonprofits care for approximately 70 percent of all inpatient cases in acute care hospitals and for half of the inpatient mental health and substances-abuse treatment. Home health care services are also dominated by nonprofits and they take care of almost a quarter of the patients in nursing homes. Around half of the people belonging to health maintenance organizations belong to nonprofit HMOs.

Total revenues (including government grants, user charges, and private contributions) of the charitable organizations totaled over $800 billion in the United States in 2000. Private philanthropic contributions amounted to $200 billion. Charitable giving has hovered around two percent of GDP for the last 40 years. This, of course, understates by a considerable measure the importance of individual contributions—the large volume of unpaid volunteer services is not included since its real value is almost impossible to estimate.

The Role of Civil Society

The existence of the Third Sector demonstrates that it fills an important need in modern economies. In addition to its benevolent contributions, some other nonprofits like the Ku Klux Klan or extremist militias have a less than benevolent purpose.

There is a powerful propensity for the civil society to multiply and grow as a country becomes more developed. People use their freedom to pursue other interests when they no longer feel that their day-to-day survival is threatened. The prevailing culture obviously has a large influence on this process. The Anglo-American tradition of decentralization and individualism favors a wider spectrum of civil society activity than the German or French historical experience of reliance on state bureaucracy but the civil society has grown everywhere.

Peter Drucker argues that the Social Sector provides a sphere where people can act as citizens and create a community for themselves. People seldom live in the towns they were born and raised in. The modern family usually consists at most of two parents and one or two children and often the family itself is impermanent. But people still have social needs that only some kind of community action can provide. The social challenge arising from the anomie and ailments of a rootless society—drugs, parental irresponsibility, purposelessness, etc—need to be met. The work-organization today is not a satisfactory social unit while government is so big and complex that responsible citizen participation is almost impossible. The social sector, on the other hand, gives individuals in the modern economy a way to escape anomie and a way in which they can make a difference in society and recreate community. [Drucker 1994, 53-80]

De Tocqueville observed that voluntary associations met a vital need in American society since feudal entities such as parishes and identifiable classes did not exist. The associations provided intermediary buffers in the leveling and egalitarian American society between the individual and the potentially tyrannical majority. The associations were an illustration of the true meaning of self-interest (as discussed in Chapter 2)—Americans were individualistic but not necessarily greedy. They pursued their own purposes in many private pursuits but combined in voluntary associations to pursue collective interests or altruistic objectives.

A useful procedure to help sharpen the understanding of the Third Sector is to look at those nonprofit organizations that provide services that are also provided by profit-making firms or that could be provided by such firms. Why it is that nonprofits exist in a field if there are actual or potential profit-making firms that could provide the same services? There is in fact a large set of nonprofits that compete successfully in head-to-head competition against firms that are run for a profit. The nonprofits thrive because they have a kind of fiduciary relationship with their clients. When it is difficult or impossible for a client to evaluate the quality of the service he is getting, the client has more confidence if the profit-incentive is absent.

Sixty percent of the hospitals in the United States are nonprofits and most or all of the outstanding hospitals are nonprofits. Patients trust Massachusetts General, Johns Hopkins, because they know that raising profits is not the highest priority.

Commercial blood banks were once quite common. People who sold their blood were usually people who had few or no other ways of earning money. That is, aside from students they tended to be petty criminals, drug addicts, drunks, and the destitute. They may also have tended to have high rates of blood infected with syphilis, hepatitis and HIV. But as safety of blood became perceived as vital, since the late 1980s the selling of blood has been banned in most high income countries and reliance has been placed on voluntary blood donations.[2]

An alternative way of securing trust in the quality or character of the service provided is, of course, for the state to intervene through regulation of a profit-making enterprise. But this entails a cost. It is often more efficient to have an enterprise that does not have an incentive to cheat or to provide poor service than to hire watch-dogs to keep an organization from using every means in its striving for profit-maximization. There are other additional reasons for the state to abstain as we discuss in a later section of this chapter.

---

[2] See Titmuss 1997.

A similar set of considerations is involved in the charities that help the poor and needy. When you make a donation to a charity to feed the hungry, to protect children, aid battered women, etc., you would not feel secure that your contribution would reach its intended beneficiaries if the charity were a profit-making enterprise. In 1993, the United Way, a nation-wide charitable organization in the United States, lost contributors when it became known that the chief executive was receiving a salary and perks, comparable to those received by executives in profitmaking enterprises. Donors regarded it as scandalous and perceived it as siphoning off money from the charitable causes they intended to support.

One large set of nonprofit institutions is motivated by ideological purposes. This includes churches, religious-run institutions such as schools, day-care centers, hospitals, etc. These are manned by people who have an affinity for the particular ideology concerned and are mainly supported by such people. What matters here is not an absolute standard of economic efficiency in performing the task but a sort of monopolistic competitive standard: you are willing to pay somewhat more for a school that teaches the "right" sort of ethical and religious behavior even though it may cost more or be more careless in handling expenses than the school down the street. One can go through the usual economic analysis in working all this out.

There are a multitude of other organizations in the Third Sector that almost defy categorization—the association of members of boards of trustees of symphonies that are designed to help trustees better perform their duties through exchange of information and experience; organizations to defend the interests of tenants, of the elderly, of consumers; to put pressure on public or private bodies to achieve public purposes (to prevent pollution, to purchase land for conservation, etc).

And, of course, there are the private, endowed universities and colleges that employ large numbers of the economics profession. It is an interesting reflection on the way in which the obvious is overlooked that academics for so many years neglected to observe that the way they made their own living was an exception to the economic theories developed for the economy.

Rationale of Nonprofits

Economics has theories explaining the *private profit-seeking economy*, the basis for its existence and how it behaves. In the *public sector*, there are theories centering on the government provision of public, collective-consumption, and merit goods, based on the inadequate argument that government is necessary because the market fails or is wanting as a producer of such goods.

The kit of tools that economists possess were mainly developed for analysis of the market economy. Some of them may be useful outside of the economy. But unlike the character in Mark Twain's story who owns only a hammer and therefore sees everything as a nail, economists need to be wise enough to know when they need more than their usual tool kit. Just as the public sector requires an additional set of theories beyond those that apply to the market, civil society is also in a class apart. The conventional economic paradigm can not cope completely and successfully with the civil society organizations since they have purposes other than private gain as their objective. [Douglas 1983]

The usual approach of the economist to the nonprofits is to ask, "What is the particular inadequacy or failure of the market that is responsible for the existence of this anomaly?" But this initial assumption that private nonprofit organizations exist because of failure or inadequacy of the market-economy is too obtuse. *All organizations exist because of market failure.* If the market were perfect under the economist's assumption of perfect competition, it would organize the cooperation of all participants instant-by-instant, day-by-day, to produce and distribute any amount of output determined by supply and demand. There would be no permanent relationships among the people concerned.

What is different about the nonprofit is that the *profit-motive* is inappropriate for the purposes sought by the founders.The different sectors of the economy—private, public, nonprofit—have different codes, ideals and values. The business sector idealizes the rugged individual, the self-made man, the person who is driven by the "bottom-line".

The essence of the civil society is that its values are not those of the market but belong rather to the moral code that predates modern capitalism. The bonds of solidarity, morality and trust, loyalty down and up, come from the feudal ethic and the teachings of traditional religion. People have a large spectrum of motives that may lead them to devote their lives or resources to other purposes than the economic maximization of pecuniary gain. The nonprofits of civil society are the instruments through which people act when they give a higher priority to other drives than the economic.

The nonprofit sector is based on voluntarism, charity, the ideal of service to the community, religious impulses. People who are drawn to work in such organizations commonly realize that it will require some sacrifice in earnings but this is offset by the knowledge that they are making a contribution to society, that their work is benevolent to the community, or consistent with their religious values.

Dennis R. Young has made a fascinating study of the main types of behavioral motivations that are involved in creating and managing nonprofit organizations. This, it should be noted, is in contrast to the usual economic assumption that all behavior is driven by a single maximizing motive. Young has classified organizers and managers of nonprofits as *believers, poets, or professionals*.The basis of the classification is the particular ideal, concept, or idea that the organizer or manager is pursuing. The *believer* has a cause—religious, civil libertarian, social justice—that he is willing to devote his life to. The *poet* is an artist wanting to create something that has positive social value and that he can claim as his own creation. The *professional* is interested in the pursuit and trying out of new ideas. [1986,162-8]

The civil society plays an important, largely unstudied, role in determining how well the market economy functions.

These organizations have a great impact on the society and economy. The environmental organizations are an outstanding example of success in the magnitude of the changes they have secured in government and business policies. Voluntary organizations produce social values and external benefits that cannot be provided through the market. Donors to these organizations believe that a for-profit organization either could not be trusted to carry out the social function or that it would siphon off too much of the income before being used for the social benefits intended. The market is therefore reserved for those activities that provide clearly defined and easily measured private benefits and costs.

Professor Robert Putnam found that the regions of Italy that had the more advanced economic development and more successful government services were those that had the stronger social sectors. His conclusion was that it was the dense networks of social engagement that resulted in better government and better economic growth. "It wasn't that wealth produced choral societies; it was that choral societies produced wealth." [Webb 1995, 11] Probably, I would venture, rather, that, as is so commonly true, the two interacted and reinforced each other. In any case, it is likely that a community's social connectedness, as a significant part of its social-capital, does have a real impact on its economic prosperity.

The two great centers of high technology in the United States, Silicon Valley in California and Route 128 in Massachusetts, owe their location and their success to their respective civil society institutions. Silicon Valley has surpassed Route 128 largely because it has had more support from its societal environment than Route 128 has had from its civil society.

Stanford and Berkeley produced world-outstanding engineers and scientists who lead Silicon Valley's creative, burgeoning enterprises while the state and community colleges trained the thousands of skilled technicians manning them. Route 128 has Massachusetts Institute of Technology but Harvard downgraded its engineering school many years ago. The public colleges in Massachusetts have always been starved for funds. Silicon Valley has a rich and intricate web of other social institutions—trade shows, business associations, hobbyist clubs, computer bulletin boards, etc. In Massachusetts, the organization of the industry, the High Technology Council, devotes itself to lobbying for lower taxes. [Saxenian 1994]

As in many other respects, the countries of the former Soviet bloc in their attempts to create a market economy and a functioning democracy are illuminating in sharp relief characteristics of our economies and societies—which are so familiar to us that we are unaware of their importance. The Eastern Europeans have demonstrated that the civil society is of major importance. It is President Vaclav Havel's belief that for a successful transition, the economy and the democracy needs the mediating structures of the civil society. Only this can build a collective conscience—a commitment to the general interest. A naked market economy with nothing but individual interests pursued for profit cannot secure the loyalty necessary for a successful economy and democracy. The relative ease that the Czech Republic had in establishing a functioning democracy and a market-enterprise system compared to Russia is directly related to the historically greater development of the Czech civil society before it was submerged by the Communist state.

Because of the shortcomings of Russia's civil society its forced march to a new economic and political system is leaving millions on the roadside, disoriented, insecure, with loss of jobs and loss of income, preyed on by criminals.[3] Market capitalism without a strong civil society becomes *mafia capitalism*, a modern instance of the results of Hobbes' war of all against all.

It is *in* the civil society and *through* the civil society that people are educated, mobilized and empowered to control the democratic state and the market economy. It is the institutions and associations of the civil society that also provide much of the richness and joy of life in modern times.

Since the activities of nonprofit organizations are not driven by the objective of maximizing profits why does the state not take on the responsibility that profit-seeking organizations cannot meet? Since the nonprofit is designed to produce social values or semi-public goods for its members or the public, why doesn't the government take over the activity? One reason, of course, is the existence of an ideological belief that it is intrinsically nobler when a private charity performs a function than when a government does. But there are other reasons.

In particular cases, there may not be sufficient public agreement that a particular social value should be sought or that there are sufficient external benefits to be derived from this activity. Consequently, in such cases governmental action does not occur but the people who do see the need may organize a private nonprofit to achieve the ends sought. Or, a minority of people may have a strong preference for considerable resources to be devoted to a purpose that the majority would support only weakly. Again, a nonprofit organization is the answer.

Another set of constraints that induce governments to leave a field to nonprofits derives from the rules that democratic governments usually must operate under. Democratic governments have to treat all people in a designated category alike. A nonprofit, instead, can tailor its action to the special needs of each individual client. In some cases (such as Alcoholics Anonymous or the humanist Rational Recovery (RR) Self-help Network), effectiveness depends on volunteers. In AA or RR the very fact that the volunteer working with the person to be helped is himself a former alcoholic is a important ingredient in effectiveness.

---

[3] This insight, I derived from Franklyn D. Holzman.

Governments using public funds have to keep records and follow civil service rules in recruiting officials; in short, they have to be bureaucracies. And, therefore, in some activities they would be ineffective.

The nonprofits, even though they are largely concerned with providing collective, public goods, cannot coerce people to finance them. In some cases, the state does step in and finance them out of taxation or lends them some coercive power permitting them to levy fees. It is sometimes more economical for the state to use a voluntary association. In the United States, some religious associations run hospitals, nursing and retirement homes, day care centers. These activities are financed partly by contributions to the religious groups and partly by government grants. The Family Planning Association provides help to women, again partly financed by contributions and partly by government grants.

In Massachusetts, for 30 years the commonwealth government has been contracting out much of public welfare—care of mentally sick, homeless, family counseling, supervising troubled families, drug abuse treatment—to nonprofit associations who compete for the government grants. In these instances, the government attempts to secure the flexibility and initiative of nongovernmental organizations while meeting governmental responsibilities. Since what is involved is the provision of services whose quality and quantity are difficult to control, the government devolves this responsibility to nonprofits. Profit-making enterprises making such decisions would be regarded as too cold to the needs of the clients being served. Managers of the nonprofits work for a fixed salary, eliminating the temptation to shortchange the client for the managers' own profit. The nonprofit also has a board of local citizens that is likely to be closely in touch with community needs. The board is a better judge of how well the nonprofit is performing than a bureaucrat supervising from the center. Finally, since the funds from the state usually fall short of meeting the needs, the caring nonprofit runs fund raising campaigns to secure donations from the community to supplement the money from the state.

Putting the provision of the services outside of the government bureaucracy brings in an element of competition and choice. Since the manager and staff of the nonprofit are employees of the nonprofit rather than of the state, there is much more flexibility in the pay and benefits they receive— usually less generous than in the regular state civil service. They also do not have the same degree of security of tenure possessed by civil service workers. In short, the arrangement makes possible a considerable exploitation of the nonprofit workers as compared to the civil service.

Using a nonprofit to provide a good or service may also help a government to avoid political difficulty. A government may decide that funding a particular medical research will be beneficial for society. However, such research may require using animals in experiments and animal rights advocates would be up in arms. A nonprofit involved in medical research might be picketed but does not fear voters turning it out. Government contribution to a nonprofit provides some measure of political insulation for the elected officials.

Nonprofits, finally, outside the usual government constraints, can be flexible and innovative in experimenting in meeting new social needs. If after time a majority consensus develops and the need is one that government can meet, the government can then take over the responsibility.

Recognizing the contribution that the nonprofits make to the general welfare, governments encourage them through granting them certain privileges. In the United States, they are exempt from income taxes on their revenue, have lower mailing rates for their organizational business. The government also indirectly subsidizes by allowing an income tax deduction (for people who do not take the standard deduction) for gifts to nonprofits that are ruled to be socially worthy. At the same time, the state requires that the organization stay faithful to its mandate. Specifically, it must remain nonprofit and there must be no distribution of profits to owners, members or managers.

The nonprofits often can use social pressure. Charities may be allowed to run their fund-raising campaigns at a corporate or governmental work-place with the top managers taking the lead in organizing the soliciting of funds. Colleges use their alumni organizations to get individuals to raise money from their classmates. People are mobilized by other charities to ask for money from their neighbors or friends: "I'd better contribute to her charity because I am going to be asking her to contribute to mine." Some people give for the opportunity to memorialize themselves or others. Every college knows that the easiest way to secure a large donation is for "bricks and mortar" which will be named after the donor or his nominee. Thus people contribute because they want to earn the esteem, gratitude, or applause of others.

All these motives do not tell the whole story. There is much that people do to support nonprofits that cannot be fully explained by these reasons alone. People give blood, give voluntary contributions of money and time to organizations from which they neither ask for nor receive any external *quid pro quo*. They do this because "It's the right thing to do"; "It's only fair to help others who have less"; "It's what my religion requires", etc. In short, people often act on one or another altruistic, motive.

Nonprofits, however, are not immune to predators or parasites. Predators disguise themselves as legitimate charities and raise money by mimicking the names and fund-raising techniques of the bona fide organizations. Others run legitimate nonprofit organizations but exploit them by siphoning off revenues into their own pockets, directly, or by having them buy services or commodities from firms they control at exorbitant prices.[4]

---

[4]A nonprofit state subsidized school for retarded children in my own town of Brewster, to all intents and purposes, was well-run but costs rose sharply each year. The increases were due to rising rents and higher costs of various services. An investigative reporter, helped by a whistle-blower, discovered that the suppliers were secretly owned by the directors of the school. In this way, the directors were siphoning off profits for themselves.

Measures of Performance

The usual economic criterion or measure—profits, "the bottom-line", "the verdict of the market"—by which the success of ordinary corporate organizations can be judged is not applicable to Third Sector organizations. They have to have another measure of success/failure.

Organizations are concerned with inputs, process, outputs, and outcomes. The two main criteria that organizations, which are not driven by the profit motive, can use to measure their success, are *outcome* or *output*. The World Bank, while in form an intergovernmental organization, functions much as an member of the Third Sector. In its first quarter century it focused on outcome as the measure of its success or failure. Beginning with Robert S. McNamara's presidency in 1968-82, the Bank began measuring its success by its output, that is, by the volume of its loans. The Bank's experience in using these two different measures of success is instructive.

When *output* is chosen—in the Bank's case, loans—it can be closely controlled and measured. It fits in with the approved business theory of "management by objectives". It can be easily quantified and easily controlled from the top: the subordinate either met his target or he didn't. It lends itself to centralized management. It is, in short, highly attractive for managers who like to run a tight-ship. It is not, however, the optimum objective for organizations.

The early Bank, in contrast, took the economic development of its members for its guide. That is, it took as its criterion of success, *outcome* or results.

Outcomes, unlike outputs, are much more difficult to measure. Progress in promoting the development of a member country depends necessarily on a cooperative, intimate working relationship with the member country. Progress depends not only on what the Bank does but even more on what the country does. It required therefore that the Bank engage very closely and directly with the government and the member country. Bank staff had to be led, rather than managed, by top management. Staff had to be motivated to do their best, since there was no easy quantifiable measure of success or failure.

When lending volume output became the measure of success, a system of monthly statistical reports on the progress of the lending program of each division provided objective, impersonal centralized super-vision from the very top. Staff was managed rather than led. New members of the staff would complain that they had been in the Bank for two or three years and had never even seen the President. This also ramified downwards with staff members sometime never having met the vice-president in charge of their region.

In its first quarter century, Bank presidents were very conscious that the Bank could provide only a small marginal addition to the capital resources of a country. To help countries develop, the Bank almost instinctively realized that Bank help had to be used as a means to secure improved economic management of resources in the borrowing country.

Economic development comes through making more effective use and improved management of all resources—existing capital as well as new capital, manpower, land, and other natural resources. A greater supply of capital may be essential to make possible taking the necessary measures to improve economic performance. The point is that concentration on increasing the *amount* of capital as the central element in economic development represents the wrong approach to getting faster growth.

Outcome is not an easy objective to work with. It calls forth the need to exercise ingenuity and creativity. The Bank management was very aware of the fact that there was no one simple solution to securing results and it was therefore very open to ideas and initiatives, as the record shows. By the end of the first quarter century after Bretton Woods of the Bank's existence, it was universally judged, with only minor dissent, to be a success. It had created the International Finance Corporation, the Economic Development Institute, the International Development Association, and pioneered a whole sheaf of other creative and innovative initiatives to aid its member countries in their economic development.

Robert S. McNamara on becoming president of the Bank in 1968 announced in his first major policy address that the Bank would double the amount of its lending over the next five years. Setting up the volume of loans as the measure of success for the Bank, and, internally for the loan officers, meant that other aspects of Bank activity in helping LDCs became subordinated. Getting loans out got priority. In the first quarter century when outcomes were the goal, in contrast, it was the *refusal* of the Bank to lend to Spain until major reforms were instituted that contributed to the rapid take-off of the Spanish economy in the 1960s.

Escott Reid in evaluating McNamara's first five years in office (1968-73) observed that in spite of the President's statements (that the Bank was devoted to aiding the poor and improving the distribution of income in the less developed countries) there was little evidence of any help to the poor in Bank lending. Bank officers were convinced that McNamara's overriding goal was the volume of lending. They did not believe that he would reduce drastically lending to any country that did not tailor its program to helping the poor. Further, when he subjected the officers of the Bank to great pressure to double the volume of lending, they were compelled to abandon the more complex and time-consuming projects that were designed to give priority to providing jobs and a better distribution of income. [795-797]

With lending *output* as the goal, easy projects are chosen, large projects over small, quick-disbursing over slower, simpler over complex, single beneficiary over many beneficiaries. The effort to use Bank projects as a means to secure improved economic management of the country's resources was weakened and largely disappeared in practice.

In a 1982 note on Robert McNamara's presidency, I commented,

> Putting the emphasis on the need to achieve lending targets resulted in
> what some bitter Bank staff called 'reversal of roles.' The loan officer's
> career was dependent on the willingness of borrowers to accept loans.
> The official Bank line...was that the quality of Bank projects was as high
> as ever. But this is not to the point: a power project during the McNamara
> years was undoubtedly a good project but the real question is whether the
> Bank negotiators were as successful as they would have been earlier in
> getting improvements in rate policy, for instance. [*Foreign Affairs* Spring
> 1982, 952]

I was too sanguine. Not only was the endeavor to improve the
economic management undermined, in the drive to achieve lending targets
even the quality of Bank projects deteriorated. According to an internal
Bank study, the Wapenhans Report (1992), 20 per cent of active Bank
projects had major problems which could cost their failure if not corrected.
That is, Bank investments totaling as much as $28 billion could be wasted.
It is significant that the report attributed much of the problem to a failure to
appreciate the importance of policy and institutional factors.

It is not only the project loans that soured. In 1980, the Bank
began a new program of Structural Adjustment Loans (SALs) which made
up as much as a fifth of Bank lending in some years. These so-called
"policy-based" loans were fast-disbursing and not related to any project.
They supported the borrowing country's balance of payments while the
government was supposed to carry out structural reforms. These loans
were made to countries anxious for Bank financing but, in spite of their
promises, unable, administratively or politically, to carry out the policies
they agreed to as conditions of the loans. The program helped increase in
the volume of lending. But studies made of the results have had difficulty
in finding instances of restructuring successes.

On the occasion of the celebration of its Fiftieth Anniversary in
1994, the Bank management realized that it had major problems to
overcome. The Bank president, Lewis Preston, announced that the pressure
to lend had been a mistake: "Every guy in this bank thought he was going
to get promoted based just on the number of loans he could get approved.
It was a crazy way to run a railroad." [Zagorin 1994, 55]

In 1993, the Bank's new policy agenda, *Getting Results*,
recognized that the Bank's effectiveness in terms of development impact is
crucial and that improving this would not be easy: "Bringing about the
institutional changes required...will require sustained leadership from
management .., and strong and continuous support from the board *in
attaching as much importance to lending results as to lending volumes.*"
[my emphasis] [World Bank, 17]

On June 6, 1994, one of the Bank's Managing Directors, Sven
Sandstrom, told a Bank staff meeting that, after surveying the progress of
the past 25 years.

... I think it's much more widely accepted in senior management, the Board, shareholders, that we need to give more attention to the actual results and the development impact. [*Bank's World* August 1994, 6]

Clearly, the Bank management in 1993-94 rediscovered that the early Bank criterion of *outcomes* as the objective of the organization was the correct one for a nonprofit organization.

Many Third Sector organizations fall into the same trap as the World Bank and adopt output rather than outcome as their measure of accomplishment. As illustrated in the case of the Bank it is administratively far more attractive. It also is psychologically appealing, not only for managers but for many other people. Many religion-motivated persons, for example, like Gandhi even give priority to the process itself.

It is the action, not the fruit of the action, that's important. You are expected to do right. It may not be in your power, it may not be in your time, that there will be any fruit. But that doesn't mean that you stop doing the right thing. The virtue comes in doing it.

Albert Schweitzer's hospital at Lambarene was not as well-equipped nor as effective in curing patients as a modern hospital that existed a few miles away, but that did not bother him nor most of the pilgrims that came to pay homage to him and his works. Process and output as objectives provide satisfaction to the members or the management of the organization. They are less useful to society outside of the organization. While government may wish to grant the privileges of nonprofit association to religious and other organizations that are so oriented, their contribution to the overall welfare of the community may be minimal.

8　The Professions

> *That any sane nation, having observed that you c ould provide for the supply of bread by giving bakers a pecuniary interest in baking for you, should go on to give a surgeon a pecuniary interest in cutting off your leg, is enough to make one despair of political humanity.* — George Bernard Shaw.

Most economists, even those in business, think of themselves as being "professionals". Society depends on the professions to cope with the problem Shaw identified in the opening citation. There is no single motive driving the professions—self-interest, altruism, desire to serve humanity, wish to contribute to knowledge and human progress, pride in accomplishment, jealously, envy, etc. are all present. Still, the professions, ideally, are an outstanding antithesis to the assumption that every individual is driven to maximize his own personal economic gain.

One of the most important characteristics that sets the professional off from other workers is that the member of the profession is expected to place the interest of his client, patient, or pupil above his own financial interests. A profession has much in common with the Calvinist "calling". It isn't just a business, an "occupation", or a trade. It is something more—it is not something which is done simply because one has to earn money—that is, merely a response to the pure economic motive. It is affected with the public interest. In paradigm, a profession is a vocation: searching for perfection in one's work, upholding standards, and serving humanity. In Harvard Law School Dean Roscoe Pound's view, to be a professional is *...to pursue a learned art as a common calling in the spirit of public service—no less a public service because it may incidentally be a means of livelihood.*

In the modern high-income countries we are surrounded by professionals. As Abbott observed, "The professions dominate our world. They heal our bodies, measure our profits, save our souls." [1988,1] As usual, it is impossible to define what a profession is with sharp boundaries. From the historical and sociological research on the professions, there is generally a consensus that a profession is an occupational group with a special skill—usually an abstract skill that requires extensive training—that is applied not in a routine fashion but as required, case by case. A profession tends to be institutionalized: it usually has its own professional association, professional examination for qualifying, a university-level professional school, national journal, an ethics code, and, often, a governmental-sponsored or authorized licensing exam. These characteristics apply mainly to the English-language areas of the world.

On the continent of Europe, the state plays a much bigger role. In

France, when a profession is recognized by the state it takes organizational form through governmental regulations. Since Napoleonic times, the Conseil d'État has controlled the specifics of jurisdiction and the professional function of each profession. In the legal professions, entry is strictly controlled by the state, and a qualified candidate enters only by the purchase of the office from an existing holder or his heirs. [Abbott, 16-17, 27, 63]

While professional or earlier guild ethics have a long history—for doctors stretching back to ancient Greece—the multiplication of professions in the United States, for example, began in the last third of the nineteenth century. Then, modern universities and graduate schools were organized. New medical schools provided scientific training. In law, graduate law schools and the American Bar Association came into existence. The professional academic associations existing today in economics, history, engineering and other fields were organized at that time. Similar developments occurred in Britain, also in the nineteenth century.

Guy Benveniste has pointed out that professionals have become the largest single category of American workers and that most American workers now aspire to secure some of the status professionals have conquered. The recognized professions include doctors, nurses, social workers, lawyers, clergy, architects, engineers.With the success and prestige achieved by the original professions, many other occupations have attempted to copy their type of organization. And, so we have the professions or pseudo-professions of morticians, plumbers, electricians, sanitary engineers, accountants, financial analysts, etc.

There is not much good statistical information on the people that might be classified or classify themselves as professionals. In the United States, there are probably around 10 million people that might fit in this category. Professional earnings tend to fall in the high-income brackets.

The professions separate themselves from other workers by maintaining that their work requires extended training or special education, the mastery of an esoteric, difficult body of knowledge, and mutual discipline and support of their peers. The individual is supposed to abide by the explicit codes of conduct and ethics that govern relationship between the professional and the clients he serves. [Benveniste 1987]

Professionals practice their livelihood subject to the judgment of their peers while recognizing that their actions are to be directed to the benefit of their clients and the community and not primarily for their own wallets. The ethical professor does not award the highest marks to the pupil that pays him best. The ethical doctor selects the treatment that is of maximum help to his patient rather than the one that most profits the doctor. Service to the client and the best interests of the client are expected to override concern for the professional's own selfish ends. [Moore 1985]

One notable example of a profession that lives up to this ideal is the dental profession. The dentists embarked on a program advocating public health measures such as fluoridation of drinking water which reduced dental decay (and their own incomes) and worked diligently and successfully to educate the public on better care of teeth and gums. These activities tended to reduce dentists' income and fewer dentists were required. As a result, from 1986 to 1993, six dental schools closed, the remaining 54 schools reduced the numbers of their students, and applications for admission fell by almost a half in the ten years 1983-93.

While the professions are a recognition that people can be motivated by other than selfish-self interest, motives are mixed. Certainly self-interest is present. Shaw echoed Adam Smith, that professions are conspiracies against the public. The professions usually attempt to control competition among their membership. In part, this is driven by the selfish motive of preventing price-cutting but there is also the old aristocratic motive that the status of the professional is one that is above such lowly practices. There is no such restraint on competition against other professions or in protecting the profession from outsiders. Doctors insist on controlling writing of prescriptions, nurses are forbidden to trespass. Solicitors in England and notaries in France control the process of legal property transfer.

The professions have grown and multiplied in response to a real need. The modern economy and society have become vastly more complex and complicated. For survival and success, individuals need access to much more information and knowledge than any one individual can master on his own. Custom, habits, and common sense—the old guides to living no longer suffice in important parts of life. Tapping the professions' access to the various kinds of specialized knowledge thus becomes necessary. The layman's confidence that the aid he receives is motivated by the desire to help him rather than filling the pockets of the professional is reinforced by the special authority derived from the membership of the professional in the certified community of experts represented by the profession.

Adam Smith condemned Oxford because the teachers' salaries are "independent of their success" in teaching. Today, professional ethics are relied on to put the interests of the students above the ease of the masters.

For the individual, membership in a profession provides some protection from the insecurities of the unceasing change and confusion of the impersonal market economic system. It also gives him personal status in society, provides an association to protect him and look after his interests, and provides a way of having a career that is more secure and less structured and less rigidly disciplined than in ordinary business. Professionalization of the work force is also encouraged by the fact that the culture of modern high-income economies accepts and values professions.

The very contribution that the professional makes through his specialized knowledge and the trust that he invokes from his professional ethics gives the opportunity to the professional to use this power for his own or his profession's ends. The cultural authority they wield as experts in uncommon knowledge and skills can enable them to set themselves above and apart economically and socially from the rest of the people. How this temptation is handled depends on many factors, of which the personal ethics and philosophy of the professional are among the most important.

9   Social Capital:
The Cultural Infrastructure

... officials began to arrive, civil servants with their families and, after them, artisans and craftsmen for all those trades which up till then had not existed in the town. ...what most astonished the people of the town and filled them with wonder and distrust was not so much their numbers as their immense and incomprehensible plans, their untiring industry and the perseverance with which they proceeded to the realization of those plans. The newcomers were never at peace; and they allowed no one else to live in peace.

... They measured out the waste land, numbered the trees in the forest, inspected lavatories and drains, looked at the teeth of horses and cows, asked about the illnesses of the people, noted the number and types of fruit-trees and of different kinds of sheep and poultry. (It seemed that they were playing games, so incomprehensible, unreal and futile all these tasks of theirs appeared to the people.)

... What was this restlessness which continually drove them on, like some curse, to new works and enterprises of which no one could see the end. —Ivo Andri´c, describing the reaction of the Bosnian Muslims to the advent of Austro-Hungarian rule in 1878.

Economists, like many other social scientists, in trying to create pure, timeless, and placeless theory often base themselves on the unconscious, unvoiced cultural assumptions of our own society. These we naively assume to have universal validity. They are so embedded in our environment and so familiar that they are invisible to our conscious thought. Imprisoned in our own modes of thought and social perception, we ignore and become incapable of understanding or even acknowledging the existence of any alternatives. Consequently, we tend to assume without question that our economic theories are universal and fully descriptive of all human economic behavior everywhere and at all times.

Human behavior is affected by biological and genetic inheritance and by our cultural and institutional environment. Unlike insects, we are born with "incomplete" genetic programs. We are not obliged, as ants are, to obey our genetic blueprints in every detail of our behavior. The way we act is not the consequence of an internally-fixed program of genes but of a continuous psychic development within our social structure. As human beings we need training to teach us how to live and survive in our daily lives. Our culture inculcates the values by which we live. It provides the shared sets of ideas, beliefs, values and understandings that bind a society together and guide us in progressing from one stage of life to the next.

And, it is especially important for economists to note, our culture teaches us the ways by which we know, organize, and interact with our economic, social, and physical environment.

> That in all societies man's economic actions consist of choosing is beyond question. ... the outcome of the economic choice is expressible as a vector $X(x_1, x_2, ..., x_n)$, the coordinates of which are quantities of some commodities. Now, some economic choices are *free choices,* that is, the individual is as free to choose one of the alternatives as if he had to choose a card out of a deck .... But the most important choices usually are not free in this sense.... in its general form the economic choice is not between two commodity vectors, Y and Z, but between two complexes (Y, B) and (Z, C) where B and C stand for the actions by which Y or Z is attainable. Ordinarily, there exist several actions, $B_1, B_2,...,B_k$ by which, say, Y may be attained. ...What on the average one will do depends on the cultural matrix of the society to which he belongs. The point is that whether the outcome of choice is Y or Z depends also upon the *value* the actions B and C have according to the cultural matrix of the economic agent. To leave an employer with whom one has been for some long years only because another employer pays better, certainly is not an action compatible with every cultural tradition. The same can be said about the action of an employer who lets his workers go as soon as business becomes slack. [Emphasis in original] [Georgescu-Roegen 1971, 125]

Economists have generally accepted that individual human capital exists and is important; that investment in improving human resources can be productive. In the modern world, the human capital at work in high-tech or biotech enterprises is far more important than the physical capital embodied in plant or machinery. In Silicon Valley and at Microsoft, the crucial assets walk out the door when the workers go home.

Economists need also to accept that *the social-infrastructure is social human capital.* Our cultural environment is the *socially-constructed reality —the mental architecture—* within which we live. It is the stored, largely unarticulated, information people acquire on the ways to live in their community, economy, and society. It can be thought of as the set of strategies that a society uses to organize and to explain to itself its way of existing. A society evolves its particular culture to try to cope with its world and this human social capital identifies a group or people to itself and regulates its behavior.

The culture of a people consists of: the patterns of perception and thought that children acquire while growing up; the habits and human relationships that the people regard as natural and given. It is the accepted knowledge—the whole complex of shared assumptions, beliefs, attitudes, morals, customs, traditions that characterize a society or social group. It consists of the complex, thick networks of connections, values, norms. It provides the knowledge of how to relate to one another; of how to work in the economy, of the ways of thought, and the value system to be governed by.

A culture is in continual re-creation over the generations and may be in slow or more rapid flux depending upon the society and the times.

Once the perception is grasped that culture is part of social human capital, its importance to economics is more easily accepted.

An individual's human capital may directly contribute to productive capability or it may be responsible for leading him to downgrade economic success for spiritual satisfaction. And, as is to be expected of a human being, a person will most likely have a mix of different motivations and acquired abilities and disabilities that will influence how well he does economically. Similarly, the culture of a society, its social human capital, may be more or less effective in making the society economically productive.

There is no such being as a human who is independent of culture. Our human worlds are constructed through education, historical and political processes; they are not timeless, unchanging and unchangeable structures of nature. Because most of us are immersed in our own culture from infancy on, it is easy to confuse our own local culture as representing universal human nature. One of the rewards from encountering another culture is that its strangeness is not only fascinating but it informs us a lot about ourselves. Exploration turns out to be also self-exploration.

It is obviously impossible for this chapter to do more than to try to convince the reader that it is essential for economics to be aware of and to take into consideration the cultural matrix—the social human capital—which shapes and determines how economies function. Almost every aspect of the analysis and examples given in this chapter could easily be expanded to book length.[1]

There is no indication that human beings have had any genetic improvement since we evolved to our present form some 50,000 years ago. We are still virtually the same creatures as the savages who happily ate grubs off rotten logs in Pleistocene times. All the enormous progress that we have made, from the cowering barely-surviving pre-savages of our origins to today's globally-dominant species reaching for the stars, has come from our accumulation of social human capital built up and passed on through the generations. A Cro-Magnon born and raised in America today would blend into our society without difficulty. The differences between our world of computers, jet planes, cellular phones and the Cro-Magnon's native world have come from cultural evolution.

Cultural evolution—the creation of social human capital—works

---

[1] A number of studies on the relationship between culture and economic performance are now available and worth referring to. Among these are Max Weber's classic, *The Protestant Ethic and the Spirit of Capitalism*, and, in recent years, works by Lawrence Harrison, James Fallowes, David C. McClelland, and R. D. Mallon and J. V. Sourrouille.

through the transmission from one generation to another through imitation, teaching, and learning of skills, of the whole body of knowledge, the shared past, and the values and attitudes that influence behavior. The culture of our society is a dominant force in determining the kind of economy we have and its rate of growth.

In order to understand an economy and how it works it is necessary to understand the culture in which it operates and which has shaped it. In a civilized society, the drive of self-interest and the competitive "war of all against all" are controlled by the culture. The rules, codes and restraints are internalized through the culture and are observed voluntarily. The costs of law and order and social discipline, such as police, prisons, regulatory enforcement, are thus kept low.

Anthropologists and psychologists recognize that the behavior of each person is (1) partly unique, (2) partly characteristic of other people sharing the same social capital, and (3) partly common of all human beings. [Brandes 1987, 84,108,148] The usual economics assumption that economic theory explains the behavior common to all human beings, therefore, (even if the assumption were justified) would account for only one of the three bases from which human behavior stems.

Cultural Contrasts in History

During the whole of our existence as a species, communities have developed their own special and different cultures. Only a little more than two centuries have elapsed since Adam Smith was alive and the modern industrialized market economy began. It is sobering to realize that, on the other hand, the Pharonic Egyptian economy, organized not by exchange-relationships but by religious-bureaucratic command, lasted *28 centuries* from around 3100 BC to 332 BC when it was overthrown by the Macedonian Ptolemies.

The caste system established in India some 4000 years ago still divides Hindus into brahmins (scholar-priests), kshatriyas (warrior-landowners), vaishyas (traders), sudras (workers), and untouchables and thousands of sub-castes. Caste determines what you can eat, drink, and wear, and how you can earn your living. This so-called "Hindu equilibrium" while helpful for survival and for maintaining a stable society in the past, today impedes economic development.

For most of recorded history, the Confucian mandarin-run country of China was more civilized, more developed, and more prosperous than the West. It is only since 1500 that Europe managed to surpass China economically— with the initial and critical help of three major Chinese inventions: printing, the compass, and gunpowder.

For most of recent human history, human beings have lived in societies and economies characterized by social order and hierarchy: that is, in societies organized on the basis of status—societies in which people *knew* their "place". Government, the religious authorities and the moral code taught obedience to authority and the passive acceptance of one's lot in life. With the decline of feudalism, new ideals of self-improvement arose along with the rise of the middle class. As perfectly exemplified in Benjamin Franklin's *Autobiography,* this new model preached diligence, thrift, self-control, punctuality, and hard work—all directed to helping an individual to rise in the world economically. Today, most people in market economies, to a greater or a lesser extent, live in a world dominated by market psychology. That is, people, now, live in societies and economies in which people have to *make* their "place".

Perhaps the quickest way to get attention to the importance of culture in economics is to illustrate what an enormous difference there is between us and another people in another age in some aspect peculiarly meaningful to economists. For instance, we regard the importance of quantification as practically self-explanatory. Sometimes, as shown by the endless quoting of trivial statistics by TV commentators at football games, we appear to be in the grip of quantification-mania. But notice how quantifying was abhorred by the ancient Israelites at around 1000 B.C.

And Satan stood up against Israel, and provoked David to number Israel. King David, against the opposition of his top military leaders, ordered that a census be taken of men of military age in Israel and Judah. The census was taken. David, belatedly, realized that he had thereby sinned greatly. David then prayed God to absolve him of this grievous sin. As penance, the Lord God gave him the choice of three punishments: seven years of famine for his kingdom, six months of being hunted by his enemies, or three days of pestilence. David chose the three days of pestilence. In administering the punishment, the angel of the Lord slew through disease, 70,000 people. And this was a mitigation of the punishment because the Lord took pity on Jerusalem and stopped the angel of death at the gate to the city. [1 *Chronicles* 21:1; 2 *Samuel*: chapter XXIV]

At that time, "numbering" the people was such a great sin that 70,000 had to die to expiate it. (The repugnance to quantifying may be more than just cultural—possibly responsive to some deep impulse in human nature. A player at a roulette table regards counting his chips as bad luck. Primitive societies appear to shy away from it. The Masai of Kenya and Tanzania still today continue to regard "counting" as bad luck.)

In the United States, *math anxiety* is much more prevalent among girls than boys. So much so that some people have hypothesized that fear of math is a natural genetic peculiarity of the female sex. In Japan, the old samurai tradition, typical of a feudal mind-set, dictated that a warrior disdained money and so did not carry it. In modern Japan, as a result, managing money is *women's work.* Women are generally expected to manage the household budgets, doling out the husband's allowance. Consequently in Japan, *math anxiety* is not regarded as a female characteristic. Boys are sometimes held to lower math standards than girls. A Japanese commented: "If there weren't lower math standards for boys than girls, our best universities would be filled with women." [Davidson 1993, 75-6; in Steinem 1994, 206-7]

In Ancient Greece, from which so much of our civilization stems, slavery was so basic an institution that no free Greek could imagine an economy without it. The life of the citizens in the city-state with all their duties and pleasures would have been impossible without the labor of slaves on the farms, mines, and in the home. Slavery was unquestionably accepted even though it represented a possible peril even to free men. Although most slaves were probably barbarians (i.e. non-Greeks), if a Greek city were conquered its surviving inhabitants might be sold as slaves. Even in time of peace, a Greek might be cast into slavery. Some sources report that Dionysus, the tyrant of Syracuse, had Plato seized and sold into slavery from which he fortunately was rescued by a friendly purchaser. Slavery was so much a part of life that Aristotle even tried in his *Politics* to defend slavery as "natural".

In the classical world, it was also conventional wisdom that trade was, either inherently or in practice. nothing but cheating and fraud. Horace called trade, *unnatural* and *impious*. The pagan philosophers and the early Christian fathers agreed in condemning the pursuit of the middleman's profit in commerce as *avarice* and *sin*. St. Jerome put it succinctly: "All riches proceed from sin. No one can gain without another man losing". [Viner 1991, 39-40]

Many economists regard the capability of making accurate predictions as the essential attribute of any branch of learning that claims to be a science. Milton Friedman, in particular, has argued that it is only successful prediction that matters in an economic hypothesis. I strongly disagree [1983, 4-6], but the point here is that no one worries that predicting the future is unacceptable social behavior. A few centuries ago, however, in medieval Europe making predictions was regarded as a grave sin. As Dante described in his *Inferno*:

> Come il viso mi scese in lor più basso,
> mirabilmente apparve esser travolto
> ciascun tra il mento e 'l principio del casso:
> Che dal reni era tornato il volto,
> ed indietro venir gli convenia,
> perchè il veder dinanzi era lor tolto. (Canto XX, lines 10-15)

According to Dante, people who have dared to try to interfere with God's plans by making predictions of the future are doomed to spend eternity in Hell with their heads screwed around to face backwards. On the same rationale, some scholastics were worried that marine insurance was sinful since it also interfered with carrying out the will of God—when God had willed a loss for somebody, his intent should not be frustrated through insurance.

A feudal noble despised money and held in contempt anyone who was motivated by monetary gain. His personal identity and social position was established by his birth. This inherited status gave him the social confidence, the social standing, and the potential for a freedom of thought and action far greater than that available to anyone condemned to grub for his daily bread. Some of this feudal attitude is still an active ingredient today in former feudal societies and still has economic results. (See Chapter 10 on Britain and Japan).

The non-feudal United States is not immune: rich families with *old money,* who are above the need to grub for money, regard themselves, and are often so regarded by others, as socially superior, The saying "Everybody loves a lord" is demonstrated by the respect still manifested by many to anyone with an inherited title. An ex-president of the United States, Ronald Reagan—the former leader of a world superpower—eagerly accepted an honorary knighthood from the Queen of England. The Japanese, in contrast, had to pay $2 million to get him to Japan.

The truth is that such a high proportion of our beliefs and attitudes is cultural not genetic, that one has to examine carefully any assumption held as to what is universal human nature. "Almost every Englishman", according to Sir Kenneth Clark, "if asked what he meant by 'beauty' would begin to describe a landscape, perhaps a lake and mountain...." An American, a Japanese, would do the same. Seeing beauty in nature is so much a part of our modern culture that we ignore the fact that it is not an innate human quality. In the Middle Ages, nature was associated with wild beasts, robbers, evil spirits and demons. It was something to endure and avoid. In China, on the other hand, in the Sung dynasty (960-1279), in the same period, nature was divine and an object of veneration. It was not until the Renaissance in Europe that European artists discovered nature. In the 1500s Venetian artists began to paint pastoral landscapes with shepherds, musicians, and nude goddesses. From this point on, with artists depicting beauty in nature and with Rousseau and romanticism inculcating reverence for nature, we began to believe that admiring the sea, mountains and lakes is a natural instinct. [Hobbs 1992, 4-5]

The *Annales* school of historians teach that history should study the deeper structural determinants of human behavior like the physical habitats in which people lived and the abiding attitudes (*mentalités*), affecting human behavior. These are regarded as more important than the old primary subject of history—the chronicle of events. wars, diplomacy, politics. Whether this argument is valid or not, to understand an economy one needs to know the structural construction of the economy and the *mentalités,* the culture, that is, the social human capital of the society.

Some economists have tried to apply economic theory to explain human behavior and relationships outside of the economy. Impersonal economic forces and the assumption that people behave as *economic man* may explain much human behavior outside of economics. However, there must be something else than economics involved, if with the same economic forces at work, in Japan, unlike in the United States, there has resulted a society with virtually no homeless families, few single parents, little indulgence in narcotic drugs, and cities where one can walk day or night without fear of mugging, robbery, or rape. And, in Germany, with the same impersonal economic forces at work, there has resulted a country with safe streets and parks, free university education, universal health care, effective public transportation, the best-trained work-force in the world, and a successful teamwork of labor, capital and government that transformed the country from a mass of ruins at the end of World War II into the economic giant that it is today.

Even Canada—a country that most Americans tend to assume is nothing but an extension of the United States—demonstrates behavior sharply contrasting with its neighbor. An Australian, Jill Conway Ker, who is a historian and acute observer, on moving from the United States to Canada was struck by the differences she found there: a society more concerned with justice and order than acquisitiveness. Canadians regard law and tradition as the basis of civilized society, not the natural rights of individuals. The urban social order works—people can walk in city parks without fear for personal safety. The country functions with a high standard of public honesty and "a commitment to achieve fairness while respecting difference". [1994, 70, 136, 170-1, 174]

In the United States, homicide rates are always consistently lower in the northern border states from New England to the Pacific Northwest than in the southern tier. In New England, the culture is against violence. The old *lex talionis* is still part of Texas law. A husband is allowed to kill his wife's lover caught in *flagrante delictu*. In Texas it is legal for everyone to carry concealed weapons even into churches, unless the church specifically forbids it. In the North, states rarely execute prisoners, almost all the Southern states do.

As usual in most matters affecting humans, causation runs both ways in the relationship between the economy and the culture: the economy influences the cultural matrix and the culture influences the economy. Effective economic policy needs to be aware of the effect of the ruling culture on how the economy works, how far it poses a set of constraints and the possible set of opportunities it offers.

In some instances, economic ends may be attained either by economic means or by modifying the culture. The culture, and the institutions which reinforce and reflect it, are like the economy—created by human action and susceptible to change by human decisions. The government officials in the East Asian economies believe that many of the concepts and theories of Western conventional economics are culturally limited and not universals applying to all humanity. They are convinced that moral suasion and social pressures may be as effective as material rewards in influencing behavior. [Vogel 1991, 99-100] Lee Kuan Yew calls his successful Singapore economy (which in some 30 years of independence, became a center for international financial services, a corporate tax-haven, and grew from a per capita of $1,000 to $24,000) *East Asia Confucian capitalism.*

Culture as an Economic Force

The importance of culture as social human capital can also be perceived in observing the different economic results different ethnic and cultural groups achieve in the same or very similar environment. There are, for example, profound economic differences among Chinese, Indians and Malays in Malaysia. In Penang, the majority of the people are Chinese—the only province in Malaysia where this is true. Penang has become the focus of high-tech manufacturing in the country; Intel, Motorola, Hitachi, Phillips, Advanced Micro Devices, Thomson, Sony are all here. In building a plant in Penang, the managing director of Otis, bluntly explained why the island was chosen over Kuala Lumpur, Penang is "more Chinese". [*The Economist* May 22, 1993, 39]

The Lebanese in West Africa, the Gujaratis in East Africa, the Chinese in South East Asia, the Jews in Europe, the Ibos in Nigeria, the Jehovah's Witnesses in Zambia, the *balokole* (the "saved ones") in Uganda—are all ethnic or religious groups who were more successful than others in the same regions. The *haute société protestante* in France used to dominate business and finance. Still today, French Protestants, two percent of the French population, are disproportionately leaders in business, civil service, and intellectual life. Clearly there must be some influence at work beyond what conventional economic theory recognizes. [Bauer 1981)

The perception that the culture of a country or ethnic group is intertwined with its economic development is now fairly generally accepted by development economists. The United Nations in proclaiming the years 1988-1997 the *World Decade for Cultural Development* laid down as the first objective of the Decade: acknowledgment of the cultural dimension of development.

Sometimes the influence of a particular culture on an economy is startlingly obvious. In erecting a new office building in a country with a Chinese culture, it is wise to consult a *feng shui* expert to be sure that supernatural forces are right—otherwise the building may remain empty of tenants. It is also good sense not to try to make big decisions in the *ghost month* in the Chinese lunar calendar. People avoid risks during this period.

Through studying other cultures than our own we can discover whether a particular economic behavior characteristic of a group of people is inherent in human nature or is due to the culture where it is found. Unless we are aware of these cultural differences we may wrongly assume that our particular national cultural behavior is universal—inherent in all human nature. To understand how an economy functions and grows it is necessary to understand the culture within which it is embedded and which may have a large impact on the economy.

The culture of a society colors the attitude toward work and the value given to different kinds of work; it weights the way in which people decide between present and future satisfactions. It establishes the socially-accepted goals for individuals. These are not the same over time for all individuals, social groups, societies or even for the same society. In some societies unlike the American, the individual is taught to believe that he is subordinate to the welfare of the state, to the religious or ethnic community of which he is a member, or to whatever is regarded as representing an eternal power that transcends the comparatively short temporal life of the individual.

The different pace of economic development in different countries over the last two centuries has shown that countries vary in the extent that their traditional modes of behavior and customs hinder or facilitate speedy adoption of new technologies and new types of economic organization. [Sundrum 1983] The Japanese success in building the world's second largest economy with a culture that has relied on motivations directly opposed to much of what standard economics assumed to be "natural behavior" underlines the need to reconsider our old approach.

Even the acquisitive instinct, that modern economics regards as so fundamental, has to be fostered in human beings by the culture. When the aborigines in Australia first came into contact with people from the rest of the world in 1788, they had no notion of or feeling for private property. Their great ceremonies were designed to reinforce communal bonds and sharing. The same general importance given to communal values is still manifest in much of Eskimo or Inuit culture. For each of these simpler societies, it turns out that private ownership of goods is not a genetic emotion but a concept that had to be learned from contact with outsiders. [Hughes 1987, 9-16; Carey 1987, 12]

The basic concept of exchange—of one commodity for another—is also not innate but learned. Apparently, in many, perhaps most. primitive societies, the first purpose for objects apart from one's own use was for gift-giving not trading. In the 1930s, tribes of stone-age highlanders in New Guinea, who had believed they were the only human inhabitants on earth, were discovered by explorers from the rest of the world. The explorers found that the highlanders particularly prized pearl shells which were used for gift-giving. A *big man* in rank and prestige was not the one who had accumulated more shells than anyone else but the one who had given away more than anyone else. [Connolly and Anderson 1987]

In eastern Africa away from the coast, as the new colonial administrations from 1870 on attempted to establish a money economy they discovered they had to teach the people the basic concept of economic exchange. Farmers were instructed or coerced into planting a cash crop, such as cotton. When the cotton was picked the farmer would deliver it to the door of the gin and often then leave without collecting any money. Even as late as 1960, this still happened in new cotton-growing areas up-country in Uganda. The idea that you exchange a product for payment was incomprehensible.

What was natural and understandable was the delivery of goods or services as tribute to the chief (in those tribes that had chiefs—not all had). African tradition taught a very limited idea of property rights which did not include the notion of private ownership of land. Communal cooperation in hunting, clearing the land, and building was the custom. All this contributed to the socially-expected flow of tribute to the chief who decided whatever redistribution was needed.

In the high-income countries of the West we have largely forgotten how the cultural consciousness of the average person changed in the transition from the pervasive agricultural economy of the past to the modern industrial societies. The less-developed countries are still struggling with these changes and accompanying traumas. In the course of successful industrialization humans have to force themselves to learn to live methodically by the clock rather than by the uncertain vagaries of nature and the whims of human impulse. People have to be willing or driven to accept the stern discipline of the factory or office and to give up freedom over their day and work. In this transition, quantitative thinking and money values overbear and displace qualitative discrimination, weaken moral values, and inject stress into daily life.

The time-discipline that we in industrialized societies regard as an important virtue is a cultural attitude that has been inculcated in us. The more natural approach is illustrated by the behavior of peasants in the Middle Ages. In the village of Montaillou, now part of France, around the end of the thirteenth century, people were not necessarily lazy but took many days off and celebrated a large number of saints' days. No inordinate incentives were felt to get work done.

> People were fond of having a nap, of taking it easy, of delousing one another in the sun or by the fire. Whenever they could they tended to shorten the working day into a half day. [339][2]

The same absence of time-discipline is seen in what we regard as more primitive human beings—that is, people who are closer to the instinctive core of human behavior. Here is how a group of Athabascan hunters in northwestern Canada operate: after discussing whether to fish for trout or to hunt for moose, they finally agree they will go next morning.

> But come morning, nothing is ready. No one has made any practical formal plans. ...more often than not—something quite new has drifted into conversations, other predictions have been tentatively reached, a new consensus appears to be forming. As it often seems, everyone has changed his mind. [Brody 1982, 36]

---

[2] Even after the transition to a high-income, industrialized, market economy has been completed some people seek haven from the *rat race* by moving to areas like Cape Cod where I live. Here on the Cape, life is guided more by the changes in the seasons than driven by impersonal market forces.

The same lesson of how unnatural the rigid discipline of the clock is inherently for human beings is brought home repeatedly when you live in an African country which is still largely untouched by much economic development.

The culture dominant in an economy affects economic performance. If the level of honesty and trust is high, economic agents can rely that commitments will be honored. Transaction costs are thereby lowered. If people have to continuously protect themselves against being cheated the economy suffers. In many countries the felt need to distrust people outside the family restricts the growth of enterprises—nothing beyond the span of control of family members can be undertaken. The economic performance of a society is directly related to its level of trust.

The work ethic in an economy is also an important economic force. This scarcely needs discussion, it is so obvious. If a worker takes his responsibilities seriously, requires little or no supervision, is creative in carrying his tasks and improving the process or product, the economy is more productive. As an expatriate manager complained to me from frustration with his workers in a poor subsistence-level region: "At home, we say, 'Give me the tools and I will finish the job'. Here, it's 'Give me the job, and I will finish the tools!'"

All economies in the past and most still today assign different duties and functions to people on the basis of their gender. Some of this may be due to biological differences between the sexes but most is dictated by the prevailing culture. Most societies have had rigid cultural divisions between what is considered to be *Man's Work* and what is considered to be *Woman's Work*. In most African countries, growing food is women's work. When increasing population density requires more productivity per acre the women with no free labor time in reserve may not be able to meet the challenge. Since providing food for the men comes first, children and women may not get enough to eat. The result is malnutrition of children and consequent future impoverishment of the society.

In Western economies till very recently, gender dominated the very base of capitalism; that is, property rights. A woman's economic and legal identity was usually subsumed in her husband's. Any property she brought to the marriage was his; any debt she owed he was responsible for. Men also controlled every avenue of achievement.

Humanity is only now in the middle of a transformation that is changing the economic and legal meanings of gender and the place of men and women in the society and the economy. It is only very recently that women have begun to have the autonomy and freedom that economic theory assumes is possessed by every individual.

Every individual chooses voluntarily or involuntarily the value system by which he will govern his life. In the modern high-income countries the individual is under immense cultural pressure to make economic acquisition his major goal. However, it is still possible to escape the *iron cage* of the modern money-driven economic order. [Weber 1958, 181] As in the past, a person can adopt a religious calling which usually entails a life of respectable poverty. Poverty is also typically the fate of most people who choose the aesthetic life as musicians, artists, actors, authors. Rich pecuniary rewards are rare and exceptional. (Leonard Bernstein's father was concerned about his son's welfare when he counseled his son to set aside his music and use his college career to learn something useful which could be reasonably expected to help him make a living. His son stuck with his music and the father later remarked, "How did I know that he would become Leonard Bernstein?")

People choose the intellectual life and become professors, philosophers or scientists because thus they can make their life meaningful even though they know that in these occupations they are likely to have economic rewards below those of successful bond salesmen or used-car dealers. Rank in this aristocracy of rational knowledge is not measured by money gained but by the intellectual contribution made.

People who go into the public service, work for a nonprofit organization, or become a member of some profession, make the choice to put some other objective ahead of pecuniary gain and to that extent opt out of the part of the economy where success is primarily measured by money earnings. They refuse to play the game where as one American billionaire put it, *Money is how you keep score.*

Brian Urquhart, a great international public servant of the post-World War II period, tells in his autobiography how the calling of public service was ingrained in him during his school days. The daily services in Westminster Abbey with the language of the prayer book, the guidance of the masters in conduct and civility, the code of conduct among the students, all contributed to it. Although non-religious he learned, remembered and was guided by the prayer of St. Ignatius Loyola:

> Teach us, good Lord, to serve thee as thou deserves;
> to give and not to count the cost;
> to fight and not to heed the wounds;
> to toil and not to seek for rest;
> to labor and not to ask for any reward,
> save that of knowing that we do thy will....[Urquhart 1987]

The classical Roman ethic of service to the state was important historically and is still important in many countries. The British still successfully attract top Oxbridge graduates into the civil service. In France, the brightest lycée graduates go on to the Grandes Écoles and are trained essentially for service to the state. Since World War II, the graduates of the École Nationale d'Administration hold key governmental positions no matter what government is in power. As of 2000, an *énarque*, as they are called, was president; another, the prime minister (belonging to an opposition party); as were half of the ministers in the cabinet and, most of the ministerial *directeurs de cabinet*. All the leaders of the three main political parties were *énarques*. The *énarques* and the graduates of the other elite schools after some years in top posts in government move on to the big banks and industrial corporations as top managers. The head of the confederation of employers was a classmate of the prime minister at ENA and almost half of the heads of the top 200 corporations in France also graduated from the school.

Even in the United States the public service ethic exists for some people: it was this that motivated General George Marshall, one of America's truly great men of all time. Harvard University's attempt during the 1980s and 1990s to build up the Kennedy School of Public Administration to train students for public service, depended in part on the hope that the classical motive of service to the state could be sufficiently instilled to counter the prevalent material hedonism of American culture.

Remnants of the feudal code also persist in modern states. The society created by feudalism had a profound effect on later social attitudes. While a lord had certain rights, they were linked to certain obligations to his overlord and to the men under him.. It was this ingrained sense of responsibility and service that was involved in Bismarck's invention of Social Security. Rules of fair conduct and fair play; respect for rules, laws and regulations; respect for one's opponents; willingness to observe and apply the same rules to one's side and to one's opponents; loyalty to one's company and to one's country—all these stemming from feudalism are all needed and need to be observed by enough people to make an economy function. [Barzini,182-3]

It also appears reasonable to conclude that the aftermath of feudalism in Japan had something to do with the development of the attitudes and institutions that helped Japan, the first among the non-Western countries to transform herself into a modern nation-state, to adopt the technology and economic institutions of the West and to compete with it successfully. [Reischauer 1970, 112]

There are many ways an individual acquires important culturally-shaped attitudes affecting economic behavior. Among these are child-rearing practices, for example. some American families require their children to earn pocket money by doing household chores and teach their children to save a part of it. Education (over and above the acquisition of economically-valuable skills), management practices in enterprises, and the media are all influential. [Appiah 1994, Harrison 1992] Also important in shaping a person's culture is the kind of leadership a society throws up in the economy, in politics, and in social life The startling economic success of the Ivory Coast in the sixties, seventies and eighties compared to Ghana when both countries have very similar resources bases was largely explained by the difference between the characters of their founders: the Ivory Coast's pragmatic Houphouet-Boigny as against the charismatic Kwame Nkrumah in Ghana.

Religion

The influence of religion is an important force in forming the culture of people even in the high-income countries and has been a dominant element in some periods and regions. Religious beliefs historically have been intimately entwined with or the basis of the system of ethics practiced in a community. (Of course, it is perfectly possible for a system of ethics, as in Confucianism and in much of modern society, to exist without a religious basis.) The system of ethics has important economic implications. The religious values of a society also affect the economy directly. They greatly influence people's attitudes towards work, saving, creativity, cooperation. History and the economy are not the product of economic forces alone. Human will and belief have great impact and these are greatly shaped by religious belief.

It is well-known that Calvinism is probably the religion most consistent with the fundamental economic assumptions of mainstream economics. For a sharer in the Calvinist world view, the desire to be one of the elect and so escape the fires of hell is overwhelming. Economic success reassures you that you are among the elect. The emphasis on individuals studying the Bible for themselves led to widespread literacy in Calvinist (and also in other Protestant countries). Consequently, Calvinist beliefs and the culture in a Calvinist country strongly reinforce the individual's pursuit of his economic self-interest. As our Marxist friends would say, it is probably not an accident that Adam Smith wrote his *Wealth of Nations* in Scotland, a strongly Presbyterian country.

Catholic doctrine originated in pre-capitalist societies. Having outlived both the Roman society based on slavery and the feudal economy resting on serfdom, the Church has never lost sight of the fact "...that life in society has neither the market nor the State as its final purpose...." It is not surprising that the Church has never completely accepted conventional economics' emphasis on maximizing selfish self-interest and individualism. The beginnings of modern capitalism met with hostility from writers of Catholic background such as More, Jonson, Donne, and Pope. And Catholic countries lagged behind Protestant Europe in the early years of capitalist development.

While Church doctrine now approves of a market economy, it must be an economy in which freedom in the economic sector is "...circumscribed within a strong juridical framework which places it at the service of human freedom in its totality...." The Church remains opposed to idolatry of the market; it approves of the market as the most efficient instrument for utilizing resources and effectively responding to needs but it must be appropriately controlled by the forces of society and the State. Workers must be treated as more than suppliers of labor: they have the right to be treated as persons through increased sharing in a supportive community of work, to have the opportunity to grow in skills, to form trade unions, to have a living wage, to be protected from *the nightmare of unemployment* by unemployment insurance and retraining programs capable of ensuring a smooth transition from one employment to another. [Pope John Paul II 1991] While the economies in a number of states have been influenced by Catholic economic doctrines, the German social market economy is probably the most successful.(See Chapter 10)

Judaism and Islam are religions of commandment and of law. In both, codes of law derived from the religion have been worked out over the centuries. These codes contain rules about ritual and civil conduct and inevitably affect economic behavior. In medieval feudal Europe, when the values of the *City of God* were placed above material hedonism and other values of this earth, the economy suffered. Similar forces can be seen in some aspects of Judaism and Islam today.

One of the striking facts of history has been the ability of Jews to win above-average economic success wherever they have lived *in modern times*. Certainly one part of the reason is the history of their persecution as non-Christians.

In the Middle Ages Jews were barred from farming and the medieval guilds refused to let them into the crafts. The Christian governments kept Jews from participating in the feudal land-tenure system. Trade and money lending were the only occupations left to them; their main livelihood had to be in commerce or finance. Since the Church forbade Christians to lend money at interest, rulers recruited *Court Jews* to sin for them and to carry on whatever money exchange was needed. This forced-training in the use of money and in coping with market forces, while a handicap in a society based on inherited privilege, gave Jews an advantage when feudalism was replaced by capitalism. The Jews had been forced into the very occupations which gave economic advantage in the new developing commercial and industrial market world.

(Credibility to this line of reasoning comes from the somewhat parallel experience of the Chinese in South-East Asia. In Indonesia, for example, Chinese descendants regarded as second-class and persecuted citizens learn that money gives security. Opportunities in government and the military are closed to them. To survive, the Chinese are forced into success in commerce and entrepreneurship.)

Another aid to Jewish success stems from their culture as it was shaped from their religion. A Jew has to be literate to be a Jew. The women in the past were less literate than the men but still much more literate than the other women in the societies where they lived. This emphasis on literacy and training the mind through learning must be at least part of the explanation for the giftedness of some and the above-average economic success of most of the Jewish people. [Arendt 1978, 18] Corroboration of this theory appears to be provided by the similar success in the last generation in the United States of those Asian-Americans whose greater emphasis on literacy and learning similarly gives them economic advantages over others in the population.

Not all the influence of Judaism is positive for economic success.

While the very location of Israel is directly due to the religious-based attraction to the area, the economic success of Israel is due to the predominance of secular Jews. The influence of the ultra-Orthodox Jews tends to be counter-productive: men retire from the economy to spend their lives studying religious matters. Traffic through Orthodox areas is not condoned on the Sabbath;[3] non-Orthodox foreign Jews are insulted and turned off from contributing financially.

Just as in the case of Judaism, some of the tenets of the fundamentalist Islamic beliefs hamper modern economic development. While the general picture so far looks bleak as most of the discussion that follows will show, there are some elements in Islam that could turn out to be positively helpful. As Charles Issawi has noted, Islam is after all the only world religion founded by a successful businessman—but in a pre-modern society.

Islam in many respects is a puritanical religion: It forbids the use of intoxicants. It bans gambling. Through its yearly fast it trains people in achieving command over their bodily wants. Such behavior can have significant positive economic effects in the right circumstances. There are, on the other hand, many well-recognized negative economic aspects.

The study of the Koran depending mainly on rote and memory does not encourage widespread literacy or development of reasoning powers. It does inculcate a feeling of the lack of human control over events and, therefore, of responsibility for them. A central theme in the Koran is that all-powerful Allah has ordained everyone's life and determined everyone's fate. "Nothing can befall us but what Allah hath hath destined." (Chapter 9, verse 51) "No people can forestall or retard its destiny." (Chapter 15, verse 5) [Berger 1964, 27]

Every remark about the future by religious Muslims is accompanied by "inshallah" (as God wills it).[4] This is not the best approach for planning.

The content of *al-iqtisad al-Islami*, that is, Islamic economics, is in dispute among Muslims. There is a liberal mainstream that views Islam as favorable to economic and earthly concerns, encourages commerce, upholds the right to hold private property, recognizes the individual's right to pursue self-interest in economic activities mitigated by a strong personal recognition of the need for social solidarity and altruism. It also sanctions intervention by the state in the economy to deal with matters that the private economy cannot cope with. Another radical, populist line of thought is that Muslims should try to create a society of brotherhood, to unite and promote social and economic equality for all. For this the state needs to

---

[3] El-Al, the Israeli airline, is not allowed to openly fly on the Sabbath—when I visited Israel on World Bank business, the Saturday flight I took out was not listed in the timetable.

[4] Our driver in Malaysia nearly succeeded in killing my wife and me by deciding to pass a truck on a curve on a two-lane road. An auto from the opposite direction barely avoided a head-on collision with us by driving off the road. Our driver was not in least upset, he shrugged his shoulders and muttered, "Inshallah".

take a leading activist role in the economy with public ownership as the primary way property is held. [Valibeigi 1993) In the general approach to the economy, one cannot, therefore, judge Islam as being inherently or necessarily a negative force.

Much of the behavior in Islamic countries that is sometimes regarded as counter to growth (lack of discipline, disregard of time-rhythm, focus on family loyalties, contentment with traditional status, lack of ambition, etc.) is typical of preindustrial societies everywhere.

The isolation and lack of education of women are negative factors. In Muslim countries, there is a strong bias if not a strict prohibition against women working for pay outside the home. The available labor force is thus halved and the economic potential severely restricted.[5] Women, confined to the house and isolated, are also likely to have many children—the opportunity cost of a child is lower. And the children, then, are brought up by uneducated women with all the adverse economic consequences this entails. The importance of schooling for women in advancing economic development and curbing population growth has been demonstrated over and over in many countries. Houphouet-Boigny, the president of the Ivory Coast, succinctly made the point when he commented that development of his country depended on "Producing three generations of educated women".

Islam regards all uncultivated agricultural land and all natural resources as belonging to the public. The nationalization of all oil reserves in the Middle East was, therefore, consistent with Islam and to be expected as soon as the countries felt sufficiently independent of imperial control. Since Islam does not recognize separate spheres for life, religion and the state, state entrance into and control of the economy is perfectly natural.

Islamic principle forbids the payment of interest on a loan. Interest is defined as securing a guaranteed profit on capital. Thus Islamic investors can not own bonds which pay regular interest payments but they may own common stocks which can lose or earn money for their owners. The need to avoid charging interest can depress economic growth whenever there is strict observance of the Koran (Qur/an). For example, in 1986, this principle caused some problems in Saudi Arabia. The drop in oil prices created difficulty for many borrowers and some decided to refuse to pay interest on their bank loans. Banks were justifiably hesitant to take the recalcitrant borrowers to court. In several cases, judges ruled the the banks must repay all the interest they collected from a debtor in the past. Bank lending as a result was greatly inhibited.

The sacred texts do not make the extension of credit impossible. Profitable trade is condoned in Islam so many Muslim countries have de-

---

[5] This discrimination is also bad for men in the Middle East Arab Muslim countires. A boy, privileged because of his sex. loses drive for achievement. Malaysia and other Muslim areas are different—suggesting that this effect may be due to older cultures that Islam has overlain.The unearned wealth in the oil-rich Arab countries adds to this effect. [I owe this observation to David Landes.]

veloped a system of Islamic banking based on the sharing of risk and profit rather than the payment of interest. A transaction that elsewhere would be handled as lending at interest is instead structured as some kind of exchange. A variety of partnership-like arrangements have evolved to substitute for loans. In broad terms, no interest rate is set, instead the lender and borrower agree how the profits or losses are to be shared between the two from the venture to be financed. What is agreed is not a rate of interest accruing over time but a ratio between what is lent and what is repaid and the time factor may be flexible or renegotiable.

Deposits in a bank are set up as shares receiving a portion of the bank's profits. Instead of making loans, the bank finances the purchase of a car, for example, and sells it, taking a profit, to the customer with the payments to the bank spread over time. In making a loan to a firm, the bank may receive a contractual share of the profits earned by the firm or in the profit generated by the particular project financed by the bank. Home buyers make a down payment, just as in the West. Instead of the credit institution financing the remainder of the price through a mortgage, the bank buys the rest of the house and leases it to the buyer. The buyer then pays rent plus somewhat more to increase his equity in the house. After 30 years, say, the owner-resident takes full ownership of the house. However, if the owner does not keep up the payments, he does not run lose all his equity in the house. The equity is divided between the owner-resident and the bank according to how much each has contributed.

An Islamic bank has religious advisers to ensure that the bank respects Islamic law. An Islamic bank is not supposed to finance enterprises involved with alcoholic beverages, tobacco products, gambling or arms manufacture.

The disadvantages of Islamic banking, clearly, are not insuperable. Some western banks operating in Islamic countries provide *Islamic* windows that provide services consistent with the sacred texts. There could even be some advantages to Islamic-banking through its encouragement of equity finance over debt. It may make lenders be more concerned with the profitability rather than the collateral of firms they lend to.

The real stumbling block is the inconsistency of Islamic banking with the business culture in Islamic countries like Iran and Pakistan. For profit-sharing loans to be practical the bank has to be able to trust the profit-and-loss accounts of the firms. But firms to avoid taxes, generally understate their income and overstate their costs and the bank winds up, cheated of its return. The advantage of interest-bearing loans over profit-sharing turns out to be that a loan based on collateral avoids the need to trust the accounts of the borrower. Finally, of course, countries can find another way around the interest-prohibition by reinterpreting it as prohibiting usury, not normal interest.

The recent upsurge of Muslim fundamentalism in many Islamic countries that demands the abolition of lending with interest is, consequently, anti-modernizing and anti-secular and is bound to be a strong anti-growth force wherever it becomes an important political factor.

In Pakistan, the Supreme Court ruled in December 1999 that "any amount, big or small, paid over the principal in a contract of loan or debt is 'riba' [i.e. interest] and prohibited by the holy Koran, regardless of whether the loan is taken for the purpose of consumption or for some production activity". The Court went on to say that "the present financial system, based on interest, is against the injunctions of Islam...and in order to bring it into conformity with sharia, it has to be subjected to radical changes" by 2001. [Asghar 1999, A10]

The fundamentalist movement in Islam is not unique. Similar phenomena are occurring in all three Abrahamic *religions of the Book*: Judaism, Christianity and Islam—that is, a discrediting of modernism; complaints about the fragmentation of society, its *anomie*, the absence of an overarching ideal; and a demand for recovering a religious foundation for society and government. Successful in Afghanistan, fundamentalism has shown results similar to those of the societies (Nazi Germany, Communist Soviet Union, Khmer Rouge Cambodia) that were ruled by a all-embracing political ideology. The official class of interpreters—the Party in totalitarian states, the clergy in medieval Christian Spain, or Afghanistan—have all the answers. Everything important has been predetermined. Such societies are inimical to reason and independent thought and lead, ultimately and inevitably, to economic stagnation. [Kepel 1994]

Confucianism is not strictly a religion but an ethical code, political philosophy, and a guide to social conduct.. The ethical teachings of Confucius emphasize devotion to parents, family and friends, the importance of benevolent and moral government devoted to the maintenance of justice and peace. They instill respect for study and learning and the recognition of competence. They emphasize social harmony, taking into account the need of everyone to maintain self-respect, saving *face*.

The various tenets of Confucianism have turned out to be beneficial to modern economic development in the new circumstances of the post World War II world. Its central values of education, merit, work, and frugality have motivated economic progress in the countries it influences. The devotion to the family works to induce family members to help the family: unessential consumption is discouraged and savings and the education of children are encouraged. The stress on social harmony mitigates social strife. The teachings of Confucius also led to the development of a meritocratically selected bureaucracy in all countries influenced by them. Such a bureaucracy in the Chinese Empire based on a land-owning ruling class was an important influence in keeping the economy unchanging. In recent years, however, similarly-chosen bureaucracies in the new circumstances of Japan, South East Asia, and South Korea have become important engines of economic progress. (See Chapter 10)

Buddhism is a religion without a god. While there are now numerous versions of Buddhism, they all share the fundamental teachings of Gautam Buddha. These can be stated briefly, if imperfectly, as follows:

There are Four Noble Truths.

1. All human life is suffering.
2. Suffering comes from desire.
3. By eliminating desire, we end suffering.
4. Enlightenment, the end of suffering, is achieved by following the Middle Path. This avoids the extreme of seeking happiness through the pleasures of the senses and avoids the other extreme of seeking happiness through self-mortification in asceticism.

The Four Noble Truths lead the believer to Nirvana: perfect knowledge of the Truth, happiness—serenity, freedom from desire—and escape from rebirth and the relentless Wheel of Life. [Rahula 1979]

Buddhism appears to be in direct contradiction to the fundamental tenets of conventional economic theory and to hedonistic market capitalism. Orthodox Buddhism is strong in Burma, Cambodia, Chittagong in Bangladesh, Laos, Sri Lanka, Thailand. Another main branch, which developed later, is present in China, Japan, Mongolia, Tibet. Buddhism is also growing rapidly in the United States though it is still a relatively minor religion in terms of relative numbers.

There has been relatively little consideration of the economic impact of Buddhism. Certainly, it has been a major or even dominant factor in the economy of Tibet over the centuries. By converting the Mongols from predatory conquerors to peaceful nomadic herdsmen, it was a major economic influence in Mongolia's development. It probably has been a force in inhibiting capitalistic development in other countries. Whether this has been good or bad in terms of the welfare of the peoples concerned is not definitively clear.

Corporate Culture

Every corporation evolves a specific culture of its own and this has an important economic effect on how it operates and its impact on the economy. How well two corporate cultures meld can be decisive in determining the success of a corporate merger or acquisition. When General Motors acquired Electronic Data Systems in 1984 it decided that it was wise to allow EDS to continue to function as an independent company in order to preserve the EDS innovative culture. Just the same, it did not work out well and the head of EDS, Ross Perot, turned out to be so out of step with the GM managers that they finally paid him several hundred million dollars to leave the company. When GM acquired Hughes Aircraft Co. in 1985, it was taken for granted that GM was doing so precisely to acquire its risk-taking culture. Hughes encourages its employees to pursue "harebrained schemes", to take risks andto do things that have never been done before. Because of this, Hughes does not do well at mass production and tends instead to look down at repetitive occupations like making autos. [Darlin & Harris,14]

The biggest American bank merger up to 1992, between Bank America and Security Pacific, resulted in a clash of vastly different corporate cultures. Bank America was centralized, run-by-the-rules, and ultra-conservative. Security Pacific was decentralized and freewheeling. After the $4.6 billion merger, so many of the Security Pacific managers left or were forced out of the new bank that the process was termed "ethnic cleansing".

The 1993 merger of the two warehouse-club giants, Costco Wholesale Corp.and Price Co. failed due to the clash of cultures. After 10 months, the board of directors gave up, kept the Costco executives in the warehouse-club business, but spun off its real estate business into a separate company to be run by the former Price team.

The World Bank and the International Monetary Fund were both created at the same conference at Bretton Woods in 1944. According to their charters, both have the same general system of governance: ownership by governments, weighted-voting, ultimate authority in a Board of Governors, day-to-day control of the management and staff by a Board of Directors. But the cultures of the two organizations have evolved very differently. The Fund has the stability and hushed tones of a central bank; the Bank is constantly changing, dynamic, and, at times, chaotic. In my 28 years in the Bank I worked in five different departments—only one of which still exists. My friends in the Fund passed their entire career in a single department.

Motorola and Minnesota Mining and Manufacturing (3M) are two of the most successful high-tech companies in the last decades of the twentieth century. Both rely on a culture that fosters internal debate, freewheeling and autonomous business and research units, and the vigorous competition of ideas. In a Motorola plant, teams participate in hiring and firing co-workers, decide on their own training and in cooperation with other teams schedule their work.

It is almost a truism that an entrepreneur who can successfully launch a new business is rarely able to mange it once it has developed beyond the initial stage. McClelland and Burnham identify the need for achievement or "the desire to do something better or more efficiently than it has been done before" as characteristic of people who successfully start new small businesses. [McClelland & Burnham 1976]

Such a drive is consistent with "self-interest" but not necessarily with selfishness. The achievement motive drives people to act in ways that do not necessarily lead to good management or the highest profits. People who have this drive usually want to do things themselves since it is their own achievement that motivates them. But a manager's job is to motivate other people to carry out what needs to be done. Management, in fact, is often defined as reaching objectives through other people. McClelland and Burnham argue that successful managers have a need for personal power but the need is "socialized"; that is, directed toward managing others' behavior for the benefit of the organization and not limited to the manager's personal aggrandizement. In short, successful managers are not inevitably the pure selfish actors contemplated in conventional economics.

All this, however, presupposes a culture that encourages or at least accepts change. The managements of the large successful American corporations in the early post World War II years became arrogant in their belief that they were superior to any possible international competitors. The Japanese after World War II were desperate. Their factories had been destroyed, the sources of their raw materials in the old Empire had gone, and the reputation of Japanese goods was bad. They turned for guidance to W. Edwards Deming, an American industrial engineer, who preached the doctrine that quality of product and a harmonious workplace took precedence over short-term profit. The Deming Prize awarded to a company for excellence of quality became the greatest honor a Japanese company could win. As for American corporate leadership, Deming commented with scorn, "The one thing we must never export is American management—at least to friendly countries" [Halberstam 1984, 4] It took at least twenty years from the 1970s to the 1990s before American companies in the old manufacturing industries changed their corporate culture enough to be able to compete with the Japanese on an equal basis.

As a previously-successful goods-producing economy becomes dominated by services, the culture becomes stressed. In material-goods production, there is the possibility to measure the concrete contribution made by an individual and reward it correspondingly, more or less accurately, Measuring contributions and scaling rewards accurately is much more difficult in the provision of human services. In addition, the provision of such services is intimately linked to the human being providing the service. The economic success of a direct service provider may depend on the ability of an individual to persuade customers to choose him rather than his competitors. His personality, appearance, attractiveness become important without regard to the economic value of the service he provides. The individual thus feels the pressure to reshape himself or to conceal himself behind the projection of an attractive image to others. It is not surprising that many such people who are economic successes are deeply unhappy and, in their turn, contribute to the growth of the services economy by compulsive patronage of psychiatrists or become self-destructive drug or alcohol addicts.

In the modern complex organizations, there are vast areas where it is impossible to measure and reward precisely the behavior of individuals. Yet how well the economy runs depends on how well each person lives up to his or her particular responsibilities. Even more, how satisfying or how frustrating everyday life is for everybody depends on how people do their jobs even though they may not be rewarded for that last bit of courtesy or thoughtfulness.

Everyone has experienced the maddening behavior of petty corporate or government bureaucrats exploiting their small field of discretion to try to bully you in some detail of the business you have with them. The experience is often even worse in dealing with French or Italian petty bureaucrats. (This common experience is one of the reasons people instinctively prefer to deal with small units of government and small owner businesses.) In Japan, the culture calls for people to do their best without regard to reward and this eliminates much of this kind of unpleasantness. In some less developed countries petty bureaucratic annoyances are avoided through paying small bribes. In these latter countries, an economist will note, annoyance is avoided by using market incentives; in Japan, through cultural means. However, even the most avid free market economist experiencing both situations is likely to prefer the Japanese solution.

Concluding Remarks

The culture of a society has been created by human beings and can be changed by human beings. If the future of an economy is being crippled by a smothering culture, an aware national leadership can try to change those features of the culture that are hurting—through the schools, the press, and all the other ways available in the country to bring about changes. Japanese history is rich in examples in the way in which particular cultural behavior was changed. The number of children that a Japanese family desires to have since World War II compared to pre-WWII is one example. An American tourist in Europe or an European tourist in America is struck by the way in which smoking in public places has become a social "no-no" in the United States while still fully respectable in Europe.

Even without changing a culture, it is often possible to contrive ways to make its influence economically positive instead of negative.

Just as culture influences an economy, the economy may influence culture. As a stagnant economy begins to grow, incentives change and may affect some aspects of the culture to make it more welcoming to economic growth. In Sub-Saharan Africa, family ties are strong. This tends to discourage individual enterprise and initiative, as the burden of family obligations rises with the economic success of an individual. However, many African successful businessmen have learned to appear poor, hungry and needy to their families. Like the Chinese before them, other Africans are learning to convert extended family connections to assets. Some families pool their tiny savings to send a bright child to higher education. In Nigeria, Ibo workers away from their villages, tax themselves and club together to send funds home to their village to finance improvements. Others club together to finance the starting of a small business. [Kamarck 1972 Second printing, 64-8] There are other striking examples as well: the rapid emergence of successful industrial and then exporter entrepreneurs from a precapitalist society given the opportunity of a new national economy from the formation of the new nation of Pakistan.[6]

---

[6] I owe this point to Gustav Papanek.

The neoclassical model ascribes economic growth to the increase in the supply of capital and labor with technological change as an exogenous factor. Recent theorists have tried to include the technical changes within the growth function. Even with this new so-called "endogenous" approach the models are still crippled by tunnel vision. There is much more involved.

In the early years of the World Bank when we were trying to establish a rational basis for decisions on lending and on policy advice to countries throughout the world, we found that pure economic analysis was not enough. To attain a better prediction of a country's economic future it was important to secure an understanding of how a people and governing elite handled change and the challenges of adversity. It was as important to get acquainted with a country's literature, social customs and other perceptive evidences of its social capital as with its economic statistics. I learned over and over that there are many reasons why some countries and ethnic groups do better economically than others. Economic management, climate, natural resources, geographic location, chance, and culture are all involved to lesser or greater degree. A country with a culture that encourages cooperation and productive initiatives, that puts a high value on work, education and training will tend to do well. Countries that are tradition-bound, that tolerate or even encourage social conflict, that accept or admire successful predators will do poorly. And, the specific culture, the social human capital, of a country or of an ethnic group is a major influence in every case. [Kamarck 1970]

10 National Cultures

Think on the greatness of your city night and day; cast your eyes on her beauty and splendor, and let them sink deep into your soul till you conceive a passion for her, and become, as it were, her lovers, and are filled with devotion for her. —Pericles, funeral oration.

In the world today, in most countries the prevalent culture is a resultant of most of the major forces sketched in the preceding chapter—surviving preindustrial attitudes, religion, materialistic hedonism, and particular national or ethnic histories. In the less developed countries the mixture is changing before our eyes. The material hedonistic element has been growing stronger as the success of the characteristic elements of what is known as "American mass culture" attests. However, the backlash of Moslem fundamentalism in Islamic countries as well as the continuance in the high-income countries of some of the anti-success attitudes of the sixties generation indicate that it is not inevitable that national cultures evolve in the direction of emphasizing economic growth.

Put in more familiar economic terms, a nation's social human capital provides the social infrastructure and the social constraints that have major deterministic effects on the fate of the economy.

An important dimension of any effective national economic policy has to be the consideration of how the prevailing culture influences the national economic goals and what, if any, cultural changes need to be encouraged. The rest of this chapter will illustrate briefly through highlighting a few examples how certain salient features of particular national cultures affect their economies. This is far from a comprehensive analysis, of course. A thorough job would require a book-length treatment for each culture sketched here.

Great Britain and Northern Ireland

As Margaret Jacob has shown, the Scientific Revolution of the sixteenth and seventeenth centuries depended on the culture and political conditions of Great Britain [1988]. This led directly to the Industrial Revolution that fundamentally transformed the British economy from 1750 to 1850. For both, there had to be a distinctive social and political milieu. For the origins of industrialization, particular cultural and political conditions were as necessary as economic considerations. Britain also exemplifies how the impact of a particular cultural characteristic can at one time be favorable to economic growth and later in changed circumstances retard it.

154

The status-conscious British society, perversely, was an initial help to economic growth. Dissenters and Quakers led in the creation of the Industrial Revolution in Britain. Legally barred from Oxford and Cambridge and the existing elite occupations (the Church, military and the public service), they could turn their minds and energies to inventing machines and building factories. The Unitarians in Manchester— barred from filling their heads with Hebrew, Latin and Greek at the ancient universities—turned instead to science. They fostered scientists like Priestly, Dalton, and Joule, and helped found the British Association for the Advancement of Science and the University of Manchester, the world-leader well into the twentieth century in physics. [Dyson 1989, 39-40]

Britain led the world into industrialization and was the dominant economic power for around a century. It then experienced a century-long relative industrial decline to around 1980; since then, British living standards have roughly matched those of other Western European countries.

There are several reasons offered for Britain's relative slide.[1] Certainly the cost and exhaustion of being a major player in two world wars, a generation apart; the end of empire; a class-ridden anti-business culture; and an educational system ill-fitted for modern economic growth, all played a part.

Britain's long dominance also discouraged it from changing those features of the economy and culture that were a drag on its growth. Success breeds complacency. Britain failed for over a century to shift resources out of the initial industries of industrialization in which it became uncompetitive into more technologically advanced industries. Old firms with long industrial traditions made adapting to new conditions difficult and Britain's long delay in joining the Common Market protected them from invigorating competition.

In his classic *Sovereignty at Bay,* Vernon commented:

> Those who have the courage to generalize on the subject describe amateurism as a major characteristic of British heads of enterprise. The amateurism is evidenced by the lack of vocational preparation on the part of businessmen, and by the preference of executives for a leisurely work pace and a limited degree of personal involvement. Like most clichés, these generalizations have their striking exceptions, especially in recent years. But there is not much doubt that they also retain considerable validity. [Vernon 1971, 217]

A British Foreign Office professional observed, in trying to help British companies win foreign contracts,

> ... that even if one had an important report affecting a matter in which

---

[1] See Kindlelberger (1996) "Britain, the Classic Case" in *World Economic Primacy,* 125-148, for a more comprehensive review.

hundreds of thousands of pounds were involved, it was impossible to talk to any responsible person in the firm concerned except on Tuesdays, Wednesdays and Thursdays—perhaps Friday mornings; from Friday to Monday business seemed to be at a standstill. [Kelly 1952, 207]

The most common explanation for Great Britain's relative economic decline is that it is due to the British *anti-industrial culture*. This "cultural critique" argues that British society is actively prejudiced against business. To be "in trade" is to be looked down upon. Surgeons, in the nineteenth century, could not call themselves "Doctor", because their work suggested manual labor. A physician's wife could be presented at court, but not a surgeon's. Solicitors received fees from their clients, so they were in trade. Buffered by the solicitor from the vulgar, the barrister was a gentleman and his wife could be presented in court. [Pool 1993]

After Humphrey Davy (1778-1829), recognized as the greatest scientist of his day, was knighted and married, he devoted much of his energy to trying to emulate the aristocracy. This vain endeavor was destructive of his dedication to science.

Wealth and property were respectable and socially-legitimate only when these came from inheritance rather than from competitive hustling. Successful English businessmen retired early to estates in the country. They tried to imitate the life of the horse-riding landed-gentry. Their sons were trained to be gentlemen not businessmen. They were enrolled in the public schools, like Eton, Harrow, Winchester, where they were taught aristocratic values and went into the public service, the Church or the military.

There is certainly substance to this critique.The Confederation of British Industry, for example, reported in 1992 that in Britain, manufacturing has to "...struggle to attract the country's best young people". A study to discover what career the children of successful men in industry took up found that out of the 40 children of the 26 company chairmen and chief executives participating in the study, only five went into industry. *[The Economist* November 14, 1992, 64; Wiener 1981; Rubinstein 1993]

Astute writers depict the same theme. The poet W. B. Yeats boasted that he had *blood/ That has not passed through any huckster's loin*. In a Somerset Maugham short story, a successful businessman has been made a baronet and has acquired an Elizabethan mansion with a spacious park. Although he has won acceptance in the county, he is a poor rider in following the hounds; he has excellent shooting but he is a bad shot; he has a golf course but is an indifferent golfer. He has set his mind that his son and heir, George, would not go into business but would be "an English gentleman". He was taught to shoot as soon as he could hold a gun; he rode a pony from the age of two. George was sent to Oxford with a large allowance and was completely idle there; the baronet does not care.

You know, I've got an idea that nowhere in the world now is the Greek ideal of life so perfectly cultivated as by the English country gentleman living on his estates. I think his life has the beauty of a work of art. ["The Alien Corn"]

But the aristocratic feudal anti-industrial *ethos* was also as strong if not stronger on the Continent. Where England suffered was in the fact that its landed aristocracy proved to be more permeable to the newly rich businessmen. Their sons educated at the public schools passed easily into the aristocratic ruling class. "At present if a chap goes to the right schools and universities, and passes the right exams, he has a good shot at getting an interesting and well-rewarded job pulling on the levers of power..." [*The Economist* May 2, 1998, 52]

On the Continent, in contrast, sons of businessmen were not accepted and had to stay in business. [Clesse and Coker 1997, 145, 152]

But the *culture critique* is not the whole story; it undoubtedly is part of the explanation but not all. In taking a sample survey of American industrialists I discovered that the American Ivies have little if any better record than Oxbridge in regard to the economy. The Ivy graduates who do go into industry opt for consultative jobs—lawyers, management consultants, investment bankers. The command-oriented jobholders like CEOs, come from technical schools, state universities, or from second or third class colleges, the kind that Americans call *Podunk U*: Robert E. Allen, CEO of AT&T, had his BA degree from Wabash College; in 1996, both the CEO of General Electric and of General Motors were graduates of the University of Massachusetts. William Gates, the founder of Microsoft, was sent to Harvard but dropped out. The founders of Apple Computer were also college drop-outs. The American advantage, here, is simply that bright and ambitious young have access to a wide spectrum of education.

English society has been and to a considerable degree still is an elaborate hierarchy of ranks and orders, preoccupied with finely graded distinctions of prestige ranking. People are obsessed with status. Titles, honors, descent, accent, social behavior, and dress matter greatly and determine how people are treated and regarded. Henry James observed that the hierarchical plan of English society was the great and ever-present fact to a stranger. The great Australian novel, Henry Richardson's *The Fortunes of Richard Mahony*, gives an unforgettable depiction of the class society in an English community. George Orwell commented that England was the most class-ridden country under the sun. This perception was reinforced for me, personally, over and over again during the 30 years that I worked closely with Englishmen and women in Allied headquarters in World War II and the international World Bank staff after the war.

The English class system divides the population, fosters antagonism in the workplace and reduces the degree of cooperation in coping with the changes in economic life. ...*always...the complication of class and snobbery present at every level of English society.* [James 1997, 219] The class system hampers the emergence of talent from the lower classes. It obstructs mobility; ideas are lost and opportunities are missed.

The bitterness and antagonism in British labor–management relations appears greater than in most other countries. The feeling among workers of "them" against "us" leads, as described by Arthur Koestler, to the unwritten rules of work in the factory: *Go slow; it's a mug's game*; if you seek promotion, you are breaking ranks and will be sent to Coventry. [1980, 571-80]

In recent years, companies from outside of Britain have established factories in the country. *The Economist* made a study of a factory owned by a British firm and one owned by the German firm Bosch. The British factory's managers have their plush dining room and car park, workers keep themselves to themselves and make no suggestions to management on improvements in productivity. In Bosch, workers and managers clock in together, wear the same overalls and share all facilities. Workers are proud of working at the company and come up with a multitude of suggestions for improving productivity. [February 27, 1993, 61]

The class system largely explains why Britain failed during the nineteenth and early twentieth century to improve the nature and level of education to match that of its emerging economic competitors. Before 1902, Britain had no government secondary-school system and for most of the century continued to have a smaller percentage of children completing secondary school and university-level education than Germany, Japan or the United States. The humanistic bias in education and the snobbery that extended the disdain for "trade" to applied science[2] inhibited building the adequate applied science base necessary for the development of new modern science-based products.

During the last half of the nineteenth century while American and German firms were developing professional managements to cope with the new large scale industries required for maximum efficiency, British firms continued to remain largely family-owned and personally managed. Even in some industries such as dyestuffs where the British had originally both the technological lead and the biggest market, the British fell behind the Germans. The British family firms were not primarily interested in growth. They preferred to use the profits for current income to support their English upper class life styles. [Chandler 1990; Teece 1993]

London as a world financial center, and the large flow of British savings into overseas investment (bonds and preference shares rather than direct investment) encouraged the development of a rentier psychology in Britain. [Nye 1990, 90] The priority given to financial interests still has large economic effects. In the British system of bankruptcy, the emphasis is on retrieving as much money as possible for the creditors. It is not re-

---

[2] cf. Melvyn Bragg: ... (the) *tired old British tradition of intellectual snobbery which considers all knowledge, especially science, as "trade"*. And, Sir Peter Medawar, *Our fastidious distaste for the applied sciences and for trade has played a large part in bringing England to the position in the world which she occupies today.* Both quoted in Dawkins 1998, 40]

garded as important to save the firm as a going concern. Consequently, in the deep recession after 1979, large numbers of firms closed for good and their machinery was scrapped. When demand revived the capacity was not there to meet it. In the United States, troubled firms survive by being allowed to reorganize and in the following boom the economy is better able to meet demand. [Hudson 1990]

Germany

Since the end of World War II, when the country was in ruins and occupied by the victorious powers, west Germany has become an outstanding economic success. This *Wirschaftswunder* was facilitated by fact that the Junker landowning class had been largely dispossessed by the westward movement of Poland's boundary and the older business and political leaders had been replaced by new men through Denazification.

The German social market economy, that is, an economy where economic policies are strongly affected by public social conscience, is considerably different from a pure market economy or even the present-day American competitive managerial economy. (Alfred D. Chandler, in fact, contrasts American capitalism to what he calls German *cooperative managerial capitalism*.) [1990] With one of the highest per capita incomes in the world, Germans have a quality of life surpassing in most respects that of Americans: in art and music, public infrastructure, security from crime, social safety-net, high wages, short working hours, generous vacations.

The state has taken an active leadership role in the economy for centuries. Frederick William, the Great Elector of Brandenburg, (1640-88) began, and his grandson, Frederick William I of Prussia, (1713-40) continued a policy of enlightened paternalism. Inheriting the efficient bureaucracy they had created, Frederick the Great on ascending to the throne in 1740 had the instrument to raise the economic, social and cultural level of Prussia. He imported Frenchmen like Voltaire, Maupertuis and La Mettrie to enrich Prussian intellectual life and even to head some of the administrative departments. State aid was used to create and encourage industry and trade and to improve agriculture.

In the nineteenth century, after the devastation of the Napoleonic wars Germany was finally unified by rail, telegraph, a customs union and the creation of the Empire in 1871. German universities led in the development of chemistry and physics and in their application in medicine and industry. Technical universities were created to directly train students for industry. German universities, all government-financed, began to provide education for business management as well as graduate programs in engineering. German universities and technical institutes led the United States in supplying business with scientific knowledge and trained managers, engineers and technicians.

Germans also learned from the long experience of bureaucratic management in government to create their own effective organizations run by salaried professionals. The modern industrial enterprise appeared in Germany in the late nineteenth century at around the same time as it did in the United States. By World War I, German industrial development had moved so fast that Germany surpassed Britain even in industries such as iron and steel and chemicals which Britain had pioneered and in which it had possessed the initial technological advantage.

The feudal concept of an occupation as a *calling* has survived and has been institutionalized in the apprentice system in industry. German governments take the provision of training for young workers by the enterprise very seriously. It is regarded as vital to maintenance of the quality of German workmanship and consequently to the international competitiveness of the country. The public employment agency, the Labor Office, helps place apprentices. The firm bears the full cost of wages and the cost of the in-firm training while the government provides continuing part-time academic and theoretical instruction at a state vocational school and makes sure the quality of the training is maintained. Unions are involved in every step pushing for broad and quality training. [Spring 1987] As compared to similar enterprises in France, German wage differentials are smaller, German non-manual workers are fewer and earn lower relative wages than their French counterparts.

The social character of modern German capitalism began as early as the 1880s when Bismarck's government, stimulated by the growing socialist vote, invented and introduced the first social security system to mitigate the insecurities inflicted on workers in Germany's rapid industrialization. Count Bismarck took feudal *Noblesse Oblige* seriously. Loyalty-down as well as loyalty-up mattered and he wished to treat workers as human beings worthy of respect and not as mere hands recruited in an impersonal market. In contrast, as late as 1930 in the Great Depression, when millions of American workers were out on the streets trying to survive by such pitiful expedients as selling apples on street corners, the American Federation of Labor took a firm stand in its Vancouver annual convention against unemployment insurance. Government help to the unemployed was "un-American" and not the "American Way".

At the beginning of the twenty-first century, the two dominant German governing parties, the Christian Democrats and Social Democrats, share a strong consensus on how the economy should operate. They have never believed in a naked raw capitalism with the market allowed to reign unchecked. The government is now much less directly activist and *dirigiste* than in the past but the economy operates within a framework of laws setting the rules for the competitive economy. Government itself is decentralized in the federal republic with important functions in the *Land* governments and a highly independent central bank. (See Appendix B, "German Central Bank")

The highly regulated, redistributive social economy has been managed by a "social partnership" between employers and employees within the structure of governmental legal institutions. German corporations, *Aktiengesellschaften (AG)* have two boards: a management board for the routine management of the business and a supervisory board for long-term policy. The banks and majority stockholders are usually represented on the supervisory board and after World War II, the law mandated that worker representatives have fifty percent of these seats. This *Mitbestimmung* arrangement gives workers a stake in the long run future of their enterprise. The banks have long-term relationships with the firms on whose boards they sit. The corporate boards, the works councils, employer associations and local chambers of commerce give a high priority to training and education. The commitment by workers and unions to their companies favors investment by firms in training their workers in skills building on their formal education. The result is a higher skilled work force than in any other country in the world.

This German social market economy was highly successful in mastering the reconstruction and growth after World War II. At the beginning of the third millennium, it is faced with challenges almost as taunting. It has to complete the absorption of the East German economy with its outmoded industries, low productivity, and high unemployment. At the same time, it must be nimble enough to cope with the revolutionary changes flooding in from globalization and the precipitous technological transformations. While there is bound to be a difficult period of transition, one should have reasonable confidence in the long-term success of the German economy. A reservation to this conclusion, however, stems from Kindleberger's remark: "Perhaps... the German economy, like many before it, is becoming somewhat rigidified." [1996, 171]

Latin America

The Latin American countries are many and diverse. All, however, have lower per capita incomes and lag in industrial development behind the two North American countries of Canada and the United States. There are historical reasons for this, besides the differences in culture. Much of the area of Spanish America was inhabited by Indians who had already established extractive industries and the new Spanish rulers continued to extract value rather than establish productive agriculture and industries. Central America and much of South America are in the Tropics with all the obstacles that this poses. (See next chapter) And, Spain and Portugal brought the tradition and practice of centralized bureaucratic power with the governmental powers controlled by large landowners prizing inward-looking conformity and tradition. The economy of many of the countries was based on large scale plantations and forced Indian labor during the period of Spanish rule. As a result, the ruling class maintained and strengthened the prejudice brought from Spain against work with their hands. [Harrison 1985]

The history of Argentina is significant. In 1920, Argentina ranked with Canada and Australia as a growing high-income economy. Its stock market had a high market capitalization. Its standard of living was above that of Italy and Spain. It was an attractive country for immigrants from Southern Europe. Argentina is a temperate zone country with none of the special obstacles that tropical countries have to cope with. Its soil is rich and the country is well endowed with other natural resources. The population is nearly completely European in origin with the rich Western cultural tradition. There are no deep-seated major racial or religious differences dividing the population. The ratio of population to area or resources is not high and the rate of natural population growth is low—comparable to Europe.

In 1930, Argentina provided 25 percent of the world's wheat exports, 65 percent of the world's maize exports, and 38 percent of the world's red meat. By 1976, these percentages were down to 4, 12 and 13 percent [Almeyra 1985, 34] By 2000, Argentina's per capita GDP was around a third of that of Australia or Canada. A substantial part of the explanation for the different success stories of these countries must be sought in the different cultural backgrounds of these countries.

Japan

While the Japanese economy and political system had to undergo the painful decade of the 1990s in coping with the fall-out from the over-exuberant share and land price bubble economy of the eighties, Japan's economic achievement in the last half of the twentieth century was outstanding. Between 1950 and 1992, Japan increased its share of the growing world output from 1 percent to around 15 percent. Japan became the world's second largest economic power and the world's largest creditor. The people benefited directly: Japanese children, once the shortest among the industrial countries, now have similar height standards as European and North American children. In 1950, Japanese life expectancy was only around 50 years; in 2000, at approximately 80 years, it was the highest in the world. According to a World Health Organization study released in June 2000, the Japanese people had the best prospects in the world for long active lives. The average healthy life expectancy of a Japanese child born in 1999 was over 74 years compared to 70 for Americans.[3]

The economic success of Japan should force even theory-bound economists to recognize that the evolution of a national economy is affected by its society and culture, The successful world-competitive Japanese industry did not emerge as the inevitable outcome of free market forces but was strongly guided by planned conscious effort. Since the Meiji Restoration, the Japanese goals have been, in the words of Japa-

---

[3] This measure of population health, "disability-adjusted life expectancy" (DALE), deducts from total life expectancy, the estimated years of ill health due to particular disabling ailments.

nese economist Komiya, "making the economy self-sufficient" and "catching up with the West". The defeat in World War II strengthened the resolve to become a powerful industrial and technological nation. [Komiya 1990 quoted in Gilpin 1997, 78]

The Japanese have shown a high capability to modify their behavior and adapt or transform their institutions as necessary. [Saxenhouse 1993; Lawrence 1993] Japan modernized its economy, while maintaining its fundamental culture, and adapting the pre-modern aspects of the culture into economic strengths. As Vernon described it:

> Some of the key values that dominate Japanese society today were shaped by the centuries of feudal rule that ended in 1868. ...One was the commitment to goal attainment... A second was the concept of shared responsibility within any group for the achievement of a task assigned to the group...
>
> The Japanese managed to draw another social characteristic into their distinctive feudal mix... Despite the emphasis on group responsibility and the existence of a rigid pecking order within any given group, Japanese institutions managed to reward obvious individual merit and Japanese society to tolerate considerable mobility between the classes.
>
> ...the transition from feudalism to a modern society ... occurred over decades rather than centuries. As a result, the élite ... were able to draw on some of the surviving preindustrial Japanese characteristics of group loyalty, shared group responsibility, and task-achievment orientation when managing the process of transition.
>
> The social organization that emerged to take over the task of managing Japan's industrializing society represented an extraordinary blend of the feudal family structure, the government agency, and the modern corporation. These elements have persisted in Japanese industrial society to the present, though the relative strengths of the components have shifted somewhat in the 100 years of so of evolution. [1971, 223—226]

Japan in its meteoric recovery and development after World War II was successful in generating the macroeconomic prerequisites for growth: investment in education and training, high saving and investment rates, adoption and adaptation of superior Western technologies, etc. With government guidance the private sector cooperated in picking and fostering successful new industries. The private sector invested for the long term, worked hard and trustingly to raise productivity and maintain high quality. All these facets of Japan's success are directly related to the unique character of Japanese culture.

Japan has a unique homogeneity as a nation—a single ethnic group with a single language; it has lived as an independent national unit for several thousand years. The Japanese share common life-styles and attitudes to an extent that is comparable to a family elsewhere. The overwhelming majority of Japanese believe in and share national goals.

In American culture, young people are taught in a thousand ways to internalize a competitive approach to life. The contrast with Japan is stark.

Japanese school-children are infused with the attitude that they should learn and work harmoniously with their classmates in groups.[4] [Benjamin 1997] Japanese children are taught not to deviate from the behavior of their group through social-shaming ("People will laugh at you"). Their education emphasizes that one should avoid standing out as an individual. ("The nail that stands up will be hammered flat.") Individuals should subordinate themselves to the success of the group. In brief, the Japanese culture tries to produce people who seek to *rationally maximize* a group objective not individual self-interest. [*The Economist* August 23, 1986,18-9; Fallows September 1986]. Of course, there are some Japanese who rebel against this indoctrination, but in the main it is successful.

The culture educates people to try to do their best, not because they will be rewarded directly and individually for it but because "that is the way to act". Tipping is discouraged because tipping implies that the tip-recipient would not do his best if he were not rewarded (i.e. bribed). This cultural factor, which influences workers to do their best, even if their compensation does not directly depend on it, is important in industry. Achieving and maintaining quality of product depends on the active committed participation of the workers producing it. It is this element that made possible the competitive success of so many Japanese products throughout the world. The Japanese behavior, directly counter to the assumption of rationally-maximizing individual self-interest, in this regard turns out to be more economically beneficial for an economy.

In Japan, the long period of influence of Confucianism instilled the ideal of selfless public service and an exalted regard for such service. During the Meiji restoration, the national system of bureaucratic ministries was established as the instrument of the modernizing elite to lead Japan's modernization and so to prevent Western imperialism making Japan a colony. The bureaucracy thus predated legislative institutions and the modern political system. [Keehn 1997]

The system for recruitment of top civil servants was copied from the British. The brightest graduates of the elite Tokyo University and other imperial universities are recruited into the service of the government. When top civil servants retire at 55 to higher lucrative salaries in the private sector this is regarded as a move down in status. It is called "amakudari" or "descent from Heaven". The most prestigious expect to

---

[4] Molly Smart, a thirteen year-old American girl who attended school in Japan recounts her experience: *Almost every activity at my school was group-oriented. Get with your group and do this. Get with your group and do that. Following the rules is important anywhere, but in Japan it is extremely important.* [1994]

receive well-paid top positions in government corporations, banks, insurance companies, finance firms or conglomerate companies.

The top reaches of Japanese society and economy have strong representation of men who have mostly gone to the same elite schools as the bureaucrats. Ten of Japan's post-war prime ministers have been former bureaucrats, as are usually a substantial fraction of prefectural governors and mayors. Japanese government officials have more prestige and influence in the private economy than is true in the United States.

The prejudice that the state cannot be effective in the economy, is not borne out by Japanese experience. Both in Japan and in other East Asian countries, nonadversial relations between the public and private sectors have proven effective in producing fast-growing economies with high per capita incomes. The state economic policy has largely successfully honored a social commitment: to foster cohesion and a sense of community and to minimize social envy.

Japan's is a different kind of capitalism from that of the United States. In communist countries, property was owned by the state and investment decisions were made by state bureaucrats. In the American type of capitalism, property is mostly owned by private owners and corporate bureaucrats make most investment decisions. In Japan, there is private ownership of property but the government bureaucrats exert a strong influence on investment decisions made by corporate bureaucrats.

The corporate ethos in Japanese companies also tends to differ from that of American and British corporations. In addition to the national interest, the Japanese firm tries to serve its stakeholders which include in addition to shareholders, its workers, management, the firm's banker, its component suppliers and any other firm with which it has a long term relationship. [Gilpin 1997, 79]

Japanese tend to think in terms of *commitment,* rather than of contract. Workers have a commitment to go the extra mile, if necessary, and corporations feel the same towards their workers. The tendency of American corporations to fire staff at the end of a profitable year in order to become even more profitable next year is alien to Japanese thinking.

However, the concentration by Japanese corporations and their work force on output and productivity puts enormous strains on individuals: workers work some 300 more hours a year than American workers and 400 to 500 more hours than German or French workers. Volunteer and unpaid overtime work is widespread. Leisure-time and family life are less enjoyable than in the other high-income economies. [McCormack 1997]

The Japanese act on the belief that individuals, society, and the economy live within a framework of social and economic duties and obligations. [Dore 1987] The market is a *means* rather than a determinant of goals.

MITI (the Ministry of International Trade and Industry) guides and encourages industry to invest in fields that it regards as important. If the Japanese producers, during the period when they are learning to produce a new commodity, have difficulty in competing with imports, MITI sees to it that imports are discouraged. Once the Japanese producers are able to hold their own, the government is happy to preach free trade. [Gilpin 1997, 72] To encourage an industry to cooperate, MITI may withhold licenses and legal permissions that a firm needs. MITI, of course, is not infallible, any more than American investors, and has made some mistakes in encouraging investments that later proved unwise. The over-all success of Japanese industry during the 1960s, 1970s, and 1980s, testifies, however, to the fact that its net influence must have been productive.

The World Bank has described one example of how MITI worked.

> In the late 1940s, the Japanese machinery companies had difficulty penetrating export markets. The high price of steel was a major impediment to them. The price of steel was high because the price of coal was high. MITI took action. It brought together the coal, steel, and machinery producers. The coal producers agreed to invest ¥40 billion to rationalize production to bring down domestic coal prices; the steel firms agreed to buy an agreed mixture of domestic and imported coal at lower agreed prices and to invest ¥42 billion in rationalization, that together with the lower coal prices would lower steel prices to international competitive levels. And, as a result the machinery and shipbuilding industries were able to begin major export-oriented programs. [Levy 1997, 23]

The Ministry of Finance regulates the flow of funds from banks into the business sector. The banks have been the main source of finance for industry. With firms dependent on bank loans rather than securities, it is easier for the Japanese regulatory government to control who gets capital and when. Each quarter the banks submit their lending plans to the Bank of Japan and receive "window guidance" on their strategy. The central bank is strongly influenced by the Ministry of Finance. [van Wolferen 1989, 121]

The 1989-90 bilateral trade talks provided a vivid example of the contrast between Japanese and American culture. The top Japanese were all experienced career officials and fully knowledgeable of the whole history of the bilateral American-Japanese negotiations. It would be unthinkable that they should profit from their experience and contacts by going to work for a foreign government. The Americans exemplified a success and achievement-oriented culture of individualism and egotism. The top Americans have moved in and out of government depending upon where their personal interests took them. As usual in American-Japanese negotiations, the American officials came in with the Bush administration and had little or no institutional memory. Perhaps their most important qualification for the job was that the negotiators for the American government had worked for Japanese firms before and might well do so again. The top US trade representative, Carla Hills, before this appointment advised a Japanese company, Matsushita Electric Industrial Company, in a US Government anti-dumping complaint. Her daughter, Laura, was a registered foreign agent defending another Japanese company against an anti-dumping complaint. Mrs. Hills' husband was a law partner of the head of the Washington lobbying firm for Nissan Motor. The deputy to Mrs. Hills, Sidney Linn Williams, was formerly a corporate lawyer in Tokyo representing Japanese companies. Another deputy, Julius Katz, previously headed a consulting firm that represents Toyota and the Hitachi Research Institute. [Abramson & Lachica 1990,1, A4]

Basically, the Japanese stress a different model of efficiency from that of conventional economics. Western mainstream economists are concerned with "allocative efficiency"—trying to move each resource where it earns the best return. The Japanese (and the other East Asians) emphasize "production efficiency"—optimum overall return. In purely mathematical terms the two should be identical. In human society this is not necessarily true. Any sports fan knows that having the best individual player in the league in each position on the team does not necessarily result in making the team the winner. It is the best team that wins and the best team is the one that works best together in scoring and defense.[5]

The Japanese emphasis on community helps on the shop floor as well. Before entering the workplace, workers have already learned team work and work ethics. The Japanese employment system has been built on the culture. The employer and employee are trained to feel social responsibility for one another. Japanese use the same word "ouchi" for their home and their company. Employees are generally regarded by the firm, and regard themselves, as members of a family. The pay spread between the top of the firm and the bottom is much smaller than in American and British firms. Special class perks like exclusive executive dining rooms or reserved parking spaces are not flaunted. The emphasis on the group rather than the individual means that promotion and pay is by seniority. As needed, individuals move from job to job within the company and get whatever retraining is necessary. The feeling of involvement in the success of the group is reinforced with a large proportion of pay being in the form of bonuses related to profits.

After World War II, Japanese corporations began to offer lifetime employment for most male workers. A job for life has been actually achieved only in big firms. They discourage hiring anyone who moves from another firm. The emphasis on the welfare of all builds loyalty to the company and produces more productive workers. Team-work and problem solving are stressed. The development of skills is encouraged since work-

---

[5] Learning from Japan, American business schools and corporation executives now often cite these personal skills as essential for a successful corporate career: good interpersonal communication skills; appreciating the importance of and engaging in whole-hearted team-work; and, knowing how to exercise and cooperate with leadership within a teamwork framework.

ers are expected to remain in the firm. Older workers are more willing to train younger workers since they do not fear that they will lose their own jobs to the people they train. [*The Economist* Sept. 12, 1987, 76; Dore 1987; Morita 1993, 94-7]

The lifetime employment ideal in Japan induces managements to emphasize saving jobs over maximizing short-term profits and to emphasize planning for the longer-term rather than just for the next quarter or year. Akio Morita, the chairman of Sony, says that, because of the nature of the Japanese production system, Japanese companies can accept "razor-thin profit margins that Western competitors find intolerable". Cross share-holdings within groups of firms muffle pressure for paying dividends. Japan's wealth remains primarily corporate wealth.

The emphasis on group cooperation carries over to relationships among corporations. Firms have a whole range of ties to other firms from close informal associations to memberships in a corporate family. Many of the large firms which are so effective in competing abroad are members of a *keiretsu*[6] or *gurupu,* that is, a corporate family or group. A *gurupu* like Mitsubishi consists of various industrial companies, insurance firms, real-estate agencies, trading firms, all clustered around their own banks. They are held together by interlocking directorates and interlocking stock hold-ings. Around each large manufacturer member of the *gurupu* is a system of subsidiaries, subcontractors, suppliers and distributors. The large manufac-turers usually have long-lasting relationships with their suppliers. If a sup-plier falls short of its obligations on quality or delivery, for example, a team of the large company managers is sent to help it improve.

No one is in charge of the whole *gurupu,* it is coordinated by a president's council that meets regularly. This whole constellation of firms follows the obligation to extend mutual aid and to keep as much business within it as possible. And, as Akio Morita, the chairman of Sony, has stated the result is they exclude foreign suppliers from their production systems and imported goods from retail shelves. [1993, 93]

There were six colossal constellations: Mitsui, Mitsubishi, Sumi-tomo, Fuyo, Sanwa, and Dai-ichi Kangyo Bank. [van Wolferen 1989, 46] Mitsubishi, for example, included about 160 companies in the *gurupu* proper. Its satellite firms must number in the thousands. In the financial re-structuring led by the government around the beginning of the twenty-first century, these six keiretsu were being merged into three.

Since the members of a *gurupu* tend to own one another with the banks especially holding large amounts of the shares, this frees manage-ments from the pressure to pay dividends and allows the firm to protect its employee stakeholders and concentrate on long-term goals. Consequently,

---

[6] *Keiretsu* relationships are complex and varied. Some are organized as described in the text as *gurupu*. Others are composed of one or more large firms with their subsidiaries, allied firms, suppliers, and important customers. Still others in the distribution system consist of linked retail and wholesale distributors that have been organized by manufacturers. [Lawrence 1993, 11-7]

dividends are minuscule and profits are generally ploughed back into the *gurupu*. When entering a new market, the members of the *gurupu* emphasize winning market share over profits. [van Wolferen 1989, 395-9; Lazonick 1998, 1-25]

While in producing, competition among the *gurupu* or even within a *gurupu* is very active, in distribution with the protection given to small family retailers, competition in price often is not. This results in high domestic prices for consumers. Japanese products consequently are often cheaper in New York than they are in Tokyo itself.

The semiconductor industry is a good example of how Japanese culture affects economic success. This industry was pioneered and developed in the United States in the 1950s and 1960s with the discovery and development of transistors and integrated circuits with the US Defense Department and NASA providing the crucial early market and some of the finance for research. By the 1970s the United States dominated every stage of the market from the output of semiconductor-making equipment, the production of semiconductor chips, to production of computers.

In 1970, Japan had virtually no semiconductor industry. In the mid-1970s, MITI introduced a program providing for preferential access to capital, government-sponsored research, and guidance in licensing technologies from foreign suppliers—all to help Japanese industries to advance in high-tech.

By 1986, Japanese companies had become the only producers in the world in several of the stages in the semiconductor-making process. Half the chips in the American F-16 fighter's fire-control radar had to be procured in Japan. Large parts of the American industry had become dependent on buying chip-making equipment and semiconductor components from Japan.

Survival of an American industry was ensured by the special measures the American government took to help American producers. Copying Japanese practice, in 1987 the American government sponsored a semiconductor research consortium, Sematech, of the American companies and subsidized it with an annual appropriation of $90 million. In addition the government spent around $2 billion a year in research grants on semiconductor research. Sematech helped to advance American semiconductor technology until it was in advance of the whole world. By 1994, the American industry was doing well and Sematech's board of directors decided that it could be weaned from government help and announced that it would no longer request government subsidies in the future.

A note of caution: While the Japanese economic record from World War II to 1990 was one of unparalleled success, this did not mean that Japan has succeeded in creating an ideal economy. Problems surfaced in the 1990s.

The generations-long period of rapid growth and prosperity together with an unbroken tenure of a single party in power demonstrated that the Japanese system is not immune to hubris and temptation.

During the 1990s, there was a succession of revelations of a web of corruption and abuses among some of the top financial, political and criminal elements of Japan.

While the Japanese government encouraged the successful development of world-class leading-edge industries, it protected other domestic industries that had ceased to be competitive or had never been were (steel, cement, glass, food processing). High domestic prices in Japan reflect these highly inefficient national sectors. [Katz 1998, 54-58]

The system emphasized corporate investment over increases in personal income. Government and society encouraged saving over consumption. When the land and stock market bubbles burst and led Japan into recession in the 1990s, domestic consumer demand was insufficient to produce a revival while savings tended to flow out to foreign financial markets, particularly in the United States.

The 1990s recession weakened some of the social constraints. The Japanese companies were forced, *volens nolens,* to search for ways to cut costs. This resulted in some companies down-sizing, reducing employment through early retirements and, in desperate cases, even firing people. The close relationship with some suppliers was dissolved, replaced by purchases from cheaper foreign suppliers. Even the intimate ties with some members of the *gurupu* were weakened.

These events confronted the government and ruling elite by the end of the twentieth century with the need to review all of the features of their economy which may have changed from being assets to liabilities. Any and all of the behavioral characteristics, sketched above, are subject to change when there is a consensus among the governing elites that such changes are needed for the good of the nation and the society. The one dominant and most important attribute of Japanese culture remains: while it may take a considerable period, running into years, to achieve an agreed consensus on how to confront new major problems, the society possesses a high capability to adapt its institutions and behaviors when the fundamental economic and political context requires.

China and East Asia

As late as 1500 C.E. China was substantially in advance of Europe in technology. The vitally important inventions of the early modern era: paper, printing, gunpowder, the compass, the stern-post rudder, all originated in China. The amazing long-distance ocean voyages of Vasco da Gama and his successors, opening ocean trade between the East and Europe, had been surpassed by the Chinese. From 1405 to 1433, China sent fleets of hundreds of ships with crews numbering over 30,000 in a single fleet to all the regions of southeast Asia, India, the Persian Gulf, the Red Sea, and the east coast of Africa as far south as Mozambique. Some of the Chinese ships were five times the size of Vasco da Gama's biggest. At the end of seven great expeditions, the Chinese government decided to stop, destroyed its fleet, and resumed its self-centered existence.

The explanation why the Chinese voyages had such a different result compared to those of the European is to be found in the nature of the Chinese culture, society, and state. The Chinese Empire early in its history developed an agriculture-based economy with a monolithic bureaucratic government that dominated economic activity. Service to the state was the way to wealth, Economic rewards came through scholarship and learning within the service of the state. Over many centuries individuals rose in society by passing exams. The process was self-reinforcing: A rich landowning family clan could afford to give sons leisure to study and to pay for clan schools to educate them to take the rigorous civil service examinations. Men who did well on the exams could secure office in the government. This made it possible for them to promote and enrich their family. Officials with their official privileges could protect and increase the family landholdings and protect their gentry status.

The system and culture were stable and unchanging. Confucian teaching emphasized learning, the importance of study and the recognition and respect for competence. Coming from the gentry, the officials usually had the culture of a rentier class rather than of entrepreneurs. As is probably universally true in a land-owning society, merchants were regarded as nonproductive and parasitic and kept under control by the officials. The culture encouraged successful merchants to try to move into the gentry class through buying land, intermarriage and encouraging sons to become scholars. This, in rough outline, appears to account for the fact that, although China as late as 1500 was ahead of Europe in technology and in most facets of civilization, its economy did not progress, there was no incentive to develop trade and intercourse with the rest of the world and it consequently fell behind the more volatile Europeans.

The modern Chinese Communist state tried to destroy this family system and substitute egalitarian individualist loyalty to the state in place of the family ties of patriarchy and filial piety. Hierarchy within the nation was supposed to replace hierarchy within the family and national loyalty to replace family particularistic loyalty. So far the evidence appears to be that the Communists have not succeeded in destroying the family system that made possible the survival of a Chinese society that has survived thousands of years longer than any other. [Ching, Frank 1988]

The Chinese family system in the south-eastern provinces of mainland China now focuses on business. The economy is thus based on a "trust network". Chinese businesses develop on the basis of family-run firms and personalistic networks linking them to input suppliers and markets. The family is patrilineal with the eldest son having senior status but all sons inherit equally. The firm is patterned on the family: the head of the household is the head of the firm. If the firm prospers, profits can be invested in new firms run by family members. On the death of the father, assets are divided by allocating the different firms to the sons. Over time, a network of firms is created, owned by family members, working closely together to advance the family fortunes. [Hamilton & Biggart 1992]

The East Asian countries (Hong Kong, Indonesia, Japan, Malaysia, Republic of Korea, Singapore, Taiwan and Thailand) influenced by Chinese culture, Chinese emigrants and Confucian teachings have in recent decades shown economic growth rates at multiples of those achieved in the earlier Western industrializing societies. In one generation, after independence, Singapore moved from poor to high-income status. Singapore's per capita GDP is now higher than that of its former colonizer, Great Britain. It has the world's busiest port and is a major center of global service industries. And, these high growth rates in the eight East Asian countries have gone along with low and declining inequality of incomes. The ratio between the income of the richest fifth to the poorest fifth is around 9 to 1, whereas in Brazil and Mexico the ratios are around 20 to 1.

A World Bank study ascribed *The East Asian Miracle* to the governments' using a combination of good fundamental and interventionist policies. The governments encouraged savings and investment, kept inflation low, and provided high quality education, concentrating on basic primary and secondary education. The build-up of high levels of human and physical capital was directed through market-mechanisms and direct government intervention into highly productive investments. Advanced technologies were acquired and mastered. The economy and the government worked together to achieve rapid productivity growth.

While the East Asian countries found advantages and disadvantages *per se* in being late arrivals on the scene, it does appear convincing that the Confucian influence has been an important element in why the countries were able to master the elements needed to attain their rapid growth rates. The government of Singapore overtly promotes among its population what it calls "Asian values". These are: putting nation before ethnic community and society above self; regarding family as the basic unit of society; giving community support and respect for the individual; emphasis on consensus, not conflict; and stressing racial and religious harmony. It rejects the American value of placing individual above society. Lee Kuan Yew put it this way:

> ...Asian societies are unlike Western ones. The fundamental difference between Western concepts of society and government and East Asian concepts...—is that Eastern societies believe that the individual exists in the context of his family. He is not pristine and separate. The family is part of the extended family, and then friends and the wider society. The ruler or the government does not try to provide for a person what the family best provides. [Zakaria 1994, 113]

The Asian attitude toward the family, as Lee describes it, is not unique to the East. It was common in Western Europe 400 years ago to the end of feudalism. It is identical to attitudes today in many Sicilian families as I can testify personally.

Another positive aspect of Confucian teachings is the emphasis on the value of learning. In the "little dragons" (South Korea, Taiwan, Hong Kong, Singapore), these teachings resulted in the development in each country of a bureaucracy selected on the basis of merit. This bureaucracy is highly respected in the community and has a sense of service, putting professional pride above personal material gain. The bureaucrats are realistically remunerated, shielded from political interference and accorded high status in the community. The national goal is not as in ancient China the maintenance of a stable agricultural society but industrialization. To succeed in today's international competitive market in industrial products requires high levels of coordination, knowledge of science, technology and management and of world markets.The leadership of the meritocratically-selected bureaucrats has been decisive in the success that these countries achieved over the last half-century. [Vogel 1991]

As in Japan, however, the "little dragons" were not immune to *hubris* from their continued success—allowing problems to cumulate and investment bubbles to expand. Financial liberalization in the 1990s resulted in local borrowers recklessly running up short-term foreign debt that in the end exceeded the country's external reserves (in Korea, Indonesia, and Thailand) or were high enough to threaten the reserves (Philippines and Malaysia). In March of 1997, the U. S. Federal Reserve Board raised an interest rate leading some investors and speculators to expect market interest rates in the United States to go up and the U. S. dollar to appreciate. Consequently, they started moving funds from abroad into New York. As short-term dollar funds moved out of their markets, by midsummer 1997, first in Thailand and then in other Asian markets, there resulted a herd rush for the exits. Foreign exchange rates plummeted, real estate bubbles burst, and the general economy suffered. By the middle of 1999, the Asian countries, led by Korea and Thailand, were largely recovering except for Indonesia which was in the throes of a major political crisis. [Sachs, Woo 1999]

From the perspective of the last half of the twentieth century, in spite of their difficulties of the end of the nineties, the achievements of the East Asian countries remain outstanding. [James K. Galbraith 1999, 13; Rodrik 1999, 7-11]

11 The Tropics and Economics

The human being is inseparable from its environment. — Alfred North
Whitehead

Keynes' remark that practical men are often intellectual slaves of some
dead economist is now a cliché. People are also often intellectual slaves to
the metaphor of some long-forgotten journalist—for example, the "rich
North–poor South" metaphor popular in development economics.

The proper contrast is not "North–South" but "rich Temperate
Zone—poor Tropics". The right metaphor is important because it is the location of countries in the Tropics that matters. Otherwise, research and
policy decisions to meet the special obstacles stemming from the Tropics
will continue to be as neglected as they have been for too many decades.

The neglect of climate may have been due to a reaction against
Ellsworth Huntington who argued that human achievement was directly
determined by the weather and his ideal climate bore a strong resemblance
to that of New Haven. But as Charles P. Kindleberger pointed out,

> The arguments against Huntington are telling, but the fact remains that no
> tropical country in modern times has achieved a high state of economic
> development. This establishes some sort of presumptive case—for the
> end result, if not for the means.[1965, 78]

Kindleberger put his finger on the issue: it was right to reject
Huntington's explanation but not the reality of the malevolent influence of
tropical climate. Accepting this reality as given, I took advantage of the
wide-ranging knowledge and experience available to me in the World
Bank to investigate why the tropical climate hampered countries in their
economic development. The results were published in 1976 as a World
Bank sponsored book, *The Tropics and Economic Development*. Economists, however, almost universally continued to ignore the obvious fact of
the association of tropical climate and poverty. Professor Rati Ram, however, after making an empirical investigation" of my "provocative" pro-
posal that a county's geographical location in the tropics handicapped its
ability to develop, concluded that:

> ... the relationship of almost every measure of a country's well-be-
> ing with its distance from the equator appears remarkably strong. In many
> cases, the distance variable alone can explain nearly half of the cross-
> country variation in income and other measures of well-being. [1443,
> 1997]

174

In the last few years, nine other economists applying sophisticated econometric tools have independently discovered that, yes, a country's location in the Tropics is strongly related to its poverty.[1]

This is an important finding but standing alone what policy recommendation does it imply? One cannot advise a government that it should move its country into a temperate zone. *Only if we understand what it is about the tropical climate that creates the obstacles to development can suitable policy actions be taken.* We need to know what are the forces at work that are responsible.

The causes of this phenomenon cannot be explained by using pure economic theory. An economist-hedgehog is useless in coping with this highly important fact that affects the living standards of hundreds of millions of people. It takes an economist-fox supplementing economics knowledge by drawing on other disciplines to bring out the issues involved and to advise what can and should be done.

The Special Problems of the Tropics

Tropical climatic factors severely hamper development through their impact on human beings themselves, on agriculture and, to a lesser extent, on mineral development. Economic activity is directly and adversely af-

---

[1] Henri Theil and Dongling Chen developed a simple latitude model to explain per capita GDPs based on purchasing power parities and found: *This comparison suggests that latitude may be viewed, statistically speaking, as the principal component of the rich/poor distinction among the countries of the free world.* [Theil & Chen 1995, 327]

Theil and Chen carried this study further: *The major conclusion to be drawn...is that affluence tends to decline when we move towards the Equator from the temperate zones in either the Northern or the Southern Hemisphere. Needless to say, this tendency is not without exceptions nor is it constant over time.. Nevertheless, its existence as a tendency in the non-Communist world in the last several decades cannot be denied.* [Theil 1996, 28]

Charles I. Jones and Robert E. Hall studied "Levels of Economic Activity Across Countries" and found that: *Distance from the equator is the single strongest predictor of long-term economic success in our specification. Being located at the equator like Zaire or Uganda is associated with a reduction in output per worker by a factor of 4.5 relative to the Scandinavian countries.* [1997, 176]

Xavier X. Sala-I-Martin's "I Just Ran Two Million Regressions" determined that: *Absolute Latitude (far away from the equator) is good for growth.* [1997, 181]

Jeffrey D. Sachs and Andrew M. Warner found that: *Countries with tropical climates and landlocked countries have lower steady-state incomes and, therefore, lower growth from any initial level of GDP per capita.* [1997, 187]

Paul Collier and J. W. Gunning write: *Sub-Saharan Africa is predominantly tropical. There is some evidence that this has reduced African growth...*[1999, 72]

fected through the widespread extent and impact of tropical diseases on people; tropical agriculture suffers in the quality of its soils, its rainfall, and from its multiplicity of pests and diseases; and mineral discoveries are handicapped by tropical conditions.

The tropical obstacles to economic development do not represent absolute barriers. As they are overcome or bypassed, the whole process should become easier: as a country advances in economic development, the proportion of GDP produced in agriculture drops and the importance of the climatic factors affecting agriculture drops correspondingly. Research can mitigate or eliminate climatic problems of farmers. Growth in GDP simultaneously permits greater allocation of resources to health problems and the impact of climate thus will be further reduced.

The most important special characteristic of the Tropics is that because of its continuous heat and the absence of frost, life and reproduction go on throughout the year. The great executioner, winter, is absent. No winter temperatures constrain continuous plant growth or the continuous reproduction and growth of all kinds of life: weeds, insects, birds, parasitic fungi, spider mites, eelworms, microbes, and all kinds of viruses, pests and parasites on humans, their animals, and their crops.

Life over most of the Tropics takes on an infinite multiplicity of forms. Fierce competition results and only a few individuals in every generation of any species survive in any one place. The conditions are ideal for rapid evolutionary change to adapt to any new opportunities. It is not at all surprising that human beings first evolved in the Tropics and that this is also true of new diseases like AIDs and Ebola.

In the Tropics, the high temperatures allow large populations of insects to live for much of the year and the extrinsic incubation periods are reduced to the minimum. Insects are poikilothermic, their body temperature largely controlled by the temperature of their environment, affects their speed of development. The parasites carried by insects are also poikilothermic. Their development within their insect host varies depending on the temperature. The life cycle of bacteria, protozoa, and other pathogens is also ecothermic. In temperate zones, the aquatic stage of mosquitoes takes weeks, in the tropics, days; and the extrinsic incubation period of the pathogen, yellow fever virus, for example, varies from three weeks to a few days, depending entirely on the mean temperature. [Gillett 1974] The yellow fever epidemics in the United States when, for example, 11,000 people died in New Orleans in 1853 or more than 20,000 died in several towns in 1878—all occurred in summer. (The year 2000 West Nile encephalitis threat in New York and New England ended "with the first killing frost".)

Human Diseases

Since the invention of air-conditioning, heat and humidity can be controlled in offices and factories. The very provision of air-conditioning in such environments strongly argues that high temperatures and high humidity hurt productivity. Agriculture is not air-conditioned and it is the dominant economic activity in the Tropics. As long as agriculture remains important, this alone would slow down the pace of economic growth.

In today's high income countries, it is reasonable to assume that the state of health of the population can be ignored for most purposes of economic analysis. This assumption is unwarranted in poor countries in the Tropics. Ill-health affects a person's learning ability, initiative, creativity, energy, attitude toward work, and capacity for heavy or sustained work or thought. In the poor countries of the Tropics, most people are affected: always, for substantial periods, or at critical times by poor health.

Studies find high percentages of people in the Tropics harboring various kinds of parasites, usually around two infections per person. Among the parasitic worms that afflict very large numbers are hookworm (ancylostomiasis, infecting a billion people), roundworm, whipworm, tapeworm, pinworm, and Guinea worm, and various varieties of filariasis (250 million people infected).[2] Bilharzia or schistosomiasis affects some 200 million people. The widest spread disease is malaria. WHO estimates that in 1998 there were 238 million clinical cases of malaria, 82 percent of these in Africa; it killed 1,110,000 people, 87 percent of these in Africa where the most deadly variety of malaria is prevalent. [WHO 1999, 99, 115]

The Tropics favor the multiplication and reproduction of parasitic species and the vectors that spread them. Even those diseases, which are present in both temperate and tropical climates, are harder to resist in the Tropics. Bacillary dysentery, which can occur almost anywhere, depends on the house flies. The speed with which the fly multiplies depends on the temperature. At 16°C, it takes 44 days for the fly to develop from egg to adult; 16 days at 25°C; and 10 days at 30°C. The result is an exponential increase in number in the Tropics compared to the Temperate Zones.

Some idea of the magnitude of the health problem facing the Tropics can be indicated by the River Blindness, elephantiasis, and trachoma eradication programs.

Although river blindness (Onchocerciasis) has been a leading cause of blindness in Africa and Latin America, it is much less important compared to most tropical diseases. It affected only (!) about 20 million people in West and East Africa and in limited areas in southern Mexico, Guatemala, Venezuela, Brazil, Colombia, Ecuador, and Yemen. Several species of blood-feeding black fly (one appropriately named Simulium damnosum), by biting human beings, spread a nematode worm in its microfilaria form. A related fly afflicts northern New England, Canada and Siberia. But in these latitudes the fly cannot carry the parasite because temperature governs the duration of the parasite's cycle in the vector.

In the hot tropical climate, the worms reach adulthood and mate in

---

[2] For details see Kamarck, *Tropics and Economic Development*, 57-80.

their human host. The adult female, the thickness of a human hair and about half a meter long, lives mainly below the skin, and produces millions of microfilariae during her 15 year lifetime. These migrate through the human body and may produce lesions or wounds in the skin and in the eyes, causing partial or total blindness. The flies reproduce near flowing or turbulent water. Hence, the incidence of this disease near rivers and its popular name of "river blindness".

River blindness is not fatal but by destroying the sight, it turns productive adults into a burden on their community and it forces people to move from fertile alluvial river valleys into less fertile hills.

The World Bank, WHO (World Health Organization), and UNDP (United Nations Development Program) began in 1974 to try to eradicate river blindness in Africa. This has had some success in eradicating the fly from some limited areas. But, success may only finally be achieved in the first decade of the this century. By serendipity, it was discovered in 1987 that Mectizan, a drug that Merck & Co. used to treat a parasitic infestation in livestock, is also effective against river blindness. The drug paralyzes the parasites that cause the disease and has virtually no side effects.

WHO trials found that if 95 percent of the people in a river blindness infected area take Mectizan once a year over a 12 to 14 year period, the life span of the worm, the disease can be eliminated. Merck is contributing the drug at no cost to the program making possible its use everywhere. Beginning in the 1990s, the Inter-American Bank has taken the lead together with the Pan American Health Organization in a similar program for the Americas. In 2000, more than 18 million people in Africa and Latin America were receiving the medicine.

The total cost in trying to eradicate just this one relatively less important disease has been $550 million over the more than two decades of the program even though nothing had to be spent on drug research and the effective drug is being donated by Merck.

In early 1998, the British pharmaceutical company SmithKline Beecham announced plans to join in a 20-year program in partnership with the World Health Organization to try to eradicate elephantiasis (lymphatic filariasis). About 120 million people in the Tropics and Sub-Tropics suffer from disability from this disease with a total of one billion people at risk. The company, in addition to a cash contribution, has agreed to donate an anti-parasitic drug, albendazole, for the eradication campaign.The plan is to provide one dose a year over at least five years to all the people in an entire geographical region to eradicate the disease in that region. It will take 20 years to treat all of the millions of people concerned to eradicate the disease. The total cost mainly shared by the company, WHO, the World Bank, and the Arab Fund for Economic and Social Development is expected to cost from $500 million to $1 billion.

A smaller trial program is underway to eradicate trachoma in Ghana, Mali, Morocco, Tanzania and Vietnam. Trachoma infects more than 150 million people and blinds around six million people in Afica, the Middle East and tropical Asia. The partnership here is between Pfizer, the Clark Foundation, and WHO. Pfizer found that a single dose of its drug Zithromax (azithromycin) would cure 78 percent of trachoma infections. It is not yet known whether the dose needs to be repeated again after a year or whether a series of annual doses will be needed. Pfizer has agreed to donate some $60 million worth of the drug to treat 3 million people over a period of two years.

Agriculture

Farming in the Tropics is not like farming in the Temperate Zones. Here's what it's like in Latin America's low Tropics:

> (The farmer clears the) land he intends to plant...two to five acres—depending on the number of machete swingers in his family...(He) burns over the whole piece of land he is going to plant. (After he plants his corn) when the rains come, everything...bursts forth...every conceivable weed, insect, and pest, along with the corn....Finally the corn approaches maturity. Then come the weevils that begin eating the new kernels. So do the birds....([It is a) miracle that the long-cultivated burned-over acres produce any corn at all—not to mention the worn-out farmer himself. He probably has a bit of chronic malaria, also some amoeba and a variety of other debilitating "hitchhikers" festering in his system. Nevertheless, the average...peasant farmer produces twelve bushels to the acre—about what his ancestors produced a thousand years ago.
>
> Contrast this to an American farmer in the Midwest, around 1900, for example, before the use of modern equipment, fertilizers, herbicides, and improved seeds. The severe winter suppressed weeds and pests. With the help of a horse the farmer could cultivate a bigger piece of land than the Tropical farmer.
>
> When he planted his corn ... (g)ermination was a slow process for both corn and weeds. ...plants grew slowly at first. Thus he could cultivate his fields several times before the soil warmed up, eliminating most of his weeds. ...when...the plants began growing faster, no further cultivating was necessary because the corn was now high enough to shade out any late-sprouting weeds ..nutrients had not yet leached out of the virgin soil. And because of lower temperatures the organic matter was not broken down by soil organisms as it is in the tropics. Even with unimproved seed the Midwest farmer...averaged thirty-two bushels of corn to the acre, two and one- half times as much as the tropical peasant farmer of today... [Paddock 1973, 171-173, quoted in Kamarck 1976, 32]

Poor countries are usually highly dependent on agriculture. As the conditions and the problems of tropical agriculture are different from those of temperate zone agriculture the research and the technologies that have made temperate zone farming so productive are not directly appropriate to the Tropics. Temperate zone research was directly designed to minimize the weaknesses and exploit the strong points of farming in the Temperate Zone. Until the creation of the network of tropical agricultural research institutes in the 1970s at the initiative of the World Bank, practically all the research that had been done on tropical crops was limited to a few export crops.

The Tropics are not *temperate,* that is "moderate". Compared to the Tropics, the climate of the Temperate Zones is much more even, equable, and reliable. It is not only the greater incidence of tropical hurricanes and typhoons that differentiate the Tropics, even the normal rains and the fierce sun are stronger than the rains and the sun of the Temperate Zones. No inhabitant of the Tropics would write Wordsworth's poems about gentle nature.

In the Tropics, rainfall rather than temperature determines the seasons. The variation of rainfall from year to year and within the year is considerable and unpredictable. Rainfall in the Tropics is usually too much or too little. Average annual rainfall means little when one year may receive three times as much rain as the next, or when it does not rain evenly throughout a given season of the year but falls in torrents within brief periods. The extremes are often almost absurd: in July of one year over four meters of rain fell on Luzon, on which much of the economic effort of the Philippines has been concentrated. The rice crop on one million acres was destroyed. Also lost was 30 percent of the sugar crop, which is a large part of Filipino export earnings. Even yearly variations over so large a river basin such as the Volta, which drains over 100,000 square kilometers in western Africa (an area comparable in size to Great Britain) are very great. At Akosombo, near the Volta's mouth, the flow averages 3,500 to 9,800 cubic metes a second at the peak and only about 30 cubic meters at the low.

Drought tends to come in the hottest and windiest part of the year, so that loss of water by evaporation and transpiration is high.

The ideal conditions, in which the right amount of water is available in the right place at the right time, are only rarely achieved under natural conditions in the Tropics.

In the semi-humid Tropics, the period before the rains break is the driest and hottest time of the year.This makes the farmers' preparation of the dry, hard ground for planting particularly arduous. By comparison, Temperate Climates experience cold weather precipitation that exceeds evaporation; the soil thus becomes charged with a reserve of water for the new growing season. Moist soil is easier to work.

In the semi-humid Tropics, when the rains come and the soil becomes easier to work, everything has to be done at once. The pattern of rainfall and the relation between precipitation and rates of evaporation also result in frequent drought or flood. Productive periods must be sandwiched between these droughts and floods. Consequently, proper soil and water management and careful timing of farm operations are vital. The different water regimes of the Tropics also require different approaches to such things as the application of fertilizers and different techniques of plant protection.

Because of the multiplicity of species and the rapid evolutionary potential of the Tropics, there is a high probability that any new plant or animal introduced into an area by humans will soon be attacked by some rapidly multiplying enemy. A crop initially successfully established always runs the considerable risk of attracting some new pest that suddenly appears or has learned or evolved to take advantage of the new opportunity. Without a "close season" for plant growth, all sorts of pests may thrive all the year: not only weeds, but the parasitic fungi, insects, spider mites, eelworms, bacterial and virus diseases that make drastic reductions in crop yields. Take, for example, maize which is an important crop in South America, the United States, and eastern and southern Africa; out of 25 major insect pests that afflict the crop, 21 are a cataloged as present in Africa as compared to 5 in the United States. [Hill 1975, 443-4] Even after harvest, serious losses can result from storage pests and rats.

Some enemies may largely wipe out a crop, while others that are not lethal, but nevertheless insidious, may cause severe crop damage. Among the most spectacular predators are the locusts that from time to time appear in swarms, of up to 80 by 40 kilometers in size, and devour everything where they land. Locusts can fly only when their thoracic muscle temperature is at least 25° so they are restricted to the Tropics.

Trypanosomiasis (nagana) carried by the tsetse fly bars half of Tropical Africa to cattle and horses. As a result, not only is there a reduced supply of animal protein available as food but it prevents the use of animal power in agriculture. *Farmers over most of Tropical Africa are dependent on human muscle power to carry out all the hard tasks in agriculture.*

Compared to temperate zone countries, there is comparatively great ignorance in the Tropics on how best to exploit and improve the soil. The tropical soils and conditions are generally so different from those of the Temperate Zone that different body of knowledge is needed altogether. The obstacles to productivity presented by tropical soils may not be insuperable; with sufficient research they may be bypassed or overcome.

In the Tropics, the soil has to be protected against the heat of the sun, which would burn away the organic matter in the soil and it has to be protected from the direct blows of the torrential rains. These, plunging on to unprotected ground, crush the structure of the soil, seal off the underlying soil from the air, and leach out the minerals or trace elements needed for plant growth or carry these so far into the earth that the plant roots cannot reach them. When the soil is laid bare and exposed to the elements, its temperature rises and the sun hastens the oxidation and disappearance of the humus. Wide variation in temperature occurring in the Tropics between day and night accelerates the mechanical disintegration of the soil. Finally, heavy rains and wind erode the bare soil.

Generally soils are poor over most of the Tropics because they contain little organic material. Tropical vegetation often looks rich and luxuriant, but appearances are deceiving. Even in dense forests, soils are usually thin and have low fertility. In the forests, decaying plants and trees constantly return to the supporting soil the elements they borrowed from it. This interchange is precarious, with very small reserves.

Over a large part of the humid Tropics the soil has turned into laterite. Through leaching, the main plant foods or assimilable bases and phosphorus have been removed from the top horizons of the earth. What is left is a reddish mottled clay, consisting almost entirely of oxides of iron and hydroxide of aluminum that tend to solidify upon exposure to air. While laterite makes useful building material, these so-called tropical red and yellow earths that cover the greater part of the humid Tropics are either agriculturally poor or virtually useless. This soil composition accounts for some of the large iron ore deposits in the Tropics and explains the large bauxite deposits mined in tropical countries for the aluminum industry.

Over the centuries, the inhabitants of many tropical countries learned how best to manage the soil conditions confronting them. Farmers in most of sub-Saharan Africa, the Philippines, the highlands and many lowland areas of Indonesia's outer islands, parts of India and Sri Lanka, and the tropical rain forests of Central and South America developed "shifting" or "semi-nomadic" cultivation. Shifting tillage, still by far the most common type of farming in the humid tropics, cultivates fields for a few years, then allows them to revert to bush jungle to restore their fertility over periods that may last as long as 25 years. Shifting cultivation makes survival possible under difficult conditions—but only at a bare existence level. This practice has also meant that often one of the main advantages of agricultural over a nomadic life—living in a settled community—is not attained.

Not all tropical soils are equally problematic—alluvial soils (along lakes, rivers and in deltas) and recent volcanic soils are more fertile. Forest soils of tropical mountains or high plateaus that are high enough to escape the great heat of lower altitudes may also be fertile and rich in humus.

Tree crops, by shading the soil and protecting it from the direct impact of rain, avoid many of the problems mentioned above and make possible permanent farms. With aggressive research beginning in colonial times, Malaya has been able to develop an efficient rubber and oil palm agriculture.

There are potential advantages in tropical agriculture that could be harnessed by research. The humid and semi-humid Tropics have 60 to 90 percent more sunlight energy for growing crops than the Temperate Zones do, even after taking account of the effects of cloudiness. Plants in tropical rain forests produce three to five times more organic matter each year than plants produce in temperate zones. The absence of winter, if pests are controlled, can extend the length of the growing season making possible growing several crops a year. The multiplicity of species and the rapid pace of evolution can help in developing new and better crops and livestock.

Livestock in the Tropics are subject to most of the temperate zone diseases—on which there is a great deal of applied research on how to cope, but also to a whole series of tropical parasitic, nutritional toxic, and organic diseases. There is still a very short history of knowledge and applied research on tropical diseases. A principal technical reason for the low-level of livestock productivity in the semi-humid Tropics, in those areas where livestock can survive, stems from the way the climate varies. The alternating wet and dry seasons cause wide seasonal fluctuations in the growth and quality of pasture. Because these areas usually lack stock watering facilities, the number of animals that can be safely carried through the dry season sets the maximum that can be carried for the whole year. Moreover, much of the weight that the livestock gain during the wet season when feed is plentiful is lost when feed is short, so the average yearly weight gain is very low. Long periods of underfeeding lower the reproduction rates of the herd and increase its susceptibility to parasitic and other diseases.

By providing water, fences and corrals, which are essential for management of the grazing areas and for controlling the high risk of disease, it is possible to achieve multiple gains in production. In some areas, pastures can be improved by using the legume plants that fix nitrogen in the soil, which have been developed for the tropical areas of Australia.

There have already been enough results from research on the problems of tropical agriculture to show that some day agriculture in the humid and semi-humid Tropics will be highly productive. Whether this becomes true in this century depends on how soon sufficient resources are devoted to research, applied technology, and training on tropical agricultural problems and the tropical medical problems of the peoples who live there.

Minerals

One of the most effective ways a poor country can rapidly increase its export earnings, government revenues, and investment is through the discovery and exploitation of a rich mineral resource. There is no rational basis for supposing that the Tropics *per se* should possess poorer or fewer mineral resources than the Temperate Zones. But the tropical countries have lagged in mineral discovery and exploitation. There are institutional reasons why this should be so—finding and developing minerals tends to be capital-intensive. Investors, consequently, prefer countries where governments are stable and the legal environment is predictable. (The oil companies are different, having a long history of coping with difficult natural and political environments.) But there are also obstacles stemming from the climate.

The geophysical and geochemical techniques for securing information about the basic geology of areas were for the most part developed for use in the Temperate Zones. The physical and chemical parameters of the humid Tropics are different so a different structure of inference is needed. Even different instruments may have to developed since extremes of heat and humidity can ruin the delicate instruments that were built for temperate conditions.

In the humid Tropics and in countries that formerly possessed a humid climate but now are arid (e.g. the southern edge of the Sahara) mineral formations are overburdened with soil. The rains and the high temperatures help rapid weathering and the formation of laterite and other soil mantles that hide the underlying rock. Minerals such as dolomite, limestone, gypsum, and salts of potassium and sodium are relatively soluble and hard to locate in high rainfall areas. Most of the minerals, other than oil, that are found in the Tropics are surface concentrations formed from the weathering action of the climate: bauxite, some iron ores, manganese and nickel, tin, and diamond placers.

Africa

It is impossible to understand the African economies without appreciating the pervasive influence of the Tropics.

Africa is the most tropical of all the continents. Over three-quarters is in the Tropics. Only countries at the top and bottom are not. The equator almost exactly bisects the continent; it is about 4000 kilometers from the equator to the northern crown and 3,750 kilometers to the southern tip.

Geography and climate isolated sub-Saharan Africa from the rest of the world and Africans from one another.

Access to and from the sea is not easy. Most of the African coastline below the Sahara is forbidding—where desert does not come down to the sea, there is mostly swamp or lagoon. The block shape of the continent is such that most of the interior is remote from the sea; of all the continents, Africa has the shortest coastline in relation to area. The continent has very few natural harbors where ships can lie safely at anchor. Before artificial harbors were built in recent years, ships had to remain at sea during the few months when it was safe to lie off shore, and cargo had to be transported in small boats to get through the surf.

Africa is by and large a plateau, with most rivers falling over the escarpment in a series of falls or rapids near the coast. It is usually impossible in Tropical Africa to penetrate the interior by sailing up rivers, as was done for example in North America. So that while the coastline of Africa was known centuries before that of North America, it was not until about a hundred years ago that the interior of Africa was mapped. European ships were off the Nigerian coast before 1500 but never knew for over three centuries that there was a major river, the Niger, emptying into the mangrove swamps and lagoons that they encountered. When the upper reaches of the Niger were explored, it was believed that the river was the Nile!

Climate was also an important factor in isolating tropical Africa from the rest of the world and most Africans from one another. Yellow fever and malaria exacted a heavy toll of death on all visitors.

> Beware, beware the Bight of Benin,
> For few come out though many go in.

Trypanosomiasis was a major obstacle. This disease carried by the tsetse fly causes sleeping sickness in humans and nagana that kills horses and cattle. This made it impossible over centuries to penetrate to the interior using animal transport. Afrikaners expanding their settlements north from South Africa in the first half of the nineteenth century were stopped at the Limpopo River valley. Here, their oxen mysteriously sickened and died.

Commerce and travel in Africa had to depend on human porters, the most costly and inefficient of all transport systems. One can get an inkling of how difficult it was from the reports of European explorers in Africa. Here is an excerpt from Stanley on his search for Livingstone in 1869:

> The distance from Bagamoyo to Simbamwenni we found to be 119 miles, and was accomplished in fourteen marches. But these marches... extended to twenty-nine days, thus rendering our progress very slow indeed—but a little more than four miles a day. ...had I not been encumbered by the sick Wanyamwezi porters, I could have accomplished the distance in sixteen days. [1872 (1960), 96-7]

That is, if not held back by sick porters, Stanley could have traveled seven and a half miles a day!

A later explorer, J. W. Gregory, in 1893, boasted that "Dr. Moloney claims the record ... for the Stairs expedition to Katanga, which traveled 1080 miles in six months all but ten days. We went 1650 miles in two days less than five months." [1896 (1960), 287] That is, the Stairs expedition's record was almost 6 miles a day while Gregory made almost 11 miles a day. These expeditions were not transporting anything except what was necessary for sustenance of the explorers and of the porters accompanying them. This is what dependence on human porters meant.

The only trade that could take place with and in most of tropical Africa was in commodities of great value and little bulk—gold and ivory—or slaves, a commodity provided with its own legs. And these were the African commodities for several thousand years. The slave trade, while supporting the African. the Arab, or, later, the European slave dealers, was destructive for any economic advancement. Africa lost people in their most productive years and it encouraged conflict between and among tribes, plunging vast areas into anarchy. A substantial trade in slaves did not end on the Atlantic side of Africa until well after the American Civil War and on the Indian Ocean side until early in the twentieth century. There are still reports of slave raiders in the Southern Sudan and in Mauritania.

It was not until the nineteenth century invention of the iron horse, the railway engine, immune to the bite of the tsetse fly, that tropical Africa could begin to come into helpful communication and trade with the rest of the world. But it was not until around the beginning of the twentieth century that railway building began in tropical Africa. It was also not until around the beginning of the twentieth century that the vector of malaria and yellow fever was discovered. (Only then also could the Panama Canal be successfully built—the mosquito having triumphed over the French and de Lesseps.) Yellow fever is now under control but malaria still claims its millions of victims.

The transport and communication difficulties by keeping Africans separated from one another over the centuries contributed to the high ethnic fragmentation that has made nation-building so difficult in the African nations in the few short decades since their independence.[3] The unfinished task of nation-building is hampered by the fact that in most of the new African nations, there are large groups of people, often a majority of the population who regard themselves, first, as members of a tribe or ethnic group, and only secondly as citizens of the new country. In all cases, there are still large numbers of people who still regard themselves as subject peoples, subject no longer to the British, French, Portuguese, or Spanish, but to the dominant tribe who inherited the colonists' position.

While some of the obstacles caused by the Tropics are no longer so daunting, enough still remain, as I have sketched above, to continue to make development in tropical Africa a most difficult task.

Conclusions

The obstacles erected by the Tropics to economic development are primarily in agriculture and in human health. These need not be insurmountable. [Ram 1999 (2)]

The sub-tropics have led the way in success stories. In 1938, President Roosevelt called the American South, "the nation's economic problem No. 1". Malaria and hookworm affected millions of southerners. Both were eradicated by the end of World War II. Air-conditioning then made hot weather tolerable. The South, with California, became the fastest economic growing region of the country.

---

[3] Cf. Collier and Gunning 1999.

In modern times, Greece was an intense focus of malaria; in some years, as much as a quarter of the population was infected. The disease was eradicated at the end of World War II and Greece has prospered. In Corsica, no one farmed on the malarial eastern plain. With malaria gone, this area was settled and produces more than half of Corsica's agricultural output.

The Tropics proper are also not forever condemned to poverty. The trading, financial city-state of Singapore avoids the agricultural quandary and since it is urban, health concerns are manageable.

The strategic weakness of the Tropics could potentially be converted into a strength. The Tropics force a rapid pace of evolution and change which creates vulnerability for humans, their crops and their animals. But this same velocity of change could be harnessed by research into producing beneficial results for humankind. Malaya, for example, basing its agriculture on tree crops—rubber and oil palm—and with a long-term active, effective research effort, has coped successfully with its tropical problems. Through research, it has greatly improved its natural rubber product and has been able to compete successfully with synthetic rubber in quality and price. And, finally, the higher rural incomes from its tree crops and the pay-off from its oilfields have enabled it to move into the industrial age.

12 Afterword

The master-economist...must study the present in the light of the past for the purposes of the future. No part of man's nature or his institutions must lie entirely outside his regard.—J. M. Keynes.

Economics needs to be a practical art that explains how the world works. After Picasso encountered African masks, he remarked to his mistress, Françoise Gilot, *At that moment I realized what painting was all about. Painting...is a form of magic designed as a mediator between this strange hostile world and us....* The only justification for economic theory is that it is an effective mediator between the economy of the real world and us.

In this book, I have attempted to show where twentieth century mainstream theory fell short in explaining the real economic world and have tried to develop an agenda that economist-foxes need for the twenty-first century. The development of science and technology has given us the ability to dominate nature. We effectively control nature through mobilizing human capabilities through the Market, the Corporation, the Civil Society, and the modern State. These cannot be grasped by a single, overarching hedgehog theory or an all-embracing model. Each requires a somewhat different mix of insights and explanations.

Human beings are complex, adaptive, learning systems. Our whole, dynamic, human economic existence—full of contradictions and conflict as it may be—results in an infinitely complex, evolving economic system which is enormously productive and inextricably intertwined with the rest of human society. One cannot understand the economy acting as hedgehogs. Economists need to exploit the knowledge and techniques of other disciplines such as history, biology, political science, psychology, and sociology.

Economics needs to shift from last century's preoccupation with psychological welfare back to the original classical focus on material welfare. We do not need to try to compare or to compute the mental state of one person as against another but rather whether A is richer or poorer than B in command over goods and services. Only on that basis, do national accounts, income distribution statistics, make sense—they are concerned with material, not psychological welfare—and can policy be rationally made. [Cooter and Rappoport 1984]

The fundamental axiom of neoclassical theory supposedly describing human behavior is a boundary limit—most people fall well short and most would not want to go to such an extreme. As a positive description and normative prescription, Adam Smith's interpretation of self-interest as including regard for others is a better guide than the self-centered self-interest of neoclassical theory.

Human beings are not driven only by a maximizing hyper-rationality; they are more likely to be satisfied with acting reasonably, i.e., following their self-interest but with a decent regard for others. There is also a perversity in human nature. Dostoevsky rightly observed that human nature can never be completely described by mathematical formalism because if it could, people would then violate the formula just to prove that they were human and not machines. People desire not only to satisfy their needs for food, shelter, sex, comfort, and enjoyment; they also crave recognition by others as being worthy of respect. The importance of *face* or *fare una bella figura*, go far beyond the cultures where these are openly acknowledged. The need to feel useful, to contribute to the success of an ideal, to do your part, to pull your weight in the team, to avoid social shame, to act as your society and community expect, to have prestige and power—are all motives that influence different people. And, economists need to be cognizant that beliefs as to how the economy works and herd psychology, all affect economic behavior.

Pursuit of personal profit, contrary to an unvoiced assumption of economics, is not always to the benefit of society. Even in the most law-abiding society, predators and parasites are present. The standard of living and the growth or decline of an economy are the resultants of the work of the productive factors, on the one hand, and the destructive behavior of the predators and parasites, on the other.

The closeness of behavior in a transaction[1] to perfect rational maximization, *ceteris paribus*, is likely to vary directly according to:

1. the size (or importance) of the stake;
2. the degree of professionalism or specialization of the agent;
3. the degree of impersonal relationships among the parties;
4. the pressure of competition;
5. the availability of useful pertinent knowledge;
6. the simplicity of the transaction.

Consequently, most transactions will fall short of conforming to the assumption.

Effective markets depend on the freedom of the individual to pursue self-interest or altruism as he wishes *but* they also depend on a system of law and an ethical and political system that constrains people from pursuing self-interest too far or by antisocial methods. Ignoring this was responsible for the disastrous results of Russia's transition from a centrally-

---

[1] Cf.: *Most economic analyses aim at explaining market transactions. Data on transactions, or potentially collectible data on transactions, are the touchstone for recognizing interesting economic analyses. However loose the connection between a theoretical or empirical analysis and transactions, this connection is the basis of the methodology of judging the credibility and reliability of economic analyses.* [Peter A. Diamond 1994, 45]

planned economy.

"Equilibrium" is an outmoded and misleading physics concept which distorts our grasp of economic reality. The economy is not a stable, balanced or unchanging system. There is no fixed point to which the economy returns if it is disturbed. Everything is in process of change, away from the present towards an unknown future. It is crucial to accept the fact that change is the very essence of the capitalistic market system—it is the very engine that drives the system and is the major force responsible for the growth of the economy. The concept of "equilibrium" should be replaced by "outcome". This carries no baggage of implication that it is necessarily desirable in itself or that it will persist or that if disturbed it will reassert itself.

The market is a useful social and economic instrument but it cannot set national and social ends—conscious human thought has to be involved. The modern global and national economies are so complex and the responsibilities unavoidably placed on the governing authorities are so exacting that economists, if they are to be useful, need to be as wily as foxes using every bit of knowledge that affects the economy in making their diagnoses and in providing policy help.

Most of the gross domestic product for several generations in the major high-income societies has been produced in business firms.

When decisions are made by and through corporate (or public) bureaucracies a different set of forces affect decisions from those that are true of the market. Firms do not always maximize profits.The organization of production through corporations is more efficient than markets but not optimal.

Even to the extent that a rational maximizing motive continues to play a part it has a different impact than assumed in conventional theory—not necessarily directed towards the interest of the firm *per se.* Consequently, the behavioral, organization, and *X-efficiency* theories on how production is organized and carried out in corporations need to be taken into "respectable" economic analysis. What is particularly difficult for persons trained in last century's economics to accept is that the special forces that are at play in corporations do not fit into the ordinary formal modeling approach of economists. This, and recognition of the contribution and drawbacks of organized cooperation should be a part of twenty-first century economics.

The high-income countries have become predominantly services-producing economies. The economics of services differ significantly from those of material goods. The dynamics of a service economy are different from those of a material-goods producing economy (just as an industrialized economy behaves differently from an agricultural one).

The public sector influences all the rest of the economy. Its responsibilities and activities cannot be cramped into the narrow axioms of conventional theory. Public Choice theory is true in some circumstances and misleading in others. The wider perspective of Chapter 6 is needed for analyzing and understanding the important functions that the state has assumed in modern times and its distinctive contributions.

Civil society, the infrastructure of civilization itself, is intimately bonded with the economy but influenced by different forces. Nonprofits are driven not by private profit but by a complex of motives and organizational factors.

In the professions, individuals work within a set of accepted ethical guide-lines and are expected to make decisions guided by what is best for their clients rather than by maximizing their own personal fortunes.

It is natural to assume that the way our society works is true in all other societies. The social human capital our predecessors have left us influences how we act in the economy as well in other aspects of our lives. Differences in this capital among countries have major consequences in economic results. The crucial role played by this has become blindingly obvious in the former Communist-run countries.

It is finally beginning to become accepted that the location of a country in the Tropics has a major negative influence on its economy. This can only be explained by disciplines other than economics.

The greatness of a chess-master is in his intuitive reasoning based on his knowledge of thousands of different patterns. An economy is infinitely more complex. It takes years of experience, a broad education, and practice to develop good economic judgment. The great, perceptive works of economics in the past by Adam Smith, Marx, Marshall, Schumpeter, Keynes, were all written by men passionately interested in the real world and dedicated to an empirical, matter-of-fact, policy-oriented framework for their thought. In the 27 years that Smith took to write *The Wealth of Nations*, two and a half years in France, and work as commissioner of customs in Scotland added to his wealth of real world experience.

> ...the part of economics that is independent of history and social context is not only small but dull. [Solow 1997, 15]

To understand an economy requires knowledge of its economic history, its economic geography: its natural and human resources, its structure of production, its position in world trade and finance. It requires an understanding and appreciation of its social and institutional infrastructure, the main constraints and critical preconditions to its economic growth. And, included as an important dimension of all this, are the capabilities—administrative effectiveness, responsiveness to challenge, ability to handle change—of the government, the leadership elite and the people. All this, has to be recognized in twenty-first century economics.

William J. McDonough, (President, Federal Reserve Bank of New York), in his Hong Kong Monetary Authority Distinguished Lecture, provided an an excellent example of a twenty-first century economic approach.

...the standard economic models are not adequate for explaining the dramatic turnaround in Asia's performance. To be sure, the growth of incomes typically depends most on technological factors and economic policies. But it also depends on a broader set of social, legal, and political institutions and policies that influence the development of economic and technological inputs as well as establish the framework within which the whole economy must operate.

Capital formation and labor supply are influenced as much by economic factors as they are by social and demographic factors. ...[The contributions of technological progress and advances in knowledge] ...depend not only on policies for capital formation—physical and human—and international trade, but also on the nation's history, culture, institutions, level of education, and degree of openness. [Annual Report 1997, 4,7]

Appendix A: Corporate Raiders

Icahn and Lorenzo

From1980 through 1985, Carl Icahn raided Hammermill Paper Co., Marshall Field & Co. J. P. Stevens & Co., Chesebrough-Pond's Inc., Uniroyal Inc., and Phillips Petroleum Co. His group profited by well over $100 million in these early raids. There was little pretense that better corporate management was the objective. [Carley June 20,1985,1]

In 1985, the Icahn group went after TWA, a major American airline. The TWA management resisted, alleging that Icahn intended to "loot TWA". To escape, the management tried to get Texas Air, controlled by Frank Lorenzo, another raider, to take over TWA. However, with the help of the main unions at TWA, who regarded Texas Air as anti-union, the Icahn group succeeded in taking control in 1986. Texas Air was paid a $18 million "break-up" fee by TWA and also made a profit of $42.6 million on TWA shares. As Texas Air had agreed to turn over 25 percent of profits to its investment banker, that left Texas Air with around $32 million in stock profits. [Carley Sept.16, 1985, 1]

Under Icahn management TWA went into bankruptcy within a few years. This is not conclusive evidence of mismanagement, of course, since all airlines during the late eighties were under pressure. TWA creditors, staff, and workers judged otherwise, however, and in January 1993 forced Icahn to relinquish control.

Under Lorenzo's management, Eastern Airlines went out of business and Continental Airlines went into bankruptcy. In 1992, Lorenzo was forced out of the airline business by creditor pressure but left with around fifty million dollars in compensation. When in 1993, Lorenzo tried to start a new airline, the Airline Pilots Association and the International Association of Machinists opposed his request on the grounds that he was responsible for the steps that led to the permanent shutdown of Eastern Airlines. The Transportation Department administrative law judge found that:

> Frank Lorenzo does not respect the law and only will honor legal commitments when forced to do so.
> Continental and Eastern, while under the control of Frank Lorenzo, regularly fell short of complying with federal regulations and directives, to the derogation of their safety and that of the traveling public.

The U. S. Transportation Department in 1994 agreed with the law judge and ruled that: *The prospect of a repeat of the [Texas Air] history is unacceptable.* [McGinley 1993, A5; Babbitt 1994. 42; Pearl 1994. A3]

Posner

Starting as a house-builder, Victor Posner, acquired control in 1966 of DWG Corporation, a Detroit cigar company. Using this as a vehicle, he took over several dozen other companies. The companies were milked to pay for his personal expenses and he put relatives and friends on corporate payrolls and boards. After a federal judge installed three directors at DWG as watch-dogs they reported to the judge that while the company had trouble finding cash to pay its creditors, Posner drew $31 million in compensation from the company over five years. He also charged the company for some personal expenses—$474 a day for meals—for a total of $173,270 in 1991 alone. He charged another company he controlled, Sharon Steel Corporation, $4.4 million to pay for his legal expenses.

Posner pleaded guilty to criminal tax fraud in one case. In 1991, in a consent decree with shareholders, Posner was removed from any active role in the DWG Corp. (since 1994 known as Triarc Cos.). On December 1, 1993, a federal judge banned Posner and his son, Steven, from serving as an officer or director of any publicly traded company. Calling Victor Posner *...contemptuous of the interests of public shareholders*, the judge said in his ruling that *Victor Posner and Steven Posner have had a long and notorious history of engaging in self-dealing and corporate waste to the detriment of the public shareholders of companies under their control.*

Many of the companies that Posner controlled have filed for bankruptcy or have been liquidated.[Sloan 1992. 86; Stewart 1993, 58; 1993, 30; Lambert 1993, A3-4; 1994, B5; Cohen 1994, A1, A4]

Riklis

Another raider, Meshulam Riklis, built his empire on some $2 billion of junk-bonds. His Rapid-American Corporation acquired companies with familiar brands like Cartier, Mark Cross, Smith-Corona, Botany 500, Playtex, Faberge, Elizabeth Arden, Dewars, Schenley, Dubonnet, Samsonite luggage. He was generous with his companies' money: The Museum of Modern Art named a gallery in his honor because one of his companies gave it a sizable endowment and several hundred works of art. He put three of his children on a company board—with each paid $300,000 a year. One company, McCrory, lost $138 million one year but paid Riklis $1.3 million in salary and other compensation. He bought the famous mansion of Mary Pickford and Douglas Fairbanks for $6.7 million and spent $27 million rebuilding it. His personal jet was a Gulfstream IV and his wife's a Boeing 727. All his companies ended up in Chapter 11 in 1991 and 1992 with most bondholders losing some or all of their investments. [Lipman 1995, A1-A10]

KKR

The biggest buyout raid in corporate history to date was the take-over of RJR Nabisco, America's nineteenth largest industrial company. It started on October 20, 1988 with the president of the company, Ross Johnson, proposing to do a LBO—a leveraged buyout, at a stock-price that would have greatly enriched him and the other senior executives involved. Investment bankers who were not in on the deal perceived that it was vulnerable to counter-offers that would be more favorable to shareholders. There were several counterproposals developed and after a swarm of byzantine negotiations the company was finally taken over 41 days later by KKR (Kohlberg Kravis Roberts), a specialist in LBOs and corporate takeovers. The total cost was over $25 billion, raised by borrowing from commercial banks and by the sale of junk bonds—to savings and loans institutions and corporate pension and employee benefit plans.

The types of obligations issued to finance the deal showed a creative imagination. They included: RJR Nabisco Holdings Corporation payment-in-kind senior converting debentures, RJR Nabisco Holding Group Inc. payment-in-kind subordinated exchange debentures, RJR Nabisco Holdings Capital Corporation guaranteed payment-in-kind subordinated debentures, guaranteed subordinated debentures, guaranteed subordinated discount debentures, guaranteed subordinated extendible reset debentures, guaranteed subordinated notes, guaranteed senior subordinated increasing rate notes.

Ross Johnson left the company with a $53 million farewell payment, Ed Horrigan, the head of the tobacco portion of RJR Nabisco, received $45.7 million. KKR paid themselves and the other investment bankers and lawyers involved a total of around one billion dollars in advisory fees and financing commissions. To help cope with the $3 billion of annual debt payments the company was now saddled with, the European food businesses were sold for $2.5 billion and Del Monte for $2.4 billion. Several thousand workers were fired. The tobacco part of the company lost market share. The headquarters were moved from the south (Atlanta and Winston-Salem) to New York and most of the managers left. [Burrough & Helyar 1990]

After the buyout, RJR had $29.6 billion in debt. After four years, the debt had been reduced to $14.2 billion with an interest bill of $1.4 billion.The company in April 1991 sold stock to the public. After paying no dividends on this stock for three years, KKR bought another company with a dismal record, Borden, by using half of the stock it still owned in RJR. In 1995, KKR unloaded the rest to Borden.

In March 1999, the company was split into three. The international tobacco business was sold to Japan tobacco for $8 billion and the money used to pay off debt. The domestic tobacco company was spun off into a separate company to be owned by the shareholders of the RJR and with $1 billion in debt. The remainder became Nabisco as it was originally in 1985.

The final results of the KKR leveraged buyout thus were: The shareholders in 1989 who were bought out in the transaction did receive a price several times higher than the prevailing market price. The investors who bought stock after it became public again in 1991, by March 1999 had stock selling at 51 percent of the price they paid while the Dow Jones industrial average had tripled. R. J. Reynolds had a smaller market share in the U. S. than before the deal and had lost the whole of its international market. Nabisco was independent again but weaker than it was in 1985. But all was not lost, the bankers that made a billion dollars in 1989 in putting the original deal together collected more millions in 1999 in dismembering the company.

Milken

Junk-bonds like those issued in the takeovers were in considerable part responsible for the Savings and Loan debacle and for the failure of firms like Guarantee Security Life Insurance Company and Executive Life. Both of these firms poured assets into soon–to–be worthless junk-bonds and the companies then collapsed into bankruptcy—defaulting on over 400,000 policy and annuity holders.The ultimete cost of the S & L cataclysm to American taxpayers will come to around five hundred billion dollars.

Michael Milken practically created the junk-bond market. By floating bonds for enterprises that could not borrow anywhere else he helped build the information highway by getting finance for Turner Broadcasting, MCI, TCI and McCaw Cellular. He also financed corporate raiders, like Posner. He floated bonds to help clients take over Savings and Loans institutions and, then, in turn loaded these up with other junk-bonds. Milken profited handsomely—in 1984-87 his firm, Drexel Burnham Lambert paid him $1.1 billion. His customers fared less well.

> Of the 104 small firms involved in public issues of nonconvertible Drexel junk bonds since 1977, 24 percent had defaulted on their debt or were bankrupt by mid-1990—five times the default rate of comparable firms, according to Dun & Bradstreet.
>
> With astonishing speed, some of Milken's biggest boosters began to collapse under the weight of the debt burdens they had embraced with such enthusiasm. Ralph Ingersoll lost control of his U.S. newspaper empire when he failed to make payments on his Drexel-generated bonds. William Farley couldn't complete the West-Point Pepperell acquisition. Even Tom Spiegel, the Milken apostle at Columbia Savings, was ousted and his savings and loan taken over by government regulators. Eventually, nearly every savings and loan that was a major player in Milken's ring of purchasers was declared insolvent and placed in the hands of government receivers. [Stewart 1992, 504]

In February 1990, Drexel Burnham filed for bankruptcy. In November, Milken pleaded guilty to six felonies, paid $1.1 billion in fines and restitution. He was sentenced to a 10-year prison term of which he served 22 months. In 1998, Milken paid an additional $47 million to settle civil charges that he had violated a lifetime ban from Wall Street. [Stewart 1993, 60]

Appendix B: The German Central Bank

The federal character and independence of the German central bank, the Bundesbank, although now strongly embedded in German culture; in origin, was an American initiative.

The history begins in Sicily. When the Allies landed in 1943, Allied Military Government closed the Banca d'Italia, regarding it as a Fascist institution, and used the Banco di Sicilia as a central bank, instead. On the mainland, as the officer in charge of central banking in liberated Italy, I found that the central bank, the Banca d'Italia, was largely free of Fascist taint and we reversed our policy. Consequently, when Colonel Bernard Bernstein left Italy at the end of 1943 to head the U.S. Finance Division in the future Allied Control Council for Germany and I followed him as his deputy in early 1945, we were predisposed to work with the German central bank, the Reichsbank. (See Kamarck, 1977, 55-63; and 1986, 37-44).

In April 1945, American troops advancing into Germany discovered the Reichsbank gold reserves at the Merkers salt mine in Thuringia in the future Soviet zone of occupation. A fleet of trucks were mobilized to move the gold stocks to the vaults of the Reichsbank branch in Frankfurt which we had taken over as American Finance Division headquarters. In surveying this treasure, we found it included looted gold reserves from the central banks of the German-occupied countries and something much worse. Included were cases of gold wedding rings, gold teeth, and watch cases, from the death camps. The Reichsbank was handling these under the code name "Melmer" for the SS. This immoral, degrading traffic turned out to be an unforgettable example of the thorough-going Nazification of the Reichsbank. The Reichsbank was under the direct control of the Government—Walther Funk, Reichswirtschaftsminister (Economics Minister) was also Präsident der Deutschen Reichsbank (President of the German Reichsbank).

We closed down the Reichsbank.

Both in Italy and Germany, the key American finance personnel in the Control Commission or Council had come out of the U. S. Treasury. Key British officers were Bank of England people. The German experience led to the unbureaucratic position of Treasury officials strongly backing the idea of a central bank free of Ministry of Finance control. The British with the natural sympathy for other central banking professionals were rather attracted to the idea of reviving the old bank. When in the summer of 1945 I drafted the U.S. policy paper for the Allied Financial Directorate on plans for a future German central bank, the paper emphasized that the bank should be independent of the central government with a decentralized structure like that of the Federal Reserve. This established American and Allied policy and the Bank deutscher Länder, the forerunner to the Bundesbank, was consequently established. Reinforced by their experience of two war inflations, the Germans continued this policy when the Bank deutscher Lånder was converted into the Bundesbank.

Annex: Excerpts from Workshop

Excerpts of the discussion in the workshop (chaired by Dr. Armand Clesse), based on a manuscript, "The Economics of the Twenty-First Century", by Andrew M. Kamarck, Harvard Faculty Club, 24 April 1998.

Introduction

A number of substantive changes (including the title!) in the final text of this book were inspired by the comments of the participants in the workshop. These have been recognized in the text. The author, of course, bears full responsibility for how they were used. Unfortunately, constraints of space forbid reproducing the discussions in full. The excerpts were severely edited to those comments that are strictly relevant to the present text.

List of Participants

Michael Ambrosi, Professor, University of Trier
Francis Bator, Professor, JFK School of Government
Anne P. Carter, Professor, Brandeis University
Armand Clesse, Director, Luxembourg Institute for European and International Studies, Luxembourg
David C. Colander, Professor, Middlebury College
Peter Doeringer, Professor, Boston University
Archie Epps, Dean of Students, Harvard College
Henri Étienne, Chargé de Mission, Ministère des Affaires Étrangères
Mario Hirsch, Editor-in-chief, d'Letzebuerger Land, Luxembourg
Jan S. Hogendorn, Professor, Colby College
Franklyn D. Holzman, Professor, Tufts University
Andrew M. Kamarck, retired Director of the World Bank Institute
Charles P. Kindleberger, Professor (emer.), MIT
Norbert von Kunitzki, President, Board of Directors, SIDMAR S.A., Gand
David S. Landes, Professor, Harvard University
Gustav Papanek, Professor, Boston University
John Powelson, Professor, University of Colorado
Bruce Scott, Professor, Harvard Business School
Paul P. Streeten, Professor, UNDP
Raymond Vernon, Professor, JFK School of Government

Discussion

A. Clesse: Yale Professor William Parker regrets that he is not able to attend the conference and writes:

> The Kamarck manuscript as far I can gauge is quite a wonderful piece of work. I have only had time to read it but I send my full and enthusiastic support for its main thrust. It appears to go into considerable detail and specificity on various institutional features on modern economy and shows great scope and learning. When I have read it more carefully, I hope I will have a more detailed critique to furnish the author. ...I hope you will convey these thoughts to all present. Congratulations on a valuable intellectual enterprise.

A. Kamarck: From spending my career on economic policy I regard economics as useful only when relevant to the real world. Twenty or thirty years ago, I would have used Milton Friedman as the foil. Nowadays, Robert Barro comes to mind. Professor Barro was invited to this workshop and I am sorry that he is not here.

D. Colander: Barro is far too easy a target.

David Kreps' and Bob Solow's articles recently in *Daedalus* on the state of economics give a more reasoned statement of where economic thinking is at this point. They are moving along the same lines as you. Kreps agrees that economists have got to start talking about bounded rationality, and start dealing with such issues.

In the complexity group there is a set of people dealing with these issues. Order arises spontaneously: people inductively learn to deal with situations. Rationality is replaced with purposeful action which is institutionally specific. So, within micro, there is a lot there. Such an approach to rationality plays a big role within business. There is a movement away from talking about grand insights about the overall working of the economy and toward talking about the specific elements of what is going on.

P. Doeringer: Economics does not require that everybody be rational. It only requires that there be a substantial number of individuals at the margin who follow that kind of rationality model. So you could see an economy that was full of irrationality but still sort of operated the way that Barro or Friedman would describe.

You would be on stronger ground almost conceding more to the rationality argument in a static cross section sense, and then considering the dynamics of the economic system and the forces that drive the way the margins move over time. At that point, the ideas, the flaws and the issues that you identify have a much more powerful influence on economic evolution than in the cross section static basis.

P. Streeten: Consistency and constancy are necessary in order to get an equilibrium solution. The best example of a rational chooser would be the disinterested, conscientious trustee. He would look solely at the interest of other people, not his own. Selfishness can be irrational. Impulsive selfishness can be inconsistent and not constant.

D. Landes: Just concentrating on a person's self-interest without taking into account the other actors involved omits a good part of the story. In the empires which controlled the lives of the majority of the world's populations for many centuries, a most important defensive reactions was to conceal your assets, and above all not invest them where future revenues became visible. The result was impoverishment, keeping the society below its potential. Everybody was behaving rationally in the light of the possibility of irrationality on the part of the ruler. If you focus only on the individual, you see a highly truncated part of the story.

F. Bator: Take all the assumptions, not empirically as a good description of the real world, but simply as a hypothesis the implications of which are interesting to explore. Take the full set, the pure theorist's ideal—the first and second theorems of welfare economics do not say that under those assumptions, the result will be the best of all possible worlds. Rather, perfect market allocation under those circumstances will produce an equilibrium that is Pareto-optimal or Pareto-efficient.

The word *optimal* is terribly misleading in this context because most people think it is the best of all possible worlds, but that isn't what it means. All it means it that it will land you somewhere on the utility-possiblity curve of the economy. In a a two-person world of Adam and Eve, depending on the initial distribution of whatever, you can have an outcome where practically everything goes to Adam and nothing goes to Eve. This can be Pareto-efficient in the sense that you cannot reconfigure any of the inputs, outputs, or distribution in such a way as to make Eve better off without making Adam worse off.

This is where the Barros of this world go so far wrong—omitting distributional ethical value judgments.

At best, even if you swallow all the assumptions, Pareto-efficiency is a necessary and not a sufficient condition for even the most restricted ethical social welfare function that is sensitive only to individual preferences. The attack, that modern welfare economics leads one to think a system of idealized markets produces the best of all possible worlds, is unfair.

This point is important to make because the usefulness of that set of formalizations, based on these wholly and empirically unrealistic set of assumptions, enables you to identify how strong the assumptions have to be in order to make the modern version of the invisible-hand theorem hold. It also begins to give you an agenda for interference with markets when markets fail and, pre-agenda, that there is at least a presumption that it might be possible to improve the results. Distribution is, of course, obvious but once you introduce externality, public goods, and all the rest, then you have to have a theory of government. Otherwise you get the foolishness of Alan Greenspan maximizing his own lifetime consumption. It leads to enormous clarification even if you do not accept the empirical validity of all the assumptions.

The best quote is from our young colleague that you have in a footnote. People who know only economic theory, who are caught up in the black box and totally give up on ordinary street-walking sense, end up talking nonsense. People who tend not to understand that machinery, also tend to end up talking nonsense. If I were thoroughly mixed-up, whom would I single out to have a half-hour conversation with? I would put Paul Samuelson and Solow with Toynbee very high on my list.

J. Powelson: It's a world of cooperation and not a world of total selfishness. The ways to maximize whatever we are maximizing are basically through cooperation with other people, and economic theory ought to take that into account. I do not think it has done that adequately.

I wonder whether any one person could judge the rationality of another person's actions. Economic theory ought to recognize that whatever somebody decides, is rational even if the person is crazy. The question is how to maximize what that person wants with a minimum of cost.

Different groups cooperating with each other, as best as they can, will achieve a reasonably good society. Not the maximum but a reasonably good society unless people with power prevent them from doing so.

M. Ambrosi: It is very refreshing to have a new and critical perpsective on economics.

The problem with economic rationality is that it is not sufficiently recognized as a cultured tool and as an acquired mode of thought. Economists must distinguish between rationality in science and rationality in man. We all know and accept that every science is based on rationality. Economists took over the maximizing models of the natural sciences but they equate maximization with intentional purposeful behavior. Nobody in physics would do that any more—the principle of conservation of energy is no longer presented as a rediscovery of the marvels of the work of the Creator. As nothing intentional must follow from maximization in physics, so in economics.

N. von Kunitzki: If your book is to be read by people that have no training in formal economics it will give them a healthy distrust of economic authors that maintain that you can have clear-cut solutions in the economic field. But for people that do have economic training, you should perhaps have drawn a line where you consider the general assumptions to be a good tool in economic analysis and the cases and circumstances where they become unsustainable. In our western economies, there is a big central range where the assumptions of rationality and of selfishness do appear to conform to economic reality.

If the general public reacts as I did when I read the title (*The Economics of the Twenty First Century*), they will expect the book to describe the basic conditions of economic life in the 21st century. You come to that in the last chapter of the book, where you draw on your rich experience at the World Bank. This chapter is descriptive of some of the problems that will appear in the 21st century. The regions that will represent a problem in the 21st century did not concern Adam Smith, Karl

Marx, nor Keynes.

A. Kamarck: To do good economics you need to know more than economics and take advantage of the insights of other disciplines, including history. Francis Bator recalled a quote from David Cutler that makes the point succinctly: *If you think only as an economist, you'll produce silly answers. And if you don't consider economics at all, you'll produce silly answers.*

A. Carter: I want to say that I agree with practically evrything you said. I could never have written this book as clearly and with such flair as you..

I would like to see elaborated what is wrong, for example, with the whole idea of selfishness. There are very interesting issues about what is the objective function of a woman as opposed to a man, of a person with public spirit as opposed to a person without public spirit.

We can argue from now until forever about "what-ifs". If you knew what people wanted to accomplish and what their value system was, would economics be right or wrong? The real issue is what kind of things can you do to know what they want. What are the social constraints? What are the objectives? What are the values? What do you have to know in order to describe an objective function? You also talk about other disciplines and how economics cannot do without other disciplines. In a way it is doing the reverse of what Gary Becker does.... I would love to see our discipline take care of some of these things and I wonder if you would not also. Rather that saying we need more sociology, economists might themselves look at what people are trying to accomplish. In sum, what would you recommend to make economics more useful, realistic or true?

P. Doeringer: I agree very much with what Anne said but it also raises the issue of how other disciplines may be imperialistic. If we were not sitting around here as a group of economists, but as a group of sociologists, the argument might well be made that sociology has done a much better job of picking up economics than vice versa.

Perhaps we should be passing the torch in the twenty-first century to some discipline other than economics. Your economics of the twenty-first century may belong to business schools or sociology departments.

P. Streeten: Bringing in history (and time), as Andy is attempting to do, can be highly subversive to economics. To give you only one illustration: The conventional textbook demand curve disappears as soon as we bring in time in an essential way. Every point on it, relating quantity demanded to price, depends on the history of this price and the quantity demanded in the past. For past experience is the basis for expectations in the future. And these expectations determine the current demand. So we need additional dimensions on a multi-dimensional diagram in order to trace different quantities demanded at different prices now, depending on the past history of the price. If it has been rising and we expect the rise to continue, we demand more now than if it has been falling and we expect the fall to continue. If you take this seriously, it destroys much of economics, as we know it.

H. Etienne: Why people act or do not act matters. The important point is that Formal Theory is not innocent. It has become the dominant religion, which is even implemented in international binding conventions and through institutions. The multilateral agreement on investments was taken to OECD from the WTO because WTO was considered by Westerners, led by the United States, as being not Walras-pure in order to have a world-wide constitution for investment, which would be Pareto-efficient. Next Monday and Tuesday these negotiations will reach an impasse. Because they did not take into account the realities of life. Investment does not depend only on the selfish capital return calculation of investors. People do not accept a dispute settlement mechanism inspired by the American Court system without safeguards provided by the Court system of the host state. Civil society refuses. That is reality and that is real economics.

F. Bator: That organizations matter goes without saying but how do we integrate institutional analysis with mainstream theory? The hard question is how to build what Simon called old-type models with the particular types of organizations that mimic the behavior or response regularities, SOPs, which show up in careful case studies.That would be useful and doable though game theoretic indeterminism is bound to remain. But combining such models of firms, unions, families, whatever, into even very simple toy-like formal models of the economy with non-fatuous implications is unimaginably hard. It is difficult enough to construct non-empty general equilibrium models with rational decision-makers in oligopolistic relations with each other.

One statement that is stuck in my mind from "The Limits of Organization": the combination of uncertainty, indivisibility, and capital intensity associated with information channels and their use imply (1) that the actual structures and behavior of an organization may depend heavily on random events—in other words, on history—and, (2) the very pursuit of efficiency may lead to rigidity and unresponsiveness to further change.

The problem is: it is very hard; we do not know how to do it; it all falls apart. How does one think in those terms and produce results?

It is important to decide what to attack and what to defend in the existing body of conventional economic theory: To distinguish between the content and implications of the method of formal theory and formal theorizing from the method of formalization and in particular building small abstract models from small assumptions and deriving their implications.

It is important to realize many important economic theories, some of the most valuable, are not based on any rigorous individual-agent optimization assumptions. Take the standard old-fashioned Cambridge Massachusetts Keynesian model. From the empirical evidence, its open economy variant is enormously useful for understanding the real world. That has old-fashioned micro foundations. A lot of the assumptions are *ad hoc*, essentially empirical observations like the effect of changes in disposable income and changes in wealth on effect current consumption.

I have more of a problem on long run reality. I do not think we know what explains the movement of the residual in total factor productivity. We know some very powerful stories from David Landes. But whether this really gives one capacity for contingent predictions, I am not sure. Backwards, it does remarkably well. I am less sure that I agree with what makes the trend.

N. von Kunitzki: Some minutes ago I criticized Mr. Kamarck's title and the structure of his book so I am very glad to say that the two chapters that we are now analyzing appear as especially brilliant and partially new to me.

The part about corporations is not really new because in his book "The New Industrial State", John Kenneth Galbraith has brilliantly treated the subject. Take the fad of today "corporate governance". Most people consider that things have completely changed since 1967. Mr. Kamarck says that this is not true. I can entirely agree with him, because of my experience of 40 years in big business.

What is really original and inspiring, is his analysis of the market. I agree that there is not one market nor one market mechanism, but that there are suboptimizations everywhere, depending upon circumstances. You cannot understand economics out of context and those who think that there is one model which is universal and one mechanism unaffected by circumstances, are wrong.

Market equilibrium might be phony. I have been in steel all my life and for many decades, the Soviet Union was the biggest producer in the world producing 160 million tons in the eighties (world production 700 million). The opening of the Soviet Union to the world market has shown that the Soviet Union never really produced 160 million tons. At the height of Soviet steel output, the country imported 600,000 tons a year from my company, SIDMAR, to build Ladas— because modern automobiles could not be built with Soviet steel. Probably, production that could have been used on the world market has never been higher than 80 or 100 million tons. So the real capacity now is probably utilized up to 75 percent. But the 160 million tons, in their times, were a reality and were part of a market equilibrium, if only because the people that made the 160 million tons of so-called steel were earning wages, buying consumer products, saving money.

The game at the Stock Exchange is, as a matter of fact, only a game with figures without any real meaning—as the crash of 1987 showed. How long will this illusion last? Perhaps the stock-exchange bubble will burst, just like the Soviet steel bubble burst. There is no real, permanent, universal market equilibrium.

M. Ambrosi: There was virtually no industrial country which did not subsidize the agricultural sector heavily. What significance could this have had for the global distribution of economic welfare? In all of the industrialized countries this arrangement gave an upward drift for prices of industrial goods in comparison to primary goods (net of subsidies to domestic producers). Thus the rest of the world wanting to buy manufactured goods from the industrialized countries in exchange for primary products faced terms of trade, which were to the detriment of the less developed nations. Now with industrialization spreading around the world, competition increases in manufactures. For established suppliers the demand functions for industrial products appear to be more elastic and they cannot exploit the rest of the world as they did before. This is an interesting aspect of globalization. It worsens the terms of trade for the old industrial products and thereby it might lower the well-being of the industrial workers who produce them.

A. Kamarck: With the wider markets from globalization the old market relationships change. As capital is mobile and labor much less so, corporations acquire more power. For example, in Massachusetts in the last few years, insurance and mutual funds corporations and an arms producer were all able, one after another, to force the state to give them special tax concessions by threatening to move out of state.

R. Vernon: Although we tend to think of the global market as containing numbers of competitors, and therefore that the classical market forces operate in some degree, the closer you get to the actual markets of the producers and suppliers, the more you have to modify that general impression. About half of the industrial output of the world is produced by three or four thousand multinational enterprises. In a product market, the product manager characteristically will identify the individual enterprises or products that he regards as his competition. The product managers do not regard themselves as market takers but as members of an interacting market with a few competitors.

B. Scott: Andrew, you wrote a chapter on the history of the World Bank and you divided it at 1970. Pre-1970, the theory was that the big problem in development was how well the country managed its basic resources, not how much aid was dribbled in. After 1970, the new mathematical wizardry from a new chief executive made the Bank more anti-development from using the new math. Your book here should have the same sort of approach: from your experience, economic development is different from economic growth. The existing economic model is a model of change at the margin—it is a model of economic growth, not development. I have rebelled against this for 25 years but did not know how I could do it. There are already beginnings of a change in the model by bringing in elements such as institutional changes and the very rapid switches of resources from one sector to another that are not included in the equilibrium model. This is the big terrain to be dealt with. I wish I had something like this to use.

A. Carter: I think the job is to learn how the world works and to inspire other people to follow in the right direction,. That is where students or economists will want to continue.

C. Kindleberger: As a footnote, philosophers do not believe in utilitarian ethics, they have a stronger view of ethics. I have another footnote: there is a German economic historian, Jacob von Klaveren, who says the most corrupt episode in the world history was the East-India Company, where they bought and sold jobs, the captains bought the supplies for the ships from their own companies, and the East-India Company does not have a bad reputation except with economic historians.

H. Étienne: In Luxembourg (and certainly elsewhere), the nonprofit organizations which increasingly depend on public subventions have been the main channels for corruption. Government officials give loans and gifts to nonprofit organizations and then there are kickbacks.

P. Streeten: I agree with Jan Hogendorn: if something isn't worth doing, it isn't worth doing well. One often hears the argument that a particular method or model or theory or statistic is not very good, but what would you put in its place? During the 1755 Lisbon earthquake (which shook Voltaire's faith in the inevitability of human progress) a peddler was selling anti-earthquake pills. When hailed before a magistrate, he pleaded in his defense: "What would you put in their place, your Honor?"

A. Carter: Many economic acts impose hardship on others unintentionally. My classic example is that of my father. He was in the windshield-wiper making business when General Motors in 1933 decided that it would sell its cars fully-equipped, and therefore my father was out of the windshield microbusiness. General Motors did not even know that he existed, and yet I felt that was really predatory behavior. There are lots of externalities of that sort.

B. Scott: If you look at rates of return on the assets or equity of the major corporations, no matter how outrageous American CEO pay is, it is more than justified compared to the performance of the Japanese. Japanese corporate returns in the 1990s were no higher than the return from investment in Japanese bonds. While ours are a double digit above government bond returns. The difference in rates of return, over a little more than the last decade, on capital between the United States vs. Europe or Japan has become phenomenal.

Now, in the States there is a market for corporate control that can mobilize 40, 50, 60, 70, billion dollars for a transaction. It is forcing a downsizing of our big companies in assets employed, in employees. In the last four years, the rates of return have gone up by fifty per cent. It is absolutely phenomenal. This is partly why we have those goofy things going on in the stock market. We have never had returns like this before—straight across the Fortune 500.

A really brutal capitalism is at work, drawing the money out the biggest firms, driving the layoffs. Net new employment in the Fortune 500 over the last 15 years is negative; net assets employed, negative; shareholder capital is being bought back, not added to. All of this is redeploying people and resources into all sorts of other businesses. It is not happening to the same degree in Europe and not happening at all in Japan.

For the first time, the market is working the way it is supposed to and the results are somewhat the way they should be when the markets work better. Your argument would be stronger by recognizing that this is going on.

R. Vernon: Europe differs markedly from the United States—less today than ten years ago—on who are the stakeholders. Europeans, until fairly recently, assumed that some of the rewards ought to go to society, to workers, or to something other than stockholders.

Virtually every large enterprise today consists of a cluster of corporations, operating in different countries with different social values. The results are very complex contrasted with the economists' implicit notion about for whose benefit this enterprise is being run and what it is that is being maximized.They have individual strategies for individual markets.The important strategies, are enterprise strategies. For example, Royal Dutch Shell in 1910 set up a subsidiary in the United States and, in its innocence, said in its report: "We set up a subsidiary in the United States, the main market of Standard Oil, to make sure that Standard Oil behaves itself in Asia. This little bit of effort on our part can keep them honest in Asia." That kind of cat and mouse game is not uncommon in a world where a cluster is controlled by a common strategy.

The point is that what may appear as potentially negative behavior of a corporation has to be examined at the enterprise level if you really want to understand it.

J. Powelson: There is nothing inconsistent with being responsible to stockholders for profit, to workers for good working conditions, to customers for a good product. What you have are interests in common.

H. Étienne: We are here at the core of the problem. The behavior described by Bruce, comes very close to effective functioning of your Formal Theory model—hedonistic short-term behavior making money now without taking the long-term into account. That is very different from Germany, for instance, where it is almost impossible to take over a company. There, to handle the cost of subsidization between branches and between the different parts of the work force, they have just enough reserves to pursue a policy of stability unlike the alternative. Once again the market economy is really a question of political choice between the German system or you have the American system.

(Unidentified): In the American style of capitalism employees have no rights, any more than animals on a farm.

B. Scott: The growing activity of people like the California pension system is forcing our big companies to a single-minded focus on the benefits of the shareholders. You shut the Renault plant in Belgium, you move it, you fire workers. Shareholders have now learned to mobilize their votes and to drastically reduce the agency problem that used to exist. It is still there in Europe with its cross share-holdings and banks being allowed to vote the stock — which we don't allow. It is still even more there in Japan.

G. Papanek: In the United States, as distinct particularly from Japan, the markets function very closely to what the traditional theory says the way they work. However, in companies where there is a lot of innovation going on, where for a period of time somebody's good idea generates a lot of extraordinary profits, the company can continue despite a lot of inefficiency and non-market behavior. In Silicon Valley there is a tremendous amount of innovation going so there can be a lot of inefficiency. Ultimately the market will work and the inefficient companies won't become Microsoft. But in the meantime there is a lot of inefficiency in the system even in a place that I have always assumed was highly efficient, the epitome of the entrepreneurial capitalist system.

A. Kamarck: The corporation is not per se optimally efficient. Yet we know the corporation is more efficient than the market, otherwise it would not exist. Its efficiency comes from having capable managers, a good corporate culture, and the synergy that come from people working together.

B. Scott: IBM turned the PC loose and allowed it to go to Bill Gates. This must have cost something like 100 billion dollars in shareholder value for IBM. It was not done because they were ignoring the shareholders; it was just dumb. It was the same with John Sculley running Apple Computer. Just colossal blunders. You have to make decisions, and there are lots that are made very badly. You can't explain nearly all of this in terms of the difference between the interests of the shareholders and those of the managers. Especially in the science-based businesses, competition is in technical standards and architecture and less and less in products in which people know how to compete.

D. Landes: Families prefer to keep outsiders from power— to have them as servants but not as decision-makers. I am struck by your figures on the increasing proportion of corporations that are run by managers from the late 19th into the 20th century.

P. Streeten: Two points about inflation. Assume two sectors; call them manufacturing and services. In manufacturing, productivity grows while in services, productivity is stagnant. The workers in the manufacturing sector get wage increases in line with their productivity growth. The workers in services do not want to be left behind and get wage increases too. The result is inflation. The non-inflationary alternative would have been to let prices fall in the productivity growth sector, which would have benefited the low productivity workers and kept the general price level stable. Though it is often assumed that growth of productivity mitigates inflation, here you can get high rates of cost-inflation as a result of differential productivity growth.

   Second, you can store coal. If miners go on strike, you can do quite well for a time by using up stocks. But electricity, postal services, or railway services cannot be stored. As a result, these workers have more bargaining power. For both these reasons (high differential productivity growth and the growing role of the service sector) we would expect inflationary pressures to be greater today. Yet, we hear that inflation has been virtually eliminated. There is a puzzle.

B. Scott: Sweden for roughly 20 years kept manufacturing wages essentially pegged to the German. The central bargaining in services had to stay in line because manufacturing was the lead sector. As time went on, the services sector became larger. At the end of the 60s and the beginning of the 70s, in political terms, services were more important than manufactures. The services did not care about wages in Germany. When the oil-price crunch came, they wanted it completely offset and this derailed the economy.

There is also a balance of payments impact. The politics and balance of payments have to be taken into account, and not just the difference in growth-rate between the two sectors and its impact on productivity.

C. Kindleberger: There are cycles, in all this. The public-choice theorists (who say that the public sector is peopled by ne'er-do-wells who just sit there, take the fruits and live well) rise in quiet times. In a period of stability there is no excitement, and people looking for interesting challenges tend to drift away. You attract good people in crisis and they leave in quiet times. People like Buchanan look at the quiet times and excoriate the bureaucrats, but I say "don't shoot the piano-player, he's doing the best he can".

H. Étienne: There are changing attitudes in the public sector. The Maastricht Treaty is openly inspired by Milton Friedman, by supply-side economics. The treaty mentions five times that the system is based on market economy with free competition. Maastricht did not prescribe privatizion; nevertheless the idea was there. In the Amsterdam Treaty, there is nothing like this. On the contrary, you find mentions of the necessity to protect public radio, the importance of public enterprises. The European Court decided six months ago that it is not contrary to the Rome Treaty to run a public company in the public interest. Maastricht was almost Pareto-efficient, now there has been a change. The paradigm did not work.

M. Hirsch: In France an attempt was made two years ago to slow down the deregulation of telecommunications by coming up with a comprehensive doctrine of public service. France seems to be the odd-man-out , because in no other country including those where a social democracy is ruling, is there much concern about what it is going to happen eventually to the public sector.

B. Scott: As an example, to illustrate the importance of social capital: Does the private sector run around the world looking for low wages? No, not very much. A company looks for more than low wages, low-cost land, or anything of that sort. It is the social capital that matters. Aside from 12 countries, foreign direct investment in others is and has been practically zero.

D. Colander: An interesting paper by Mancur Olson in the *Journal of Economic Perspectives* is relevant to social capital. He talked about what happened to wages when a number of people moved from, I believe it was Haiti, into the US. According to standard theory, U.S. wages should have fallen and Haitian wages risen. Instead, immigrant Haitian wages went up. The logical explanation is that social capital is important.

P. Streeten: There is a tendency to glamorize and idealize civil society. It can, of course, fulfill important functions when balanced by the state and the private profit-seeking sector. It can mobilize and harness voluntary enthusiasm and express felt needs. But it can also be very destructive, as we have seen in Sri Lanka, Lebanon, ex-Yugoslavia, etc. Some quite unattractive organizations such as the American Rifle Association, the Ku Klux Klan, the Mafia are part of civil society. And many civil society organizations, such as the Catholic Church or the trade unions are not known for their participatory forms of governance.

M. Ambrosi: I found it very interesting in Andrew Kamarck's chapter to look at the different cultures and religions and to see why particular societies are productive or why they are not. But capital is quite a complex concept. One complication which I would like to see dealt with in this context is to look at social depreciation involved in using social capital.

Take, for example, the American pre-Columbian culture. It had a highly productive social system: they invented, tobacco, cotton, potato, tomato, maize and so on. But it could not survive a bunch of Spanish hooligans. It had a brittle societal set up.They sacrificed hearts to the Sun god, and heads to the Maize god. This must have been a great strain on society. This might explain why a very inventive culture collapsed at the smallest external blow. The effort to maintain this society from day to day must have been so enormous that all its productivity was used up just to keep it from collapsing.

There is an interesting discussion initiated by Leopold Kohr, the theoretician who inspired Fritz Schumacher's "Small is beautiful". Kohr insisted that we must look at the *net* position of society, we must look at all the effort that goes into transportation and into all the goods we need in order to just keep society running. We cannot count those activities as net production because they are used just in order to maintain our system—they do not enhance our well- being.

J. Powelson: I am glad this chapter on social capital is in the book, and I approached it with great joy even, but I have found some disappointment in it. I think there could be something more about why cultures are different.

This chapter has a number of generalities that might be difficult to support. For instance, that Canada is a society more concerned with justice and order than acquisitiveness. Maybe it is, may be it is not?

Let's say: I give 100 dollars to Harvard College. I want to support Harvard's education. I am buying a product. If Harvard does not produce the kind of education that I think it ought. I'll give my money to University of Pennsylvania. I have to approve of the product just as I have to approve of the bananas that I buy. I pay a price and the nonprofit enterprise would go out of business if it is not using the money efficiently. So I think it does fit within the framework of mainstream economic theory.

I am not sure whether there is a social good that is more than the sum of private goods. I asked my students "What right do you have to a subsidized education?" Their invariable answer is "We do more good to society by being educated than the incomes that we earn". Is it really true? Does a doctor do more good to society than the income that he earns? This is very ambiguous and I am not really ready to accept that there is a social good that is something greater than the sum of all private goods. I am not ready to condemn the idea either.

A. Kamarck: The essential difference between a nonprofit and a regular corporation is that a regular corporation is there to make profits and its success is judged by that criterion; a nonprofit has an objective other than money-making and that is its criterion of its success. Harvard should not be judged by the money it makes.

C. Kindleberger: One economist measured "Social capability" using as his proxy, years of education. But what kind of education? The education of the British in 1820 was good for the clergy and the military and possibly for the civil service. The French high-power education at the *Grande Écoles* is something else. German technical *Hochschule* is something else. The quality of culture that is taught seems to be neglected. We can add and subtract people, count the feet and divide by two, but we mislead ourselves if we think years of education can be compared from one country to another. There is so much in the world of affairs you can't measure. Goldsmith said: "If you can't measure it, it does not exist". I think that is too strong.

D. Landes: I agree but there is still this preference for the quantifiable and the tendency, also, to treat everything as comparable, so you add or subtract them, etc. If the units are not in fact comparable, then adding and subtracting becomes next to impossible.

G. Papanek: The relationship of culture and the economy, I have found very elusive. Elements of culture are often identified as having a positive or negative effect on the functioning of the economy but this partly depends on whether the economy is stagnant or growing. An extended family system gives lots of people claims on those that are more enterprising, more risk-taking, more modern. That may be more true in a stagnant economy.

In other circumstances an extended family has advantages. In a growing economy, the extended family system can be especially effective in mobilizing capital and putting it at the disposal of the person in the family who is the most enterprising, the most able, the most willing to take risks. That, of course, has been one of the elements in the success of the extended Chinese family.

Secondly, and this is something you largely ignore, not only does culture affect the economy, the process works the other way as well. As long as industry is producing for the domestic market behind high tariff barriers most families can have all the key decisions made by family or clan members. But when you are forced to compete in the world market, you may find that you can no longer compete without professional management. You suddenly begin to get professional managers rather widely scattered throughout the economy.

When Pakistan was set up, the Muslims had never been in business in any large numbers, had never been in banking, had never been in the professions. Yet, they had within six years the fastest growing industrial sector in the world. Initially production was for the domestic market. Then the incentives were changed so that the exporting became highly profitable, and about 3,000 entrepreneurs responded, and that is all it took.

Economists find it peculiarly difficult to analyze culture and draw conclusions on whether particular cultures are favorable or unfavorable for economic development. In 1962 the *Harvard University Press* published a book by a political scientist and an economist, both Korea experts, which concluded that Korea was clearly a hopeless case. I have always been hesitant to draw conclusions about how culture affects performance because I remember these cautionary tales.

B. Scott: The right corporate culture in one set of circumstances is quite different from that in different circumstances. There is no universal right corporate culture.

A. Kamarck: I think the same is true for national cultures.

G. Papanek: There are some things, which are clearly not desirable in terms of economic success. One example that you mentioned is excluding half of the population from active participation in the labor force. But the prohibition against interest, is not as clear-cut. You cite some examples of ways around it. Another is to reinterpret the Koran and to say what is prohibited is not interest but usury. With that interpretation normal rates of interest can be allowed, and what is "normal" can be a flexible concept. But even without reinterpreting the Koran, both the Malaysians and Indonesians, both Islamic cultures, have been until recently quite successful in economic development.

D. Landes: One can find similar features in societies and corporations. For example, one of the big problems for corporations is to encourage initiative, imagination, heresy—if you like—and give credit where credit is due. But corporate bureaucracy often is counterproductive, assigning credit for ideas generated below to higher-ups. There are also societies that keep people from getting the rewards that are due. It might not be a bad exercise to study corporations as has been done for societies to find out what are the elements that promote more rapid growth in some rather than others.

In regard to Islam, excluding half the population from productive economic activities is a loss. But this discrimination is also bad for men. A boy raised to think he is privileged because he is male loses his drive for achievement. In the Middle East and Arab Muslim societies, men are operating far below their potential. But Malaysia and other Muslim areas do not behave this way. This indicates that much of the different behavior is due to older cultures that Islam has in some way come to sanction. The oil of the middle-eastern countries not only does not solve the problem but adds to the damage.Unearned wealth is bad for you. The Arab countries are paying a heavy price for a lot of it.

Bibliography

Abbott, Andrew (1988) *The System of Professions, An Essay on the Division of Expert Labor*, Chicago & London: The University of Chicago Press.

Abramson, Jill and Eduardo Lachica (1990) "Familiar Faces: In Trade Talks, Japan Knows the U.S. Team—Often Too Well", *The Wall Street Journal*, 215(38)(February 23): 1, A4.

Ackerman, Jerry (1998) "Install revolving doors at CEOs' corner offices", *The Boston Globe*, 253(116)(April 26): E4.

———(1998) "In '98, major mergers were dominant story", *The Boston Sunday Globe*, 255(180)(December 27): G3, G5.

Adams, Henry (1996) *The Education of Henry Adams, An Autobiography*, New York: The Modern Library.

Adams, John (1990) "Institutional Economic and Social Choice Economics: Commonalities and Conflicts", *Journal of Economic Issues*, 24(3) (September): 845–59.

Adelman, M. A. (1972) "Review of corporate control and business behavior", *Journal of Economic Literature*, 10(2)(June): 493–5.

Akerlof, George A. (1984) *An economic theorist's book of tales*, Cambridge, London, New York, New Rochelle, Melbourne, Sydney: Cambridge University Press.

Akerlof, George A. & Janet L. Yellen (1988) "Fairness and Unemployment", *American Economic Review* 78(2)(May): 44–9.

Alchian, Armen A. (1950) "Uncertainty, evolution and economic theory", *Journal of Political Economy*, 57: 211–21.

———& William R. Allen (1967) *University Economics*, Second Edition, Belmont, California: Wadsworth Publishing Company.

———& H. Demetz (1972) "Production, Information Costs and Economic Organization", *American Economic Review*, 62(4)(December): 777–95.

Alexander, Robert J. (1986) "Is the United States Substituting a Speculative Economy for a Productive One?", *Journal of Economic Issues*, 20(2)(June): 365–74.

Almeyra, Guillermo (1985) "Easing the Shock of Technological Change: a challenge for Argentina's agriculture", *C e r e s*, 18:2(164)(March–April): 33–8.

Alverson, Hoyt (1986) "Culture and Economy: Games That 'Play People'", *Journal of Economic Issues*, 20 (3)(September): 661–79.

American Economic Association (1999) "Minutes of the Executive Committee Meetings", *American Economic Review*, 89 (2) (May): 449-461.

Andri´ç, Ivo (1959) *The Bridge on the Drina* translated from the Serbo–Croat by Lovett F. Edward, New York: The Macmillan Company.

Angell, Philip S. (1996) "Cleaning Up—in More Ways Than One", *The Wall Street Journal*, 228(18)(December 16): A16.

Aoki, Masahiko and Hyung–Ki Kim (1995), "Corporate Governance in Transition Economies", *Finance and Development* 32(3)(September): 20–22.

Appiah, K. Anthony (1995) "How to Succeed in Business by Really Trying" (review of *Race and Culture: A World View*, by Thomas Sowell), *The New York Review of Books*, 42(1)(January 12): 29–33.

Archives of General Psychiatry (1994) "Survey of Mental Illness in the United States", 51(1)(January).

Arendt, Hannah (1978) "Hannah Arendt: From an Interview", *New York Review of Books*, 25(16)(October 26): 18.

Aristotle, (1905) *Aristotle's Politics*, translated by Benjamin Jowett, Impression of 1926, Oxford: Clarendon Press.

Arrow, Kenneth J. (1951) *Social choice and individual values*, New York: Wiley.

————Enrico Colombatto, Mark Perlman and Christian Schmidt, eds.(1996) *The Rational Foundations of Economic Behavior*, Hampshire, UK: Macmillan, Houdmills, Basingstoke.

Arthur, W. Brian (1989) "Competing technologies, increasing returns, and lock–in by historical events", *Economic Journal*, 90(394)(March): 116–31.

————(1993) "Pandora's Marketplace", *New Scientist,* Supplement, 6 February: 6–8.

Asghar, Raja (1999) "Pakistani court bars interest as violation of Koran", *The Boston Globe*, 256(177)(December 24): A10.

Auchincloss, Louis (1986) *Diary of a Yuppie*, New York: Houghton Mifflin.

Averett, Susan and Sanders Korenman, (1994) *The Economic Reality of The Beauty Myth*, (NBER Working Paper No. 4521) Cambridge, Massachusetts: National Bureau of Economic Research.

Babbitt, J. Randolph (1994) "Beware ivory tower opinions about Frank Lorenzo", *The Boston Globe*, 245(46)(February 15): 42.

Bailey, Steve & Steven Syre (1996) "Boston Capital: Stride Rite among '10 worst', says powerful California. pension fund", *The Boston Globe*, 249(37)(February 6): 37.

Balogh, T[homas] in collaboration with P. Balacs (1973) "Fact and Fancy in International Economic Relations", *World Development*, (February): 76–92.

Banca d'Italia (1986) *Ordinary General Meeting of Shareholders, Report for the year 1985*, Rome: Banca d'Italia.

Bank of International Settlements (1998) *Reports on Strengthening the*

International Financial Architecture, (http://www.bis.org/publ/index.html.

Bank's World (1994), "Staff Week, 50th Anniversary Forum", June 6, 1994, Washington, D. C.: The World Bank 13(8)(August):1–12, following p. 14.

Barber, William J. (1997) "Reconfigurations in American Academic Economics: A General Practitioner's Perspective", *Daedlus*, Winter 1997, "American Academic Culture in Transformation" Fifty Years, Four Disciplines", issued as Vol. 126, Number 1 of the Proceedings of the American Academy of Arts and Sciences: 87–104.

Bardhan, Pranab (1993) "Symposium on Management of Local Commons", *Journal of Economic Perspectives*, 7(4)(Fall 1993): 87–92.

Barro, Robert J. (1974) "Are Government Bonds Net Wealth?", *Journal of Political Economy*, 82(November–December): 1095–1117.

———(1992) "A Gentleman's B– For Bush on Economics", *The Wall Street Journal*, 220(65)(30 September): A13.

Barzini, Luigi (1984) *The Italians*, New York: Athenaeum.

Barzun, Jacques (1983) *A Stroll with William James*, New York, Cambridge, etc: Harper & Row.

Bauer, P. T. (1981) *Equality, the Third World and Economic Delusion*, Cambridge, Massachusetts: Harvard University Press.

Baumol, William J. (1967) "Macroeconomics of Unbalanced Growth", *American Economic Review*, 57(2)(May: 415–26.

———(1985) "Productivity policy and the service sector", 301–18 in Robert P. Inman, editor, *Managing the service economy, Prospect and problems*, Cambridge, New York, etc: Cambridge University Press.

——— and Alan S. Blinder (1988) *Economics: Principles and Policies*, Fourth Edition. San Diego, New York, etc: Harcourt Brace Jovanovich, Publishers.

———(2000) "What Marshall *Didn't* Know: on the Twentieth Century's Contribution to Economics", *The Quarterly Journal of Economics*, 115 (1) (February): 1-44.

Becker, Charles M. and David E. Bloom (2000) "The Mortality Crisis in the Former Soviet Union", Center for International Development, *Research in the Developing World*, 1(1)(Winter): 1-3.

Becker, Gary S. (1981) *A Treatise on the Family*. Cambridge: Harvard University Press.

———(1976) *The Economic Approach to Human Behavior*. Chicago: University of Chicago Press.

———(1995) "The Economics of Crime", *Cross Sections: Federal Reserve Bank of Richmond*, Fall:8–15; quoted in Saffran, Bernard, "Recommendations for Further Reading" *Journal of Economic*

Perspectives, 10(3)(Summer 1996): 181–188.

Bell, Carolyn Shaw (1994) "Data and the Economist", *Eastern Economic Journal,* 20(3)(Summer): 349–355.

Benjamin, Gail (1997) *Japanese Lessons: A Year in a Japanese School Through the Eyes of an An American Anthropologist and Her Children,* New York: New York University Press.

Benveniste, Guy (1972) *The Politics of Expertise,* Berkeley: Glendessary Press; London: Croom Helm.

———(1977) *Bureaucracy,* San Francisco: Boyd & Fraser.

———(1987) *Professionalizing the Organization—Reducing Bureaucracy to Enhance Effectiveness,* San Francisco, London: Jossey–Bass Publishers.

Berger, Morroe (1964) *The Arab World Today,* Originally published in 1962. Garden City, New York: Anchor Books, Doubleday & Company, Inc.

Berle, Adolf A. and Gardiner C. Means (1934) *The Modern Corporation and Private Property,* New York: The Macmillan Company.

Berlin, Isaiah (1969) *Four Essays on Liberty,* Oxford, New York: Oxford University Press.

Bernstein, Aaron (1999) "Why the Law Should Adopt More Family Leave", *Business Week,* (February 1): 43.

Bertrand, Marianne and Sendhil Mullainathan, (2000) "Agents With and Without Principals", *American Economic Review,* 90(2)(May): 203-208.

Blades, Derek W. et al (1974) *Service Activities in Developing Countries: An Analysis Based on National Accounts,* Paris: Development Centre of the Organisation for Economic Co–operation and Development.

——— et al (1987) "Goods and Services in OECD economies", *OECD Economic Studies* (No 8) (Spring), Paris: Organisation for Economic Co–operation and Development.

Blanchard, O. J. and L. H. Summers (1988), "Beyond the Natural Rate Hypothesis", *American Economic Review,* 78(2): 182–187.

———and P. A. Muet,(1993) "Competitiveness Through Disinflation: An Assessment of French Macroeconomic Policy Since 1983", *Economic Policy,* 16(April 1993): 12–56.

Blanchard, Olivier (2000) "Commentary", Federal Reserve Bank of New York, *Economic Policy Review* 6(1)(April):69-73.

Blaug, Mark (1980) *The Methodology of Economics, or how economists explain,* Cambridge Surveys of Economic Literature, Cambridge, London, etc: Cambridge University Press.

———(1997) "Ugly currents in modern economics", paper presented at conference *Fact or Fiction? Perspectives on Realism and Economics,* Erasmus University, Rotterdam, November.

Bleichrodt, Hans (2000) Review of *Rational Risk Policy: Arne Ryde Memorial Lecture Series,* by W. Kip Viscusi. *Journal of Economic*

Literature 38 (March 2000): 127-8.

Blinder, Alan S. (1988) "The Challenge of High Unemployment", *American Economic Review*, 78(2)(May): 1–15.

———(1990) "Discussion", *American Economic Review* 80(2)(May): 445.

Bloom, David E. and Jeffrey D. Sachs (1998) "Geography, Demography, and Economic Growth in Africa", *Brookings Papers on Economic Activity, 2.* Washington, D.C. 207-295.

Blumenthal, Marjorie S. (1998) "Federal Government Initiatives and the Foundations of the Information Technology Revolution: Lessons from History", *American Economic Review, AEA Papers and Proceedings,* 88(2) (May): 34-39.

Bok, Sissela (1978) *Lying: Moral Choice in Public and Private Life,* New York: Pantheon Books.

Bolton, Patrick and David S. Scharfstein (1998) "Corporate Finance, the Theory of the Firm, and Organizations", *The Journal of Economic Perspectives*, 12(4)(Fall): 95-114.

Boorstin, Daniel J. (1979) *Hidden History,* New York, Cambridge, etc: Harper & Row, A Cornelia & Michael Bessie Book.

————(1988–89) "Remarks on Receiving Phi Beta Kappa's Distinguished Service to Humanities Award", *The Key Reporter*, 54(2)(Winter):6.

Boulding, Kenneth E. (1982) "Pathologies of the Public Grants Economy" in R.C.O. Matthew & G.B. Stafford, *The Grants Economy and Collective Consumption*, New York: St Martin's Press, 3–22.

———& Thomas Frederick Wilson, eds. (1978) *Redistribution Through the Financial System*, Praeger Special Studies, New York, London, etc: Praeger Publishers.

Brandes, Stanley (1987) *Forty, the Age and the Symbol,* Knoxville: University of Tennessee Press.

Break, George F. (1980) "Tax Principles in a Federal System", 317–326, in *The Economics of Taxation*, Henry J. Aaron, Michael J. Boskin, editors, Studies of Government Finance, Washington, D. C. The Brookings Institution.

Broder, David S. (1986) "Upgrading education", *The Boston Globe*, 230(65) (September 3): 17.

Brody, Hugh (1982) *Maps and Dreams,* New York: Pantheon Books.

Browne, Lynn E. (1986) "Taking In Each Other's Laundry—The Service Economy", *New England Economic Review,* (July/August): 20–31.

Browne, Lynn E. & Eric S. Rosengren (1992) "Real Estate and the Credit Crunch: An Overview", Federal Reserve Bank of Boston, *New England Economic Review,* (November/December): 25–35.

Browning, Lynnley (1999) "Heir apparent Gifford to gain kingly bundle after Fleet merger", *The Boston Globe,* 256(9)(July 9): C1, 10.

Bryant, Adam (1997) "Calpers Draws A Blueprint for Its Concept of An Ideal Board", *The New York Times,* New England Edition, 146(50826)(June 17): D1, D 9.

————(1997) "The Search for the Perfect Corporate Board", *The New York Times,* New England Edition, 146(50873)(August 3): F1, F7.

Buchanan, J. M. (1986) *Liberty, Market and State: Political Economy in the 1980s.* New York: New York University Press.

————(1987) *Economics: Between Predictive Science and Moral Philosophy.* Compiled by Robert D. Tollison and Viktor D. Vanberg. College Station: Texas A & M University Press.

———— (1987) "Tax Reform as Political Choice", *Journal of Economic Perspectives,* 1(1)(Summer): 29–35.

Burghardt, Walter J., S. J. (1996) *Preaching the Just Word.* New Haven: Yale University Press.

Burrough, Bryan and John Helyar (1990) *Barbarians at the Gate: The Fall of RJR Nabisco,* New York, Grand Rapids, etc: Harper & Row.

Burrough, Bryan (1993), "Barbarians in Retreat", *Vanity Fair,* 56(3)(March): 190–5.

Business Week (1997) "Bloodshed and Terror in Bollywood—A True Story", September 8: 50,52.

————(1997) "The CEO and the Board", September 15: 106–116.

————(1997) "The Best and Worst Boards", December 8: 90–98.

————(1997) "Directors in the Hot Seat", December 8: 100–104.

————(1997) "The Year of the Punctured Myth", December 22, 110.

————(1998) "Special Report: Executive Pay", April 20: 64–111.

————(1998) "Lessons From Our Fast-changing World", May 18: 210.

————(1998) "Needed: A New Financial Architecture", October 12: 162.

————(1998) "Bosses Under Fire", November 30: 52–54.

————(1999) "The New Atlantic Economy", February 8: 70, 130.

————(1999) "Special Report: Executive Pay", April 19: 72–90.

————(2000) "Special Report: Corporate Governance, The Best and the Worst Boards", January 24: 143–152.

Byrne, John A. (1999) "Management, Shareholder Activists: The Teddy Roosevelts of Corporate Governance", *Business Week,* May 31: 75-79.

————(2000) "Pepsico's New Formula: How Roger Enrico is remaking the company", *Business Week,* April 10:172-184.

Calderisi, Robert (1994) "More Letters from Abidjan", *Bank's World,* 113(5)(May): 20–3.

Cannadine, David (1992) "Cutting Classes", *The New York Review of Books,* 39(21)(December 17): 52–8.

Carey, Richard Adams (1987)"On the Corner of Hollywood and Quinhagak", *Harvard Magazine,* 90(1)(September–October): 10–15.

Carley, William M. (1985) "Battle Tactics, Carl Icahn's Strategies In His

Quest for TWA Are a Model for Raiders", *Wall Street Journal*, 205(120)(June 20):1, 16.

———(1985) "TWA Pact Apparently Clears the Way For Investor Icahn to Acquire Carrier", *Wall Street Journal*, 206(54)(September 16): 17.

Cassidy, John (1996) "The Decline of Economics", *The New Yorker*, 72(37) (December 2):50–60.

Casson, Mark (1991) *The economics of business culture: Game theory, transaction costs, and economic performance*. Oxford, New York, Toronto and Melbourne: Oxford University Press, Clarendon Press.

Chandler, Alfred D. Jr. (1977) *The Visible Hand (The Managerial Revolution in American Business)*, Cambridge, Massachusetts & London, England: The Belknap Press of Harvard University Press.

———(1990) *The Dynamics of Industrial Capitalism*, Cambridge, Massachusetts & London, England: The Belknap Press of Harvard University Press.

———(1992) "Organizational Capabilities and the Economic History of the Industrial Enterprise", *Journal of Economic Perspectives*, 6(3)(Summer): 79–100.

Chang, Andrew S. (1999) "An Open Letter From a New Alum", *The Harvard Crimson*, 210(75)(June 10): A12.

Chayes, Abram (1959) "The Modern Corporation and the Rule of Law", in Ed-ward S. Mason, ed. *The Corporation in Modern Society*, Seventh printing, Cambridge, Massachusetts: Harvard University Press, 25–45.

Chernow, Ron (1998) "EndGame", Book Excerpt from *Titan: The Life of John D. Rockefeller Sr.* New York: Random House, reprinted in *Business Week*, May 18: 67–84.

Chhibber, Ajay (1997) "The State in a Changing World", *Finance and Development*, 34(3)(September):17–20.

Ching, Frank (1988) *Ancestors: 900 Years in the Life of a Chinese Family*, New York: Morrow.

Clesse, Armand and Christopher Coker, eds. (1997) *The Vitality of Britain*, Luxembourg: Luxembourg Institute for European and International Studies.

———, Takashi Inoguchi, E. B. Keehn, and J. A. A. Stockwin, eds. *The Vitality of Japan, Sources of National Strength and Weakness*, St Anthony's Series, Luxembourg Institute for European and International Studies and St Antony's College, Oxford; Houndmills, Basinstoke, etc, Great Britain: Macmillan Press Ltd; New York, USA: St. Martin's Press.

Clinton, William J. (2000) *Economic Report of the President* . Washington: United States Government Printing Office.

Coase, Ronald (1937) "The Nature of the Firm", *Economica 4* (New Series) (November): 386–405.

————(1991) *The institutional structure of production.* Alfred Nobel Memorial Prize Lecture in Economic Sciences.

Coffee, John C. Jr., Louis Lowenstein, and Susan Rose–Ackerman, editors, (1988), *Knights, raiders, and targets: The impact of the hostile takeover.* New York and Oxford: Oxford University Press.

Cohen, David and Glenn Follette (2000) "The Automatic Fiscal Stabilizers: Quietly Doing Their Thing", Federal Reserve Bank of New York, *Economic Policy Review* 6(1)(April): 35-67.

Cohen, Laurie (1994), "Daddy Dearest, Victor Posner Lies Ill As Dysfunctional Clan Feuds Over the Spoils", *The Wall Street Journal,* 224(74)(October 14): A1, A4.

Cohen, Stephen S. & John Zysman (1987) "The Myth of a Post–Industrial Economy", *Technology Review,* Massachusetts Institute of Technology, 90(2) (February–March): 54–62.

Collander, David (1992) "Retrospectives: The Lost Art of Economics", *Journal of Economic Perspectives,* 6(3)(Summer): 191–198.

Collier, Paul & Deepak Lal (1986) *Labor and Poverty in Kenya 1900–1980,* Oxford: Clarendon Press.

Collier, Paul and Jan Willem Gunning (1999) "Explaining African Economic Performance", *Journal of Economic Literature* 37(1)(March): 64-111.

Commons, John R. (1961) *Institutional Economics,* 1934, Reprint, Madison, Wisconsin: University of Wisconsin Press.

Conlisk, John (1996) "Why Bounded Rationality?" *Journal of Economic Literature,* 34(June) : 669–700.

Connolly, Bob and Robin Anderson (1987) *First Contact: New Guinea's Highlanders Encounter the Outside World,* New York: Viking.

Conway, Jill Ker (1994) *True North, A Memoir,* New York: Alfred A. Knopf.

Cooter, Robert and Peter Rappoport (1984) "Were the Ordinalists Wrong About Welfare Economics?", *Journal of Economic Literature,* 22(June): 507–530.

Cottrell, Robert (1997) "Russia: The New Oligarchy", *The New York Review of Books,* 44(5)(March 27): 28–30.

Coveney, Peter and Roger Highfield (1995) *Frontiers of Complexity: The Search for Order in a Chaotic World,* New York: Fawcett Columbine.

Cromie, William J. (1995) "Mind's Role In Healing The Body Is Probed", *Harvard University Gazette,* 90(16)(January 5): 3, 6.

————(1998) "Study Finds Two Minds in Every Brain", *Harvard University Gazette,* 94(9)(November 12): 1, 4.

Crystal, Graff S. (1991) *In Search of Excess.* New York: W. W. Norton and Company.

Darlin, Damon & Roy J. Harris, Jr. (1985) "GM, Hughes Face Culture Clash, Mixing Opposite Corporate Styles", *Wall Street Journal,*

204(110)(June 6): 14.

Darwin, Charles (1888) *The Descent of Man and Selection in Relation to Sex, new ed. revised and augmented.* New York: D. Appleton & company.

David, Ronald (1993) "The Demand Side of the Health Care Crisis", *Harvard Magazine*, 95(4)(March–April) 30-2.

Davidson, Cathy N. (1993) *36 Views of Mount Fuji*, New York: Dutton.

Davies, Adrian G. (1989) "The Economic War between the United States and Japan", *Mss.*

Davis, Tom E. (1963) "Eight Decades of Inflation in Chile, 1879–1959: A Political Interpretation", *Journal of Political Economy,* 71 (August): 389–97.

Dawkins, Richard (1998) "Science and Sensibility", *Free Inquiry*, 19(Winter 1998/99)1: 37-40.

Debreu, Gerard (1984) "Economic Theory in the Mathematical Mode", Nobel Prize lecture, December 8, 1983. *The American Economic Review*, 74(3)(June): 267–78.

——(1991) "The Mathematization of Economic Theory", Presidential address, American Economic Association, December 29, 1990. *The American Economic Review,* 81(1)(March): 1–7.

DeLong, J. B.,Schleifer, A., Summers, l. H., and Waldman, R. J. (1990) "Noise trader risk in financial markets". *Journal of Political Economy,* 98:703–38.

Delors, Jacques (1992) *Our Europe,* New York: Verso.

Dewey, John (1938) *Logic: The Theory of Inquiry,* New York: Holt.

Diamond, Peter A. and Jerry A. Hausman (1994) "Contingent Valuation: Is Some Number Better than No Number", *Journal of Economic Perspectives,* 8(4)(Fall): 45–64.

Dickens, Charles (1854) *Hard Times,* Toronto, New York, London, Sydney, Auckland: Bantam Books. Bantam Classic Edition, 1981.

DiIulio, John J. Jr. (1996) "Help Wanted: Economists, Crime and Public Policy", *The Journal of Economic Perspectives*, 10(1)(Winter): 3–24.

DiMaggio, Paul (1990) "Cultural Aspects of Economic Action and Organization", in Roger Friedland & A. F. Robertson, editors, *Beyond the Marketplace: Rethinking Economy and Society,* 113–136. New York: Aldine de Gruyter.

Dore, Ronald (1987) *Taking Japan Seriously: A Confucian Perspective on Leading Economic Issues.* Stanford: Stanford University Press.

Douglas, James (1983) *Why Charity? The Case for a Third Sector,* Beverly Hills, California: Sage Publications.

Dow, Sheila C. (1997) "Critical Survey: Mainstream economic methodology", *Cambridge Journal of Economics*, 21(1)(January): 73–93.

Drucker, Peter F. (1994) "The Age of Social Transformation", *The Atlantic Monthly,* 274(5)(November): 53–80.

Dunne, John Gregory (1992) "Your Time is My Time (To the End of

Time: 'The Seduction and Conquest of a Media Empire' by Richard M. Clurman)", Simon & Schuster), *New York Review of Books*, 39(8)(April 23): 49–55.

Dyson, Freeman J. (1989) *Infinite in all Directions*. Gifford Lectures, April–November 1985, New York: Harper & Row.

Earl, Peter E. (1984) *The Corporate Imagination: How Big Companies Make Mistakes,* Wheatsheaf Books, Armonk, New York: M. E. Sharpe, Inc.

Economist, The (1986) "America's SEC, On the insiders' track", 300 (7460(August 23): 74.

———(1986) "Chips with everything. High Technology Survey", 300(7460) (August 23): 11.

———(1986) "Let the daisies grow. High Technology Survey", 300(7460) (August 23): 18–9.

———(1986) "First, pick your parents", 300(7460)(August 23): 30.

———(1987), "Financial Services, A Nation of Financiers", 304 (7511) (August 15): 44.

———(1987) "Japan Brief" 304(7515)(September 12): 76–7.

———(1989) "BuyAmerica while stocks last" 313(7633)(December 16): 63,66.

———(1990) "American Survey, Being more productive takes hard work", 314(7642)(February 17): 25–6.

———(1990) "Flat rainbows", 314(7642)(February 17): 92, 94.

———(1990) "Daimler–Benz and Mitsubishi; A Tokyo–Stuttgart axis?", 314 (7645)(March 10): 72.

———(1991) "Nomura bows—halfway", 320(7715)(July 13): 84.

———(1992) "Japan, Pass the parcel", 322(7747)(February 22):28–9.

———(1992) "The children of toil", 325(7785)(November 14): 64.

———(1993) "Fraud–busters", 326(7796)(January 30): 74.

———(1993) "Knowing who's Bosch", 326(7800)(February 27): 61.

———(1993) "Malaysia: Powerhouse Penang",327(7812))May 22): 39.

———(1993) "If Kenya goes", 327(7815)(June 12): 47–8.

———(1993) "The black economy; Ghostbusters", 328(7824)(August 14): 55.

———(1993) "The Britain Audit: Crime, Bewitched, bothered and bewildered", 328(7826)(August 28): 56–7.

———(1993) "Taiwan: Buried Treasure", 329(7836)(November 6): 37.

———(1994) "Asian currencies: Malaise", 331(7858)(April 9):82–3.

———(1994) "The Texas computer massacre", 332(7870)(July 2): 59–60.

———(1994) "The word of the Lord", 332(7878)(August 27): 66.

———(1994) "Making a meal of mergers", 332(7880)(September 10):87–8.

———(1994) "Hands up all those hit by sleaze", 333(7887)(October 29):55–6.

———(1995) "Some old peculiar practices in the City of London",

334(7902) (February 18): 71–3.

———(1995) "Fat cats and their cream", 336(7924)(July 22nd):19.

———(1995)"Managers and shareholders, Acquisitive egos", 336 (7927)(August 12): 52–3.

———(1996) "France, Who's next?", 340[7974][July 13]:48–50.

———(1997) "Why too many mergers miss the mark", 342(7998) (January 4):57–8.

———(1997) "A charter to cheat", 342(8004)(February 15):61–2.

———(1997) "Economists as gurus", 343(8021)(June 14): 67.

———(1997) "A Survey of Russia", 344(8025)(July 12), supplement, following p. 49: 1–18.

———(1997) "Reforming the firm", 344(8029)(August 9): 16–17.

———(1997) "The real gangster films", 344(8031)(August 23):30.

———(1997) "Mad dogs and mergers", 345(8044)(November 22):18.

———(1998) "Little Countries, Small but perfectly formed", 346(8049) (January 3): 65–67.

———(1998) "America bubbles over", 347(8064)(April 18): 67.

———(1998) "BRITAIN Who wants the euro and why", 347 (8066) (May 2): 51-2.

———(1998) "The UN and drugs; Tremble, Medellin, tremble", 347(8072) (June 13): 45-46.

———(1998) "Shareholder voting, Voiceless masses", 349(8092) (October 31): 74, 79.

———(1998) "Herd on the Street", 349(8096)(November 28): 74.

———(1999) "Killing Glass-Steagall", 353(8143)(October 30): 18-19.

———(1999) "Procter & Gamble, Jager's gamble", 353(8143)(October 30): 75.

———(2000) "The taming of the shrewd", 355(8169)(May 6):75-6.

———(2000) "How mergers go wrong", 356(8180)(July 22): 19.

Eichner, Aflred S., (1983) *Why Economics is not yet a Science*, Armonk, New York: M. E. Sharpe, Inc.

Einstein, Albert (1954) *Ideas and Opinions*, New York: Bonanza Books.

Elster, Jon (1989) "Social Norms and Economic Theory", *Journal of Economic Perspectives*, 3(4)(Fall): 99–117.

Exeter, Julian and Steven Fries (1998) "The Post-Communist Transition, Patterns and Prospects", *Finance & Development*, International Monetary Fund. 35(3)(September): 26-29.

Fairbank, John King (1983) *The United States and China*, Fourth ed, enlarged, Cambridge, Massachusetts, & London: Harvard University Press.

Fallowes, James (1986) "The Japanese Are Different from You and Me", *The Atlantic Monthly*, 258(3)(September): 35–41.

———(May 1989) "Containing Japan", *The Atlantic Monthly*, (263)(5): 40–54.

———(1989) "Getting Along with Japan", *The Atlantic Monthly*, 264 (December)(6): 53–64.

————(1990) "Wake Up, America!",*The New York Review of Books,* 37(3) (March 1): 14–19.

————(1993) "Looking at the Sun", *The Atlantic Monthly,* 272(5)(November): 69–100.

Farley, James A. (1938) *Behind the Ballots: The Personal History of a Politician.* New York: Harcourt, Brace and Company.

Fenton, James (1996) "Degas in the Evening", *The New York Review of Books*, 43(October 3)(15): 48–53.

Ferguson, Tim W. (1994) "Tissues Turnaround Comes in Shades of Goldsmith", *The Wall Street Journal,* 224(51)(September 13): A19.

Feynman, Richard P. (1995) *Six Easy Pieces, Essentials of Physics Explained by Its Most Brilliant Teacher*; originally prepared by publication by Robert B. Leighton and Matthew Sands. Reading, Massachusetts, Menlo Park, California, etc.: Addison–Wesley Publishing Company.

Fidelity Investments, (1993) *Fidelity Focus*, Boston, MA, Fall.

Ford, Daniel (1988) "A Reporter at Large: Crown of Thorns", *The New Yorker* (July 25, 1988): 34–63.

Formaini, Robert L. (1997) "A review of Roy Cordato's *Welfare Economics and Externalities in an Open Ended Universe"*, *Journal of Economic Methodology*, 1(1)(June):180–185.

Forman, Judy (1996) "Loneliness can be the death of us", *The Boston Globe,* 249(113)(April 22): 25–7.

Frank, Richard G. and David S. Salkever (1994) "Nonprofits in the Health Sector", *Journal of Economic Perspectives,* 8(4)(Fall): 129–144.

Frank, Robert H. (1990) "Rethinking Rational Choice", in Roger Friedland & A. F. Robertson, editors, *Beyond the Marketplace: Rethinking Economy and Society*, pp. 53–87. New York: Aldine de Gruyter.

————Thomas Gilovich, and Dennis T. Regan (1993) "Does Studying Economics Inhibit Cooperation?", *Journal of Economic Perspectives*, 7(2)(Spring): 159–171.

————(1994) "Talent and the Winner–Take–All Society", *The American Prospect*, (Number 17)(Spring): 97—107.

Fraser, Antonia (1975) *Cromwell, The Lord Protector*, New York: Dell Publishing Company. Originally published in Great Britain as *Cromwell: Our Chief of Men* by Weidenfeld & Nicolson, London, 1973.

Freedman, Craig (1995) "The Economist as Mythmaker—Stigler's Kinky Transformation", *Journal of Economic Issues,* 29(1)(March): 175–209.

Freeman, Richard B. & James L. Medoff (1984) *What Do Unions Do?,* New York: Basic Books.

Frey, Bruno S. (1982) "The Public Choice Approach to the Explanation of

Collective Consumption" in R. C. O. Matthews and G. B. Stafford (eds), *The Grants Economy and Collective Consumption,* NY: St Martin's Press, 43– 68.

——& Reiner Eichenberger (1992) "Economics and Economists: A European Perspective", *American Economic Review—AEA Papers and Proceedings,* 82(2)(May):216–20.

——& Reiner Eichenberger (1993) "American and European Economics and Economists", *Journal of Economic Perspectives,* 7(4)(Fall): 185–193.

Friedland, Roger and A. F. Robertson (1990) *Beyond the Marketplace: Rethinking Economy and Society,* New York: Aldine de Gruyter.

Friedman, Milton (1953) *The Methodology of Economics: or How Economists Explain,* second edition, Cambridge: Cambridge University Press.

——(1983) Quoted in "The Fire of Truth: A Remembrance of Law and Economics at Chicago, 1932–1970", Edmund W. Kitch, editor, *The Journal of Law and Economics,* 26(April): 163–233.

Fromm, Erich (1947) *Man for Himself, An Inquiry into the Psychology of Ethics,* New York: Holt, Rinehart and Winston.

Fruhan, William E., Jr. (1998) *Pressures for Corporate Renewal,* Mss. AMP 154, Harvard Business School, June 8.

Fuchs, Victor R. (1977) *The Service Industries in U.S. Economic Growth Since World War II,* NBER Working Paper No. 211, Stanford, California: National Bureau of Economic Research.

Fuerbringer, Jonathan (1997) "Why Both Bulls and Bears Can Act So Bird–Brained", *New York Times* New England Edition 146(50746) March 30): Section 3, 1,6.

Fusfeld, Daniel R. (1996) "Rationality and economic behavior", *Journal of Economic Methodology,* 3(2)(December): 307–315.

Galbraith, James K. (1999), "The Levy Report Interview: James K. Galbraith Discusses the State of the American Economy and the Field of Economics", The Jerome Levy Economics Institute of Bard College *Report,* 9(May)(2): 8-14.

Galbraith, John Kenneth (1974) *The New Industrial State,* Harmondsworth: Penguin Books.

Gallup, John Luke, Jeffrey D. Sachs, and Andrew D. Mellinger (1998) *Geography and Economic Development,* NBER Working Paper Series, Working Paper 6849, Camridge, Massachusetts: National Bureau of Economic Research.

Gardner, Bruce L. (1992) "Changing Economic Perspectives on the Farm Problem", *Journal of Economic Literature,* 30(March): 62–101.

Gazzaniga, M. (1985) *The Social Brain.* New York: Basic Books.

Geertz, Clifford (1973) *The Interpretation of Cultures,* New York: Basic Books.

——(1998) "The Pinch of Destiny (Religion as Experience, Meaning,

Identity, Power, The William James Lecture)" *Harvard Divinity Bulletin*, Harvard University, The Divinity School. 27(4): 7-12.

Gell–Mann, Murray (1994) *The Quark and the Jaguar*, New York: W. H. Freeman and Company.

Georgescu-Roegen, Nicholas (1971) *Analytical Economics, Issues and Problems*. Cambridge, Massachusetts: Harvard University Press.

Gershuny, Jonathan (1978) *After Industrial Society? The Emerging Self–service Economy*, London: The MacMillan Press.

————& I. D. Miles (1983) *The new service economy: The transformation of employment in industrial societies*, New York: Praeger.

Gibbons, Robert (1998) "Incentives in Organizations", *The Journal of Economic Perspectives*, 12(4)(Fall): 115-132.

Gillett, J. D. (1974) "Direct and Indirect Influences of Temperature on the Transmission of Parasites from Insects to Man", *The Effects of Meteorological Factors upon Parasites*, Symposia of the British Society for Parasitology, Vol. 12, edited by Angela E. R. Taylor and R. Muller, Oxford, London, Edinburgh, Melbourne: Blackwell Scientific Publications.

Gilpin, Robert [1997] "The Japan Problem: Economic Challenge or Strategic Threat?", 58–88 in Clesse, Armand, Takashi Inoguchi, E. B. Keehn, and J. A. A. Stockwin, eds. *The Vitality of Japan, Sources of National Strength and Weakness*, St Antony's Series, Luxembourg Institute for European and International Studies and St Antony's College, Oxford; Houndmills, Basinstoke, etc, Great Britain: Macmillan Press Ltd; New York, USA: St. Martin's Press.

Gingrich, Newt (1999) "Scientists must speak out; we depend on it", *The Boston Globe*, 256(181)(December 28): A19.

Goble, Frank G. (1988) "Building Ethics From the Classroom Up", *The Wall Street Journal,* 211(5)(January 8) :18.

Goh, Leong Huat (1995) "From Singapore's Humble Beginning", *Proceedings*, U. S. Naval Institute, 121(1,105)(March): 90–1.

Gompers, Paul and Andrew Metrick, (1999) "Institutional Investors and Equity Prices", NBER Working Paper No. 6723, cited in Justin Fox, "Large Investors Drive Large Cap Prices", National Bureau of Economic Research, *The NBER Digest* (February): 1.

Gordon, Robert J. (1996) *Problems in the Measurement and Performance of Service–Sector Productivity in the United States*, NBER Working Paper No. 5519, Cambridge, Massachusetts: National Bureau of Economic Research.

Gramlich, Edward M. (1985) "Government services", 273–89 in Inman, Robert P., editor, *Managing the service economy, Prospects and problems*. Cambridge, New York, etc.: Cambridge University Press.

Granovetter, Mark (1990) "The Old and the New Economic Sociology: A History and an Agenda" in *Beyond the Marketplace: Rethinking*

Economy and Society, edited by Roger Friedland and A. F. Robertson. 89–112, New York: Aldine de Gruyter.
————& Richard Swedberg, editors (1992) , *The Sociology of Economic Life*, Boulder, San Francisco, Oxford: Westview Press.
Gray, Cheryl W. (1997) "Reforming Legal Systems in Developing and Transition Countries", *Finance and Development*, 34(3) (September): 14–16.
Greenwald, B. & Joseph E. Stiglitz (1986) "Externalities in economics with imperfect information and incomplete markets", *Quarterly Journal of Economics*, (May): 229–64.
Gregory, J. W. (1896) *The Great Rift Valley*, London: John Murray (extracts in Charles Richards and James Place, *East African Explorers*, London: Oxford University Press, 1960).
Grossman, Sanford J. & Joseph E. Stiglitz (1980) "On the Impossibility of Informationally Efficient Markets", *American Economic Review*, 70(3)(June): 393-408.
Hahn, Frank H. (1981) "General Equilibrium Theory", in *The Crisis in Economic Theory*, Daniel Bell and Irving Kristol, editors, New York: Basic Books.
————(1985) "In Praise of Economic Theory, the 1984 Jevons Memorial Fund Lecture", University College, London. Quoted in Tony Lawson, (1995) "A Realist Perspective on Contemporary 'Economic Theory'", *Journal of Economic Issues,* 29(1)(March): 1–32.
————(1987) Review of "The rhetoric of economics". By Donald N. McCloskey", *Journal of Economic Literature*, 25(March 1987): 110–1.
————(1992) "The Next Hundred Years", *The Future of Economics,* John D. Hey, editor, (Issue 1 of volume 101 of the Economic Journal, January 1991), Oxford and Cambridge USA: Blackwell.
————and Robert Solow (1997) *A Critical Essay on Modern Macroeconomic Theory*, Paperback edition, Cambridge, Massachusetts; London, England: The MIT Press.
Hahn, Robert W. (1998) "Policy Watch. Government Analysis of the Benefits and Costs of Regulation", *Journal of Economic Perspectives,* 12(4)(Fall): 201-210.
Halberstam, David (1984), "Yes We Can", *The Parade Magazine*, (July 8): 4–7.
Hall, Robert E. and Charles I. Jones (1997), "Levels of Economic Activity Across Countries", *American Economic Review,* 87(2)(May): 173-177.
Haltiwanger, John C. (1999) "Understanding Aggregate Fluctutations: The Importance of Building from Microeconomic Evidence", National Bureau of Economic Research *NBER Reporter,* (Spring): 4-7.
Hamilton, Gary G. & Nicole Woolsey Biggart (1992), "Market, Culture,

and Authority: A Comparative Analysis of Management and Organization", in *The Sociology of Economic Life*, Mark Granovetter & Richard Swedberg, editors, 81–224, Boulder, San Francisco, Oxford: Westview Press.

Hampshire, Stuart (1993) "Liberalism: The New Twist", *The New York Review of Books*, 40 (14) (August 12): 43-47.

Hanemann, W. Michael (1994) "Valuing the Environment Through Contingent Valuation", *Journal of Economic Perspectives*, 8(4) (Fall): 19–43.

Hannah, Leslie (1998) "Survival and Size Mobility Among the World's Largest 100 Industrial Corporations, 1912-1995", *American Economic Review, AEA Papers and Proceedings*, (88)(2)(May): 62-65.

Hansen, Robert G. and John R. Lott, Jr. (1991) "The Winner's Curse and Public Information in Common Value Auctions: Comment", *The American Economic Review*, 81(1)(March): 347–361.

Harrison, Lawrence E. (1985) *Underdevelopment Is a State of Mind*, Cambridge, Massachusetts: Harvard University Press.

————(1992) *Who Prospers?, How Cultural Values Shape Economic and Political Success*, New York: Basic Books, HarperCollins.

Harvard Gazette (1993), "Report Cites Disparities in Day Care Services Nationwide", 99(2)(September 17): 1,7.

Hatta, Tatsuo (1992) "The Nakasone–Takeshita Tax Reform: A Critical Evaluation", *American Economic Review*, AEA Papers and Proceedings, 82(2)(May): 231–6.

Hausman, Daniel M. and Michael S. McPherson (1993) "Taking Ethics Seriously: Economics and Contemporary Moral Philosophy", *Journal of Economic Literature*, 31(June): 671–731.

Hawking, Stephen W. (1988) *A Brief History of Time*, Toronto, New York, etc: Bantam Books.

Heilbroner, Robert (1990), "Seize the Day", *The New York Review of Books*, 37(2)(February 15): 30–1.

————(1990) "Analysis and Vision in the History of Modern Economic Thought", *Journal of Economic Literature* 28(September):1097-1114.

Heller, Peter & Alan Tait (1983) "Government employment and pay: some international comparisons", *Finance and Development*, International Monetary Fund and World Bank, 20(3)(September): 44–7.

Herman, Edward S. (1981) *Corporate Control, Corporate Power*, A Twentieth Century Fund Study, Cambridge, London, New York, etc: Cambridge University Press.

Hessen, Robert (1980) *Corporate Legitimacy and Social Responsibility.*, Reprint Paper 13. Los Angeles: International Institute for Economic Research.

Hicks, John R. (1946) *Value and Capital,* Second edition, Oxford: Clarendon Press, quoted in Wiles, Peter (1983) "Ideology, Methodology, and Neoclassical Economics", in Eichner, Aflred S., ed. (1983) *Why Economics is not yet a Science,* Armonk, New York: M. E. Sharpe, Inc. pp. 61-89.

———(1977) *Economic Perspectives: Further Essays on Money and Growth,* Oxford: Clarendon Press.

———(1983) *Classics and Moderns,* Oxford: Basil Blackwell.

Hill, Dennis S. (1975) *Agricultural Insect Pests of the Tropics and their Control,* Cambridge, London, New York, Melbourne: Cambridge University Press.

Hirshleifer, Jack (1985) "The Expanding Domain of Economics" *American Economic Review,* 75(6)(December): 53–68.

Hobbs, Jack (1992) "Nature in Culture and Landscape Art: An Overview", *A View from here: Heartland Landscape Painters,* Bloomington, Illinois: McLean County Arts Center.

Hobbes, Thomas (1651) *Leviathan,* Everyman's Library no. 691, London: J. M.Dent & Sons; New York: E. P. Dutton & Co. 1914 edition, 1934 reprint.

Hogendorn, Jan S. (1987) *Economic Development,* New York: Harper & Row, Publishers.

Holmström, Bengt and John Roberts (1998) "The Boundaries of the Firm Revisited", *The Journal of Economic Perspectives, 12(4)(Fall):* 73-94.

Hoover, Herbert (1958) *The Ordeal of Woodrow Wilson,* New York: McGraw–Hill.

Horton, Richard (2000) "An Autopsy of Dr. Osler", *The New York Review of Books,* (47)(9)(May 25): 36-9.

Horwitz, Steven (1995) "Feminist economics: an Austrian perspective", *Journal of Economic Methodology,* 2(2)(December): 259–279.

Howells, William Dean [1890] *A Hazard of New Fortunes,* A Signet Classic, First printing 1965. New York, New York, The New American Library of World Literature.

Hudson, John (1990) "Comment on Michelle J. White, 'The Corporate Bankruptcy Decision'", *Journal of Economic Perspectives,* 4(1)(Winter): 209–11.

Hughes, Robert (1987) *The Fatal Shore,* New York: Alfred A. Knopf.

Hulten, Charles R. (1985) "Measurement of output and productivity in the service sector", 127–130 in Inman, Robert P., editor, *Managing the service economy, Prospects and problems.* Cambridge, New York, etc.: Cambridge University Press.

Hunt, Albert R. (1999) "Clinton strikes out on health research", *Cape Cod Times,* 63(32)(February 6): A13.

Hutchison, Terence W. (1996) "On the relations between philosophy and economics, Part I: Frontier problems in an era of departmentalized and internatioalized 'professionalism'", *Journal of Economic*

Methodology 3(2) (December):187–214.

——— (1997) "On the relations between philosophy and economics, Part II: To what kind of philosophical problems should economists address themselves?", *Journal of Economic Methodology* 4(1)(June):127–151.

Hutton, Will (1994) "Back by Popular Demand", *The American Prospect*, Number 16 (Winter 1994): 50–7.

Ikenberry, David, Josef Lakonishok, and Theo Vermaelen (1995) *Market Underreaction to Open Market Share Repurchases*, NBER Working Paper No. 4965, Cambridge, Massachusetts: National Bureau of Economic Research.

Ingrao, Bruna and Giorgio Israel (1990) *The Invisible Hand: Economic Equilibrium in the History of Science*, translated by Ian McGilvray. Cambridge, Massachusetts, London, England: The MIT Press.

Inman, Robert P. (1985) "Introduction and overview", 1–24 in Inman, Robert P., editor, *Managing the service economy, Prospects and problems.* Cambridge, etc.: Cambridge University Press.

Inter–American Development Bank (1997) "Indicators of Structural Reform", *Latin American Economic Policies*, Office of the Chief Economist, 1(third quarter): 8.

Ito, Takatoshi (1997) "Japan's Economy Needs Structural Change", *Finance & Development*, Washington, DC: International Monetary Fund and the International Bank for Reconstruction and Development, 34(2) (June):16–19.

Jacob, Margaret C. (1988) *The Cultural Meaning of the Scientific Revolution*, Philadelphia: Temple University Press.

Jacobs, Jane (1969) *The Economy of Cities*, New York: Random House.

———(1992) *Systems of Survival: A Dialogue on the Moral Foundations of Commerce and Politics*, New York: Random House.

Jacobs, Michael (1991) *The Green Economy*, London: Pluto Press.

Jaffé, W., ed. (1965) *Correspondence of Léon Walras and Related Papers*, 3 vols., Amsterdam: North–Holland.

James, Estelle (1986) "How Nonprofits Grow: A Model", in Rose–Ackerman, Susan, ed. (1986) *The Economics of Nonprofit Institutions: Studies in Structure and Policy*, Yale Studies of Nonprofit Organizations, Program on Non–Profit Organizations, Institution for Social and Policy Studies. New York, Oxford: Oxford University Press, 185–95.

James, P. D. (1997) *A Certain Justice*, New York: Ballantine Books.

James, William(1902) *The Varieties of Religious Experience, William James, Writings 1902–1910*, New York, New York: The Library of America, 1987.

———(1907), "The Present Dilemma in Philosophy", Lecture I, 487–504, *Pragmatism, William James, Writings 1902–1910*, New

York: The Library of America, 1987.

John Paul II, Pope (1991) *On the Hundredth Anniversary of Rerum Novarum, Centesimus Annus*, Encyclical Letter May 1, 1991, Washington, D.C.: Office for Publishing and Promotion Services, United States Catholic Conference, Publication No. 436–8.

Johnson, Harry G. (1977) "Methodologies of Economics", Mark Perlman, ed. *The Organization and Retrieval of Economic Knowledge*, Proceedings of a Conference held by the International Economic Association at Kiel, West Germany. Boulder,Colorado: Westview Press, pp. 496-509.

Johnson, S., L. J. Kotlikoff, and W. Samuelson (1987) *Can People Compute? An Experimental Test of the Life–Cycle Consumption Model*, NBER Working Paper No. 2183, Cambridge, Massachusetts: National Bureau of Economic Research, March.

Johnson, Simon, Rafael LaPorta, Florencio Lopez-de-Silanes, and Andrei Shleifer (2000), "Tunneling", *American Economic Review*, 90(2)(May): 22-27.

Journal of Economic Perspectives (1997) "Correspondence, AEA Dues and Ethics", letters from Enrique Lerdau, Edward W. Eboch. 11(3)(Summer): 198.

Kagel, John H. and Dan Levin (1991) "The Winner's Curse and Public Information in Common Value Auctions: Reply", *American Economic Review*, 81(1)(March): 362–369.

Kaldor, Nicholas (1985) *Economics without Equilibrium*, Armonk, NY: M.E.Sharpe.

————(1996) *Causes of Growth and Stagnation in the World Economy*, Raffaele Mattioli Foundation, Cambridge: Cambridge University Press.

Kamarck, Andrew M. (1970) "The Appraisal of Country Economic Performance", *Economic Development and Cultural Change*, 18(2)(January 1970): 153–65.

————(1972) *The Economics of African Development*, Rev. ed., London & New York: Praeger Publishers. Second printing.

————(1976), *The Tropics and Economic Development*, Baltimore & London: The Johns Hopkins University Press, Published for the World Bank.

————(1977) *Politica finanziaria degli alleati in Italia (luglio 1943, febbraio 1947)*, Rome: Carecas.

————(1982), "McNamara's Bank", *Foreign Affairs*, 60(2)(Spring) 951-3.

————(1982) "The Resources of Tropical Africa", *Daedalus: Black Africa: A Generation After Independence*, Proceedings of the American Academy of Arts and Sciences, 111(2)(Spring): 149-64.

————(1983) *Economics and the Real World*, Oxford: Basil Blackwell.

————(1986) "Donato Menichella: la Commissione di controllo alleata e l'IRI, l'ECA e la Banca d'Italia", *Donato Menichella, Testimonianze e Studi Raccolti dalla Banca d'Italia.* Roma–Bari: Editori Laterza.

————(2000) "Slow Growth in Africa", *Journal of Economic Perspectives* 14 (2)(Spring): 235-6.

Kaplan, Steven N.(1992) *Top Executive Rewards and Firm Performance: A Comparison of Japan and the United States* (NBER Working Paper No. 4065), Cambridge,Massachusetts, National Bureau of Research.

————(1993) *The Evolution of Buyout Price and Financial Structure,* NBER Reprint No. 1835, Cambridge, Massachusetts:National Bureau of Economic Research. December.

Katz, Richard (1998) "What Japan Teaches Us Now", *The American Prospect*, 40(September-October): 54-58.

Kay, Neil M. (1995) "Alchian and 'the Alchian thesis'", *Journal of Economic Methodology*, 2(2): 281–286.

Keehn, E. B. (1997) "Organized Dependence: Politicians and Bureaucrats in Japan", 131–148 in Clesse, Armand, Takashi Inoguchi, E. B. Keehn, and J. A. A. Stockwin, eds. *The Vitality of Japan, Sources of National Strength and Weakness,* St Anthony's Series, Luxembourg Institute for European and International Studies and St Antony's College, Oxford; Houndmills, Basingstoke, etc,[i] Great Britain: Macmillan Press Ltd; New York, USA: St. Martin's Press.

Kempton, Murray (1992) "A New Colonialism" *New York Review of Books*, 39(19)(November 19): 39.

Kendrick, John W. (1985) "Measurement of output and productivity in the service sector", 111–23 in Inman, Robert P., editor, *Managing the service economy, Prospects and problems.* Cambridge, New York, etc.: Cambridge University Press.

Keynes, John Maynard (1925) "Alfred Marshall, 1842–1924", in A.C. Pigou (ed.), *Memorials of Alfred Marshall*, London: Macmillan,1–65.

————(1930) *A Treatise on Money*, New York: Harcourt, Brace and Company.

————(1936) *The General Theory of Employment, Interest, and Money*, New York: Harcourt, Brace and Company.

————(1949), *Two Memoirs: Dr. Melchior: A Defeated Enemy and My Early Beliefs,* New York: Augustus M. Kelley; London: Rupert Hart–Davis.

————(1951) *Essays in Biography.* New ed. New York: Horizon Press.

Kelly, Sir David (1952) *The Ruling Few or The Human Background to Diplomacy,* London: Hollis & Carter.

Kepel, Gilles (1994) *The Revenge of God: The Resurgence of Islam, Christianity and Judaism in the Modern World,* First published in France as *La Revanche de Dieu,* 1991 Éditions du Seuil, Translated by Alan Braley, University Park, Pennsylvania: The

Pennsylvania State University Press.

Kiely, Robert (1991) "White Swan, Gray Turtle", *Harvard Magazine*, 93(6) (July–August): 45–50.

Kindleberger, Charles P. (1965) *Economic Development*. Second edition, New York: McGraw–Hill.

——(1984) *A Financial History of Western Europe*, London: George Allen and Unwin.

——(1996) *World Economic Primacy: 1500 to 1990*. New York, Oxford: Oxford University Press.

Kinsley, Michael (1986) "How to Succeed in Academia by Really Trying", *Wall Street Journal*, 208(86)(October 30): 33.

Kirman, Alan (1996) "Micro–foundations built on sand? A review of Maarten Janssen's *Microfoundations: A Critical Inquiry*", *Journal of Economic Methodology*, 3(2)(December):322–333.

Kirzner, Israel M. (1997) "Entrepreneurial Discovery and the Competitive Market Process: An Austrian Approach", *Journal of Economic Literature*, 35(March):60–85.

Klamer, Arjo and David Colander (1990) *The Making of an Economist*, Boulder: Westview Press.

Koestler, Arthur (1970) "The Lion and the Ostrich", *Bricks to Babel*, New York: Random House, 571–80.

Komiya, Ryutaro (1990) *The Japanese Economy: Trade, Industry, and Government*. Tokyo: University of Tokyo Press.

Korda, Michael (1996) "Annals of Tycoonery: The Last Business Eccentric", *The New Yorker* 72(39)(December 16): 82–91.

Kornblut, Anne E. (1998) "McGovern vows revamp of child care", *The Boston Globe* 253(82)(March 23): B8.

Kramer, Jane (1992) "Letter from Europe", *The New Yorker*, 68(27) (September 21):108–24.

Kreps, David M. (1997) "Economics—The Current Position", *Daedlus*, Winter 1997, *American Academic Culture in Transformation" Fifty Years, Four Disciplines*, issued as Vol. 126, Number 1 of the Proceedings of the American Academy of Arts and Sciences: 59–86.

Kuntz, Mary (1985) "A price on your head", *Forbes*, 136(7)(September 16): 92–3.

Kurkjian, Stephen (1993) "Papers show new links between Ferber, firm", *The Boston Globe*, 244(170)(December 17): 1, 44.

Kuttner, Robert (1998) *Everything for Sale: The Virtues and Limits of Markets*, A Twentieth Century Fund Book. New York:Alfred A. Knopf.

——(1999) "The real engine of our growth", *The Boston Sunday Globe*, 255 (38)(February 7): C7.

Kuznets, Simon (1966) *Modern Economic Growth*, New Haven & London: Yale University Press.

——(1971) *Economic Growth of Nations*, Cambridge, Massachusetts:

Belknap Press of Harvard University Press.
Ladurie, Le Roy (1978) *Montaillou, The Promised Land of Error*, originally published in France as *Montaillou, village occitan de 1294 à 1324.* 1975, *Éditions Gallimard,* Translated by Barbara Bray. New York: George Braziller, Inc.
Lambert, Craig (2000) "Deep Cravings", *Harvard Magazine,* 102(4)(April):60–8.
Lambert, Wade (1993) "Posner Is Barred From High Positions in Public Companies", *The Wall Street Journal,* 222(108)(December 2): A3, 4.
———(1994) "Posner Fights Ban on Public–Firm Posts", *The Wall Street Journal,* 223(19)(January 27): B5.
Landes, David S. (1970) *The Unbound Prometheus: Technological change and industrial development in Western Europe from 1750 to the present,* Cambridge: At the University Press.
La Porta, Rafael, Florencio Lopez–de–Silanes, Andrei Shleifer, and Robert Vishny, (1997) "Trust in Large Organizations", *NBER Working Paper No. 5864,* Cambridge, Massachusetts: National Bureau of Economic Research.
Larsen, Ralph S. (2000] "Letter to Shareowners", *Johnson & Johnson 1999 Annual Report, Leading from Our Strengths.*
Latham, Robert (1983) *The Diary of Samuel Pepys,* vol. 19, *Companion,* Berkeley & Los Angeles: University of California Press.
Lavoie, Don. (1985) *National Economic Planning: What Is Left?,* Washington: Cato Institute.
Lawrence, Robert Z. (1993) "Japan's Different Trade Regime: An Analysis with Particular Reference to *Keiretsu*", *Journal of Economic Perspectives,* 7(3)(Summer): 3–19.
Lawson, Tony (1995) "A Realist Perspective on Contemporary 'Economic Theory'", *Journal of Economic Issues,* 29(1)(March): 1–32.
———(1997) "Situated rationality", *Journal of Economic Methodology,* 4(1)(June): 101–126.
Lazear, Edward P. (2000) "Economic Imperialism", *Quarterly Journal of Economics,* 115(1)(March): 99–146.
Lazonick, William (1998) *The Japanese Financial Crisis, Corporate Governance, and Sustainable Prosperity,* Working Paper No. 227, Annandale-on-Hudson, New York: The Jerome Levy Economics Institute.
Leibenstein, Harvey (1982) "Notes on X–Efficiency and Bureaucracy" in Matthews and Stafford (eds) *The Grants Economy and Collective Consumption,* NY: St Martin's Press, 191–207.
Le Monde (1997) "Les pays de l'OCDE adoptent une convention anti–corruption" (cinquante–troisième année) (16430)(24 novembre): 28.
Leontief, Wassily (1982) "Letter to the Editor", *Science,* 217(July 9): 104-

5; published in Eichner, Aflred S., (1983) *Why Economics is not yet a Science*, Armonk, New York: M. E. Sharpe, Inc.

LeRoy, Stephen (1989) "Efficient Capital Markets and Martingales", *Journal of Economic Literature* 28: 1583-1621.

Letiche, John M. (1987) "Foreword" to Amartya Sen, *On Ethics and Economics*, Oxford and New York: Basil Blackwell.

Levy, Brian (1997) "How Can States Foster Markets?" *Finance and Development,* 34(3)(September): 21–23.

Lewis, W. Arthur (1955) *The Theory of Economic Growth,* London: George Allen & Unwin.

Lichtenberg, Frank and George Pushner (1992) *Ownership Structure and Corporate Performance in Japan,* (NBER Working Paper No. 4092) Cambridge, Massachusetts: National Bureau of Economic Research.

Lind, Barry and Charles R. Plott (1991) "The Winner's Curse: Experiments with Buyers and with Sellers", *The American Economic Review,* 81(1)(March): 335–346.

Linder, Stefan B. (1970) *The Harried Leisure Class*, New York: Columbia University Press.

Linebaugh, Peter (1991) *The London Hanged: Crime and Civil Society in the Eighteenth Century,* New York & Cambridge: Cambridge University Press.

Lipman, Joanne (1995), "'I'm No Quitter', Meshulam Riklis Tries To Stage a Comeback as Pia Takes a Powder", *The Wall Street Journal,* 225 (16)(January 24): A1, A10.

Lipman, Marvin M. (1996) "Office Visit: The Power of Placebos", *Consumer Reports on Health,* Consumers Union, 8(2)(February): 23.

Loeb, Gerald M. *The Battle for Investment Survival* (1935)(1996) New York: John Wiley & Sons.

Loewenstein, George and Richard H. Thaler (1989) "Anomalies: Intertemporal Choice", *Journal of Economic Perspectives,* 3(4)(Fall): 181–193.

Lowenstein, Roger (1995) *Buffett.* New York: Random House, Inc.

———(1995) "Intrinsic Value, Turner's Pay Deal is a Lesson in Socialism", *The Wall Street Journal,* 226(67)(October 5): C1.

Lublin, Joann S. (1996) "The Great Divide", *The Wall Street Journal,* 227(72)(April 11): R1, R4.

Macaulay, Stewart (1992) "Non–Contractual Relations in Business", in *The Sociology of Economic Life*, Mark Granovetter & Richard Swedberg, editors, Boulder, San Francisco, Oxford: Westview Press, 265–83.

Macaulay, Thomas Babington (1833) "Walpole's Letters to Sir Horace Mann", (Edinburgh Review, October 1833) *Essays, Historical and Literary from the 'Edinburgh Review'*. London: Ward, Lock & Co., Limited.

MacAvoy, Paul W. (1979) *The Regulated Industries and the Economy,*

New York: W W Norton & Co.

Maddison, Angus (1987) "Growth and Slowdown in Advanced Capitalist Economies: Techniques of Quantitative Assessment", *Journal of Economic Literature*, 25(June): 649–698.

Malabre, Alfred L. Jr. & Lindley H. Clark Jr (1992) "Dubious Figures", *Wall Street Journal* 1210(31)(August 12): A1, A5.

Mallon, Richard D. & Juan V. Sourrouille (1975) *Economic Policymaking in a Conflict Society: The Argentine Case,* Cambridge, Massachusetts and London, England: Harvard University Press.

Mansfield, Edwin (1970) *Macroeconomics: Theory & Applications*, New York: W. W. Norton & Co.

————(1982) *Microeconomics: Theory & Applications,* Shorter Fourth Edition, New York: W. W. Norton & Co.

Marais, Eugene N. (1947) *My Friends the Baboons*, London: Methuen & Co. Ltd. Second Edition.

Marcial, Gene G. (1998) "That Was Just The Warm-up", *Business Week*, (December 28): 151.

Marshall, Alfred (1920) *Principles of Economics*, London: MacMillan & Co. Eighth edition, reprinted 1952.

Marshall, Matt (1995) "Germany's Law On Inside Trading Brings a Conviction" *The Wall Street Journal*, 226(35)(August 21): A5.

Maruna, David F. II (1994) "Duty, Honor, and the Commission", *US Naval Institute Proceedings*, 120(6)(June): 36–8.

Mason, Edward S. (1959) ed. *The Corporation in Modern Society*, Seventh printing. Cambridge, Massachusetts: Harvard University Press.

Matthews, R. C. O. & G. B. Stafford. (1982) *The Grants Economy and Collective Consumption,* Proceedings of a Conference held by the International Economic Association at Cambridge, England, New York: St Martin's Press.

Maugham, Somerset (1955) *The Complete Short Stories*, First published 1951, Vol. II, London, Melbourne, Toronto: William Heinemann.

Mayer, Martin (1990) *The Greatest–ever Bank Robbery: The Collapse of the Savings and Loan Industry.* New York: Charles Scribner's Sons.

Mayer, Thomas (1993) *Truth versus Precision in economics,* Aldershot, England; Brookfield, Vermont: Edward Elgar.

————(1999) "The domain of hypotheses and the realism of assumptions", *Journal of Economic Methodology*, 6(3)(November): 319-330.

McClelland, David C. (1961) *The Achieving Society*, Princeton, New Jersey, Toronto, etc.

————& David Burnham. (1976) "Power is the Great Motivator", *Harvard Business Review*, 54(2)(March–April): 100–10.

McCormack, Gavan (1997) "The Emptiness of Affluence: Vitality, Embolism and Symbiosis in the Japanese Body Politic", 112–130 in

Clesse, Armand, Takashi Inoguchi, E. B. Keehn, and J. A. A. Stockwin, eds. *The Vitality of Japan, Sources of National Strength and Weakness,* St Anthony's Series, Luxembourg Institute for European and International Studies and St Antony's College, Oxford; Houndmills, Basinstoke, etc, Great Britain: Macmillan Press Ltd; New York, USA: St. Martin's Press.

McDonough, William J. (1997) "Asia and the World Economy", The Inaugural Hong Kong Monetary Authority Distinguished Lecture, *Federal Reserve Bank of New York, Eighty–Second Annual Report, for the year ended December 31, 1996,* New York, 1–12.

McGinley, Laurie (1993) "Lorenzo's Bid to Start Airline Is Set Back", *Wall Street Journal,* 222(50)(September 10): A5.

McKinnon, Ronald I. (1991) *The Order of Economic Liberalization: Financial control in the transition to a market economy,* Johns Hopkins Studies in Development. Baltimore and London: Johns Hopkins Press.

McPherson, Michael S. (1993) Review of "Thoughtful economic man: Essays on rationality, moral rules and benevolence", Edited by J. Gay Tulip Meeks, Cambridge, New York and Melbourne: Cambridge University Press, 1991, *Journal of Economic Literature,* 31(December 1993): 1964–1966.

McUsic, Molly (1987) "U.S. Manufacturing: Any Cause for Alarm?" *New England Economic Review,* Federal Reserve Bank of Boston, (Jan–Feb): 3–15.

Medoff, James L. & Katharine G. Abraham (1984) *Years of Service and Probability of Promotion,* NBER Working Paper No. 1191, Cambridge, MA: National Bureau of Economic Research.

Meltzer, Allan H. (1995) "Information, Sticky Prices and Macroeconomic Foundations" *Review* of the Federal Reserve Bank of St. Louis, May/June 1995 issue, quoted in *Journal of Economic Perspectives,* "Suggestions for Further Reading", 209.

Michels, Robert (1962) *Political Parties,* Glencoe, Illinois: The Free Press.

Mill, John Stuart (1892) *Principles of Political Economy,* sixth edition, London: Longman.

Miller, Edythe S. (1993) "The Economic Imagination and Public Policy: Orthodoxy Discovers the Corporation", *Journal of Economic Issues,* 27(4)December): 1041–1058.

Moore, Francis D. (1985) "Who Should Profit From The Care Of Your Illness", *Harvard Magazine* 88(2)(November–December): 45–54.

Morris, Betsy (1987) "Big Spenders", *Wall Street Journal* 210(22)(July 30): 1,13.

Morita, Akio (1993) "Toward A New World Economic Order", *The Atlantic Monthly,* 271(6)(June): 88–98.

Mumford, Lewis (1973) *The Condition of Man,* New York: A Harvest Book, Harcourt Brace Jovanovich.

Murphy, Jerome (1993) "A Conversation with Jerome Murphy", *Harvard Gazette*, 98(31)(April 16):5–6.

Musgrave, Richard A. (1980) "Theories of Fiscal Crises: An Essay in Fiscal Sociology", 361–390, in *The Economics of Taxation*, Henry J. Aaron, Michael J. Boskin, editors, Studies of Government Finance, Washington, D. C." The Brookings Institution.

Myers, Henry F. (1986) "The Growth in Services May Moderate Cycles", *Wall Street Journal*, 208(58)(September 22): 1.

Myers, Milton L. (1983) *The Soul of Modern Economic Man: Ideas of Self–Interest Thomas Hobbes to Adam Smith*, Chicago & London: University of Chicago Press.

Myrdal, Gunnar (1968) *Asian Drama*, New York: Pantheon, Random House. 3 vols.

Nagel, Thomas [T.N.] (1995) "egoism, psychological", The Oxford Companion to Philosophy, ed. by Ted Honderich, Oxford, New York: Oxford University Press. 220–1.

Naipaul, V. S. (1982) *Among the Believers: An Islamic Journey,* New York: Alfred A. Knopf.

Niebuhr, Reinhold (1986) *The Essential Reinhold Niebuhr,* Selected Essays and Addresses, Edited and Introduced by Robert McAfee Brown, New Haven and London: Yale University Press.

Norgaard, Richard (1992), *Sustainability and the Economics of Assuring Assets for Future Generations*, Washington, D. C.: The World Bank.

Norris, Floyd (1998) "Q. Who Lost in Continental Airlines Deal?", *The New York Times,* 147(51,051)(January 28): D1, D6.

Nye, Joseph S. Jr (1990), "The Misleading Metaphor of Decline", *The Atlantic Monthly,* 265(3)(March): 86–94.

OECD (1999) *OECD Principles of Corporate Governance*, (http://www.oecd.org/dat/governance/principles.htm).

Okun, Arthur M. (1981) *Prices and quantities: A macroeconomic analysis,* Washington, D. C.: The Brookings Institution.

Oliver, Roland (1991), *The African Experience,* New York: Icon Editions, HarperCollins Publishers.

Olson, Mancur, Jr. (1996) "Big Bills Left on the Sidewalk; Why Some Nations are Rich, and Others Poor", Distinguished Lecture on Economics in Government, *Journal of Economic Perspectives,* 10(2)(Spring): 3-24.

Ori, Pier D'Amiano & Giovanni Perich (1978), *Talleyrand*, Milano: Rusconi.

Paddock, William and Elizabeth (1973) *We Don't Know How: An Independent Audit of What They Call Success in Foreign Assistance.* Ames: Iowa State University Press.

Page, John et al (1993) *The East Asian Miracle: Economic Growth and Public Policy,* A World Bank Policy Research Report prepared by a team led by John Page and comprising Nancy Birdsall, Ed Campos, W. Max Corden, Chang-Shik Kim, Lawrence MacDonald, Howard Pack, Richard Sabot, Joseph Stiglitz, and Marilou Uy. New York: Oxford University Press.

Pareto, Vilfredo (1971), *Manual of Political Economy,* [tr. Ann S. Schwier] NY: A. M. Kelly [original publication in French, 1927].

Parkinson, C. Northcote (1958), *Parkinson's Law,* London: John Murray.

————(1962) *In–Laws & Outlaws,* London: John Murray.

Peacock, Alan & J. A. Wiseman (1961), *The Growth of Public Expenditure in the United Kingdom 1890–1955,* National Bureau of Economic Research, Princeton: Princeton University Press.

Pearl, Daniel (1994) "Lorenzo Bid to Reenter Airline Business Is Rejected by Transportation Officials", *The Wall Street Journal,* 223(67)(April 6): A3.

Pearce, David W. (1981), *The Dictionary of Modern Economics,* Cambridge, Mass.: MIT Press.

Penrose, Edith T. (1980) *The Theory of The Growth of the Firm,* White Plains, New York: M. E. Sharpe, Inc.

Perlman, Mark (1989) "Comments 1", in Joseph E. Stiglitz et al, *The Economic Role of the State,* edited by Arnold Heertje, Oxford & Cambridge, Massachusetts: Basil Blackwell in association with Bank Insinger de Beaufort NV.

Persky, Joseph (1997) "Retrospectives; Classical Family Values: Ending the Poor Laws as They Knew Them", *Journal of Economic Perspectives,* 11(1) (Winter): 179–189.

Phelps, Edmund S. (1981), "Okun's Micro–Macro System: A Review Article", *Journal of Economic Literature,* 19(September): 1065–73.

Pines, Shlomo (1963), *Introduction to Moses Maimonides, The Guide to the Perplexed,* Chicago: University of Chicago Press.

Pitelis, C. N. (1998) "Transaction Costs and the Historical Evolution of the Capitalist Firm", *Journal of Economic Issues,* 33(4) (December): 999-1017.

Pistor, Katharina and Jeffrey D. Sachs (1998) "The Rule of Law and Economic Reform in Russia", *HIID research Review,* 11(2)(Winter/Spring): 2, 6.

Polinsky, A. Mitchell and Steven Shavell (2000) "The Economic Theory of Public Enforcement of Law", *Journal of Economic Literature* 38(March): 45-76.

Pool, Daniel (1993), *What Jane Austen Ate and Charles Dickens Knew, From Fox Hunting to Whist––The Facts of Daily Life in Nineteenth–Century England,* New York: Simon & Schuster.

Portney, Paul R. (1994) "The Contingent Valuation Debate: Why Economists Should Care", *Journal of Economic Perspectives,* 8(4)(Fall): 3–17.

Posner, Richard A. (1993) "Nobel Laureate Ronald Coase and Methodology", *Journal of Economic Perspectives,* 7(4)(Fall): 195–210.

Powell, Alvin (1998) "Taking the Pulse, Cutler monitors the vital signs of

U.S. health care system", *Harvard University Gazette*, 93(18) (February 12): 3–4.

————(1999) "Study: Parents' Presence Helps Heal Children", *Harvard University Gazette*, 95(8)(November 4): 1, 6.

Pradhan, Sanjay (1997) "Improving the State's Institutional Capability", *Finance and Development*, 34(3)(September): 24–27.

Prowse, Stephen D. (1996) "Corporate Finance In International Perspective: Legal and Regulatory Influences on Financial System Development", *Economic Review*, Federal Reserve Bank of Dallas, Third Quarter 1996: 2–15.

————(1997) "Corporate Financial Control and Governance: An International Perspective", *Southwest Economy*, Federal Reserve Bank of Dallas, September/October: 9–10.

Quine, W. V. (1987) *Quiddities—An Intermittently Philosophical Dictionary*, Cambridge, Massachusetts and London, England: The Belknap Press of Harvard University Press.

Rabin, Matthew (1998) "Psychology and Economics", *Journal of Economic Literature*. 36(March):11–46.

Rahula, Walpola Sri (1979) *What the Buddha Taught*, Second and enlarged edition, New York: Grove Press.

Ram, Rati (1997) "Tropics and economic development: an empirical investigation", *World Development*. 25: 1443–1452.

————(1999a) "Tropics, income, and school life expectancy: an intercountry study", *Economics of Education Review*, 18(1999): 253–58.

————(1999b) "Tropics and Income: A Longitudinal Study of the U. S. States", *Review of Income and Wealth*, 45(3)(September)(proof copy):1–6.

Rappaport, Steven (1996) "Abstraction and unrealistic assumptions in economics", *Journal of Economic Methodology*, 3(2)(December): 215–236.

Rappoport, Peter (1987) "Blame Labor Shortage for Inflation in Services", *The Wall Street Journal* (209)(113)(June 11):24.

Regan, Donald T. (19880 *For the Record: From Wall Street to Washington*, San Diego, New York, London: Harcourt Brace Jovanovich, Publishers.

Reich, Robert B. (1991) *The Work of Nations, Preparing Ourselves for 21st Century Capitalism*. New York: Alfred A. Knopf.

Reid, Escott (1973) "McNamara's World Bank", *Foreign Affairs*, 51(4) (July): 794–810.

Reingold, Jennifer with Brad Wolverton (1998) "When Bosses Get Rich From Selling The Company", *Business Week* (March 30): 32–3.

Reischauer, Edwin O. (1970) *Japan: The Story of a Nation*, Tokyo: Charles E.Tuttle Company.

Reuters (1993) "Bonn Tries to Fire Up Engine", Rome, Italy: *International Herald Tribune*, No. 34,367, 34/93, (August 27): 5.

Ridley, Matt (1997) *The Origins of Virtue: Human Instincts and the Evolution of Cooperation,* New York: Viking.
Rinfret, Pierre A. (1993), "Letters, The Myth of the Independent Director", *New York Times,* 142(49410)(August 1): F11.
Rodrik, Dani (1999) "East Asian Mysteries: Past and Present", National Bureau of Economic Research, *NBER Reporter,* (Spring): 7-11.
Romains, Jules (1938), *Les Hommes de Bonne Volonté,* XVI,*Verdun,* Paris: Flammarion.
Romer, Thomas (1977) "Nobel Laureate: On James Buchanan's Contributions to Public Economics", *Journal of Economic Perspectives,* 2(4)(Fall): 165–179.
Romer, Christina (1999) "Changes in Business Cycles: Evidence and Explanations", *Journal of Economic Perspectives,* 13(2)(Spring): 23-44.
Rose, Richard with Edward Page et al (1985) *Public Employment in Western Nations,* Cambridge, England; New York Cambridge University Press.
Rose–Ackerman, Susan, ed. (1986) *The Economics of Nonprofit Institutions: Studies in Structure and Policy,* Yale Studies of Nonprofit Organizations, Program on Non–Profit Organizations, Institution for Social and Policy Studies. New York, Oxford: Oxford University Press.
Rosen, Sherwin (1996) "Public Employment and the Welfare State in Sweden", *Journal of Economic Literature,* 34(June): 729–740.
———(1997) "Austrian and Neoclassical Economics: Any Gains From Trade?" *Journal of Economic Perspectives,* (11)(4)(Fall): 139–152.
Rouner, Leroy S. (1999) "Civil Religion, Cultural Diversity, And American Civilization", *The Key Reporter* 64(3)(Spring): 1, 3-6.
Routh, Guy (1984) *Economics: An Alternative Text,* MacMillan Press: London.
Rowley, Charles K. (1993) *Liberty and the State,* The Shaftesbury Papers, 4, Aldershot, England, Brookfield, Vermont: Edgar Elgar.
Rubinstein, W. D. (1993) *Capitalism, Culture & Decline in Britain: 1750–1990,* London & New York: Routledge.
Ruhm, Christopher (1998) "The Well-being of Children", *NBER Reporter,* National Bureau of Economic Research, (Summer): 27-28.
Runde, Jochen and Paul Anand (1997) "Rationality and methodology, Introduction",*Journal of Economic Methodology,* 4(1)June): 1–21.
Russell, Thomas (1997) "The rationality hypothesis in economics: from Wall Street to Main Street", *Journal of Economic Methodology,* 4(1)June): 83–100.
Ryback, Timothy W. (1998) "The Man Who Swallowed Chrysler" *The New Yorker,* (November 16): 80-89.
Sachs, Jeffrey D. and Warner, Andrew M. (1997) "Fundamental Sources

of Long-Run Growth", *American Economic Review*, 87(2)(May): 184-88.

Sachs, Jeffrey D. and Woo, Wing Thye (1999) "The Asian Financial Crisis: What Happened, and What is to be Done", mss. davos-sachswoo Asian Crisis, January 21, 1999. 16.

Saffran, Bernard (1996) "Recommendations for Further Reading", *Journal of Economic Perspectives*, 10(3)(Summer):181–188.

Sagan, Carl & Ann Druyan (1992) *Shadows of Forgotten Ancestors*, New York: Random House.

Sala–I–Martin, Xavier X. (1997) "I Just Ran Two Million Regressions", *American Economic Review*, 87(2)(May):178-183.

Samuels, David (1996) "Presidential Shrimp, Bob Dole caters the political hors d'oeuvres. Campaign Letter", *Harper's Magazine*, 292(1750) (March): 45–52.

Samuelson, Paul Anthony (1947) *Foundations of Economic Analysis*, Cambridge, Massachusetts & London, England: Harvard University Press, Tenth Printing,1975.

————(1989) "Robert Solow: An Affectionate Portrait", *Journal of Economic Perspectives*, 3(3)(Summer): 91–97.

Sandmo, Agnar (1990) "Buchanan on Political Economy: A Review Article", *Journal of Economic Literature*, 28(March): 50–65.

Saunders, Peter & Friedrich Klau (1985) *The Role of the Public Sector, Causes and Consequences of the Growth of Government.* OECD Economic Studies, No. 4/Spring 1985. Organisation For Economic Cooperation and Development.

Saxonhouse, Gary R. (1993) "What Does Japanese Trade Structure Tell Us About Japanese Trade Policy?", *Journal of Economic Perspectives*, 7(3) (Summer): 21–43.

Saxenian, Anna Lee (1994) *Regional Advantage: Culture and Competition in Silicon Valley and Route 128,* Cambridge, Massachusetts: Harvard University Press.

Schelling, Thomas (1960) *The Strategy of Conflict.* Cambridge: Harvard University Press.

Schlesinger, Jacob M. (1990) "Japan Aims to Show That Chip Market Is Open to the West", *Wall Street Journal,* 215(46)(March 7): A14.

Schultz, Abby (1996) "California Pension Fund Is Developing 1997 Governance Standards for Boards", *Wall Street Journal,* 222(58)(September 20): B5A.

Schumpeter, Joseph A. (1912) 1934 *The Theory of Economic Development, An Inquiry into Profits, Capital, Credit, Interest, and the Business Cycle.* Harvard Economic Studies, Vol 46. Cambridge, Massachusetts: Harvard University Press. First published as *Theorie der wirtschaftlichen Entwicklung.*

————(1942) 1950 *Capitalism, Socialism and Democracy,* 3rd ed. New York: Harper; London: Allen & Unwin.

————(1951) *Essays.* ed. by Richard V. Clemence. Cambridge, Massachusetts: Addison-Wesley.

————(1951) *Ten Great Economists. From Marx to Keynes.* New York: Oxford University Press.

————(1954) *History of Economic Analysis.* ed. by Elizabeth Boody Schumpeter from manuscript. New York: Oxford University Press.

Schwartz, Hugh (1998) *Rationality Gone Awry? Decision Making Inconsistent with Economic and Financial Theory.* Westport, Connecticut; London: Praeger.

Seabrook, John (1994) "A Reporter At Large: E–mail from Bill", *The New Yorker,* 69(45)(January 10): 48–61.

Sen, Amartya K. (1977) "Rational Fools: A Critique of the Behavioral Foundations of Economic Theory," *Philosophy and Public Affairs,* 6(4): 317–44.

————(1987) *On Ethics and Economics,* The Royer Lectures, Series Editor: John M. Letiche. Oxford and New York: Basil Blackwell.

————(1995) "Rationality and Social Choice", Presidential address, American Economic Association, January 7, 1995. *The American Economic Review,* 85(1)(March):1–24.

Seth, Vikram (1994) *A Suitable Boy,* New York: Harper Collins Publishers, Harper Perennial, first published in 1993 in India by Viking Penguin Books India Ltd, in the United Kingdom by the Orion Publishing Company.

Shapiro, Robert (1992) *The Human Blueprint: The race to unlock the secrets of our genetic code,* First ed. St. Martin's Press 1991, New York, Toronto, etc: Bantam Books.

Shattuck, Roger (1996) "Emily Dickinson's Banquet of Abstemiousness", *The New York Review of Books,* 43(8)(June 20): 55–9.

Shelp, Ronald Kent (1981) *Beyond Industrialization: Ascendancy of the Global Service Economy,* Praeger Special Studies, New York: Praeger.

Shleifer, Andrei and Robert Vishny (1990) "The Takeover Wave of the 1980s", *Science,* (August).

———— and Robert Vishny (1993) "Corruption", *Quarterly Journal of Economics,* (Autumn).

Schmid, A. Allan (1994) Book review of "A Framework for Cognitive Economics by Roger A. McCain" [1992], *Journal of Economic Issues,* 28(1)(March): 261-4.

Silvestre, Joaquim (1993) "The Market–Power Foundations of Macroeconomic Policy", *Journal of Economic Literature,* 31(March 1993): 105–41.

Simon, Herbert A. (1962) "New Developments in the Theory of the Firm", *American Economic Review,* 52(2)(May): 1–15.

————(1991) "Organizations and Markets", *Journal of Economic Perspectives,* 5(2)(Spring): 25–44.

Simons, Katerina and Joanna Stavins (1998) "Has Antitrust Policy in

Banking Become Obsolete?" Federal Reserve Bank of Boston, *New England Economic Review*, (March/April): 13-16.

Singelmann, Joachim (1978) *From Agriculture to Services, The Transformation of Industrial Employment*, Vol. 69, Sage Library of Social Research, Beverly Hills, London: Sage Publications.

Sissman, L. E. (1997) "The April Almanac. 25 Years Ago", *The Atlantic Monthly*, 279(4)(April):16.

Slater, Martin (1980] "Foreword", in Edith T. Penrose, *The Theory of The Growth of the Firm*, White Plains, New York: M. E. Sharpe, Inc., vi–xxxii.

Sloan, Allan (1992) "Posner deal a throwback to the '80s", *The Boston Sunday Globe*, (September 20): 86.

————(1993) "Fischbach's shocking ruination", *The Boston Sunday Globe*, 244(4)(July 4): 30.

Smart, Molly (1994) "Gaijin", *The World*, The Journal of the Unitarian Universalist Association, 8(3)(May/June): 30–1.

Smith, Adam (1937) *The Wealth of Nations,* New York: Modern Library, originally published in 1776.

————(1976) *The Theory of Moral Sentiments*, David D. Raphael and Alec L. Macfie, ed., London: Oxford University Press.

Smith, Vernon L. (1982) "Microeconomic Systems as an Experimental Science", *The American Economic Review*, 72(5)(December): 923–955.

————(1994) "Economics in the Laboratory", *Journal of Economic Perspectives*, 8(1)(Winter): 113–131.

Solow, Robert M. (1997a) "It Ain't the Things You Don't Know That Hurt You, It's the Things You Know That Ain't So", *American Economic Review,* 87(2)(May):107–8.

————(1997b) "How Did Economics Get That Way and What Way Did It Get?" *Daedlus*, Winter 1997, *American Academic Culture in Transformation" Fifty Years, Four Disciplines,* issued as Vol. 126, Number 1 of the Proceedings of the American Academy of Arts and Sciences: 39–58.

Specter, Michael (1997) "In Modern Russia, a Medieval Witch Hunt", *New York Times*, New England Edition, 146(50753)(April 5):1,4.

Spring, William J. (1987) "Youth Unemployment and the Transition from School to Work: Programs in Boston, Frankfurt, and London", *New England Economic Review*, (March/April): 3–16.

Staddon, John (1995) "On Responsibility and Punishment", *The Atlantic Monthly,* 275(2)(February): 88–94.

Stanback, Thomas M, Jr. (1979) *Understanding the Service Economy: Employment, Productivity, Location,* Policy Studies in Employment and Welfare Number 35, Baltimore & London: Johns Hopkins University.

Stanfield, J. Ron (1983) "Institutional Analysis: Toward Progress in Economic Science", in Eichner, Alfred S., ed. (1983) *Why*

Economics is not yet a Science, Armonk, New York: M. E. Sharpe, Inc., 187-204.

Stanley, Henry M. (1872) *How I found Livingstone*, London: Sampson Low (extracts in Charles Richards and James Place, *East African Explorers*, London: Oxford University Press, 1960).

Stavro, Barry (1985) "A house undivided", *Forbes*, 136(6)(September 9): 36, 40.

Stein, Jeremy C. (1991) "What Went Wrong With the LBO Boom", *The Wall Street Journal*, 217(119)(June 19): A12.

Steinem, Gloria (1994) *Moving beyond Words*, New York, London, etc.: Simon & Schuster.

Stéphane, Roger (1984) *André Malraux, entretiens et précisions*. Paris: Gallimard.

Stevenson, Glenn C. (1991) *Common Property Economics: A general theory and land use applications*, Cambridge, New York & Melbourne: Cambridge University Press.

Stewart, James B. (1992) *Den of Thieves*, New York, London, etc: A Touchstone Book, Simon & Schuster.

——(1993) "Annals of Law: Michael Milken's Biggest Deal", *The The New Yorker*, March 8: 58-71.

Stigler, George J. (1982) "Do Economists Matter?", in *The Economist as Preacher*, edited by George J. Stigler, 54-67. Oxford: Basil Blackwell, quoted in Craig Freedman, "The Economist as Mythmaker—Stigler's Kinky Transformation", *Journal of Economic Issues*, 29(1)(March): 175-209.

——(1988) *Memoirs of an Unregulated Economist*, New York: Basic Books.

Stiglitz, Joseph E. (1983) "Samuelson and neoclassical economics", *Journal of Economic Literature*, 21(3)(September): 997-9.

——et al (1989) *The Economic Role of the State*, edited by Arnold Heertje, Oxford & Cambridge, Massachusetts: Basil Blackwell in association with Bank Insinger de Beaufort NV.

——(1991) "Symposium on Organizations and Economics", *Journal of Economic Perspectives*, 5(2)(Spring): 15-24.

——(1992) "Another Century of Economic Science", *The Future of Economics*, John D. Hey, editor, (Issue 1 of volume 101 of the Economic Journal, January 1991), Oxford and Cambridge USA: Blackwell, pp. 134-141.

——(1998) "Distinguished Lecture on Economics in Government, The Private Uses of Public Interests: Incentives and Institutions", *Journal of Economic Perspectives*, 12(2)(Spring): 3-22.

Stoehr, Kevin L. (1998) "Twentieth World Congress of Philosophy: A Historical Meeting of the Minds", *The Humanist*, 58(2)(March/April): 31-33.

Stolper, Wolfgang F. (1968) "Schumpeter, Joseph A.", *International Encyclopedia of the Social Sciences*, 67-72. New York, etc: The

Macmillan Company & The Free Press.

Stone, Christopher (1976) *Where the Law Ends: The Social Control of Corporate Behavior.* New York, etc: Harper & Row.

Streeten, Paul (1972) *The Frontiers of Development Studies*, A Halsted Press Book, New York: John Wiley & Sons.

————(1986) "Aerial Roots", *Banca Nazionale del Lavoro Quarterly Review*, (157)(June): 135–59.

————(1997) "Contemporary Economics: A Critique", *Zukuntsfähige Entwicklung, Herausforderungen an Wissenschaft und Politik, Festrschrift für Udo E. Simonis zum 60. Geburtstag*, edited by Frank Biermann, Sebastian Büttner, Carsten Helm. Wissenschaftszentrum Berlin für Sozialforschung, Berlin: edition sigma.

Sugden, Robert (1989) "Spontaneous Order", *Journal of Economic Perspectives*, 3(4)(Fall): 85–97.

————(2000) "Credible worlds: the status of theoretical models in economics", *Journal of Economic Methodology*, 7(1)(March):1–31.

Summers, Lawrence H. (2000) "International Financial Crises: Causes, Prevention, and Cures", Richard T. Ely Lecture, *American Economic Review*, 90(2)(May): 1–16.

Sundrum, R. M. (1983) *Development Economics: A Framework for Analysis and Policy*, New York, Chichester, England, etc: Wiley.

Tanzi, Vito and L. Schuknecht (1995) "The Growth of Government and the Reform of the State in Industrial Countries", *IMF Working Paper*, (December) Washington, D.C.: International Monetary Fund.

Taylor, John B. (2000) "Teaching Modern Macroeconomics at the Principles Level", *American Economic Review*, 90(2)(May): 90–94.

Taylor, Lance (1993) Review of "The order of economic liberalization: Financial control in the transition to a market economy" by Ronald I. McKinnon, *Journal of Economic Literature*, 31(March): 279–80.

Teece, David J. (1993) "The Dynamics of Industrial Capitalism: Perspectives on Alfred Chandler's *Scale and Scope*", *Journal of Economic Literature*, 31(March): 199–225.

Tevlin, Stacey (1996) "CEO Incentive Contracts, Monitoring Costs, and Corporate Performance", Federal Reserve Bank of Boston, *New England Economic Review*, (January–February): 39–50.

Teoh, Siew Hong, T. J. Wong and Gita Rao, "Incentives and Opportunities for Earnings Management in IPOs", and "Earnings Management and the Long–term Market Performance of IPOs.", *UCLA working papers*. Los Angeles: University of California at Los Angeles.

Thaler, Richard H. (1988) "Anomalies, The Winner's Curse", *Journal of Economic Perspectives*, 2(1)(Winter): 191–202.

————(1991) *Quasi Rational Economics*, New York: Sage Foundation.

————(1992) *The Winner's Curse: Paradoxes and Anomalies of Eco-*

nomic Life, New York: The Free Press; Toronto: Maxwell Macmillan Canada; New York: Maxwell Macmillan.

Theil, Henri and Dongling Chen (1995) "The Equatorial Grand Canyon", *De Economist* 143(3): 317–327.

———(1996) *Studies in Global Econometrics,* in association with Dongling Chen, Kenneth Clements, and Charles Moss. Advanced Studies in Theoretical and Applied Econometrics. Dodrecht, Boston, London: Kluwer Academic Publishers.

Thomas, Lewis (1980) "On the uncertainty of Science", *Harvard Magazine,* 83(1)(September–October): 19–22.

Thomas, Michael M. (1990) "Greed", *The New York Review of Books,* 37(5) (March 29): 3–5.

Thurow, Lester C. (1983) *Dangerous Currents, The State of Economics,* New York: Random House.

Titmuss, Richard (1997) *The Gift Relationship: From Human Blood to Social Policy,* rev. ed. The New Press.

Tobin, James (1987) *Policies for Prosperity: Essays in a Keynesian Mode,* Cambridge, Massachusetts: MIT Press.

Townsend, Robert (1970) *Up the Organization,* New York: Alfred A Knopf.

Train, John (1994) "Going Into Wall Street", Harvard Magazine, 96(5) (May-June): 22–3.

Tribe, Keith (1999) "Adam Smith: Critical Theorist?", *Journal of Economic Literature,* 37(June): 609-632.

Truell and Larry Gurwin (1992) *BCCI,* New York: Houghton Mifflin.

Tuchman, Barbara W. (1984) *The March of Folly From Troy to Vietnam,* NY: Alfred A. Knopf.

Tullock, Gordon (1993) *Rent Seeking,* The Shaftesbury Papers, 2; Series Editor Charles K. Rowley, Aldershot, Hants, England and Brookfield, Vermont: Edward Elgar.

Turnbull, Colin (1972) *The Mountain People,* New York: Simon and Schuster.

Tversky, Amos & Richard H. Thaler (1990) "Anomalies: Preference Reversals", *Journal of Economic Perspectives,* 4(2)(Spring): 201–211.

———& Daniel Kahneman (1981) "The Framing of Decisions and the Psychology of Choice", *Science* 211: 453–8.

United Nations (1971) *Basic Principles of the System of Balances of the National Economy,* Studies in Methods, Series F No. 17, Department of Economic and Social Affairs, Statistical Office of the United Nations, New York: United Nations.

United States Department of Commerce, Economics and Statistics Administration, Bureau of Economic Analysis (1992) *Business Statistics 1963–91,* 27th Edition, June 1992. Washington, D. C., U. S. Government Printing Office.

Urquhart, Brian (1987) *A Life in Peace and War,* New York: Harper and

Row.
Valibeigi, Mehrdad (1993) "Islamic Economics and Economic Policy Formation in Post–Revolutionary Iran: A Critique", *Journal of Economic Issues*, 27(3)(September): 793–812.
van Eeghen, Piet–Hein (1996) "Towards a methodology of tendencies", *Journal of Economic Methodology*, 3(2)(December): 261–284.
van Wolferen, Karel (1989) *The Enigma of Japanese Power*, New York: Alfred A. Knopf.
Vernon, Raymond (1971) *Sovereignty at Bay; The Multinational Spread of U. S. Enterprises*, New York, London: Basic Books, Inc.
Vickers, Douglas (1995) *The Tyranny of the Market; A Critique of Theoretical Foundations*, Ann Arbor: The University of Michigan Press.
Viner, Jacob (1937) *Studies in the Theory of International Trade*, New York: Harper & Bros.
————(1959) "The Intellectual History of Laissez Faire", The second Henry Simons Lecture given at the University of Chicago Law School, November 18, 1959. *The Journal of Law and Economics*.
————(1991) *Essays on the Intellectual History of Economics*, ed. by Douglas A. Irwin, Princeton, New Jersey: Princeton University Press.
Vishny, Robert W. (1998) "Corporate Finance" *NBER Reporter*, National Bureau of Economic Research, (Summer): 1-5.
Vogel, Ezra F. (1986) "Pax Nipponica", *Foreign Affairs*, 64(4)(Spring): 752–67.
————(1991) *The Four Little Dragons*, Cambridge, Massachusetts, London: Harvard University Press.
Wagner, Richard E. (1997) "Choice, Exchange, and Public Finance", *The American Economic Review*, Papers and Proceedings, January 4–6, 1997, 87(2) (May): 160–3.
Waldman, Michael (1990) *Who Robbed America? A Citizen's Guide to the S&L Scandal.* New York: Random House.
Waldman, Peter and Brenton R. Schlender (1987) "Falling Chips", *Wall Street Journal*, 209(32)(February 17): 1, 24.
Waldrop, M. Mitchell (1992) *Complexity*, New York, London, etc: Simon & Schuster.
Wall Street Journal (1995) "In a Cost–Cutting Era, Many CEOs Enjoy Imperial Perks", 225 (45)(March 7): B1, B10.
————(1996) "The Boss's Pay; The Wall Street Journal/William M. Mercer 1995 CEO Compensation Survey", 227(72)(April 11): R15–17.
Wallis, John Joseph (2000) "American Government Finance in the Long Run: 1790 to 1990", *Journal of Economic Perspectives*, 14(1)(Winter): 61-82.
Walras, Léon (1965) *Correspondence of Léon Walras and Related Papers,* W. Jaffé, ed. 3 vols., Amsterdam: North–Holland.

————(1896) *Eléments d'économie pure.* (3rd edition), Lausanne.

Warsh, David (1984) *The Idea of Economic Complexity,* New York: The Viking Press.

————(1989) "Economic Principals, Where the pink slip is only an undergarment", *The Globe 235(8)* (January 8): 75, 79.

Webb, Susan (1995) "Bowling Leagues, Answer to Good Government", *John F. Kennedy School of Government Bulletin,* (Summer 1995): 10–11.

Weber, Max (1958), *The Protestant Ethic and the Spirit of Capitalism,* New York: Charles Scribner's Sons, translated from the German by Talcott Parsons, originally published in 1904–5 as *Die protestantisch Ethik und der Geist des Kapitalismus.*

Weiermair, Klaus (1986) "On the Economics of Institutional Change: An Institutional Change in Economics?", *Journal of Economic Issues,* 20(2)(June): 571–82.

Weinstein, Michael M. (2000) "Students Seek Some Reality Amid the Math of Economics", Social Science Research Council, *Items & Issues,* 1(1) (Winter): 1-3.

Weintraub, E Roy. (1983) "On the Existence of a Competitive Equilibrium: 1930–1954", *Journal of Economic Literature,* 41(1) (March): 1–39.

Weiss, Thomas Joseph (1975) *The Service Sector in the United States 1839 Through 1899,* New York: Arno Press.

Weithman, Paul J. (1989) "Sex and Sin", *The New York Review of Books,* 35(10)(June 15): 61.

Welch, John F., Jr.(1994) "To Our Shareowners", 1993 Annual Report, General Electric Company. 1–5.

————, Paolo Fresco, John D. Opie, (1996) "To Our Share Owners", *General Electric Company 1995 Annual Report,* February 9, 1–5.

Westphal, Larry (1990) "Industrial Policy in an Export–Propelled Economy: Lessons from South Korea's Experience", *Journal of Economic Perspectives,* 4(3)(Summer): 41–59.

Whitehead, Alfred North (1933) *Adventures of Ideas,* 15th printing, 1954. New York: The Macmillan company.

Wiener, Martin (1981) *English Culture and the Decline of the Industrial Spirit,* Harmonsworth.

Wiles, Peter (1983) "Ideology, Methodology, and Neoclassical Economics", in Eichner, Aflred S., (1983) *Why Economics is not yet a Science,* Armonk, New York: M. E. Sharpe, Inc. pp. 61-89.

Williams, Bernard (1985) *Ethics and the Limits of Philosophy,* Cambridge, Massachusetts: Harvard University Press.

Williamson, Jeffrey G. (1991) "Productivity and American Leadership: A Review Article", *Journal of Economic Literature,* 29(March): 51–68.

Williamson, Oliver E. (1996) *The Mechanism of Governance,* New York, Oxford: Oxford University Press.

Willoughby, Jack. (1985) "The human factor", *Forbes*, 136 (1) (July 1): 36.

Wilson, Edward O. (1992) *The Biodiversity of Life*, New York, London: W. W. Norton & Company.

Wired (1995) "Fast, Cheap, and Very Polite", 3(12)(December): 49.

Woo, Henry K. H. (1986) *What's Wrong with Formalization in Economics: An Epistemological Critique*, Hong Kong, Newark, CA: Victoria Press.

The World Bank (1993), *Getting Results; The World Bank's Agenda for Improving Development Effectiveness*. Washington, D.C.: The World Bank.

World Health Organization (1999) *World Health Report 1999*, (http://www. who.int/whr/1999/en/report.htm).

Xiao–huang Yin (1994) "China's Gilded Age", *The Atlantic Monthly*, 273(4)(April): 42–53.

Young, Allyn A. (1928) "Increasing Returns and Economic Progress", *Economic Journal (38)*(December): 527–42.

Young, Dennis R. "Entrepreneurship and the Behavior of Nonprofit Organizations: Elements of a Theory", in Rose–Ackerman, Susan, ed. (1986) *The Economics of Nonprofit Institutions: Studies in Structure and Policy*, Yale Studies of Nonprofit Organizations, Program on Non–Profit Organizations, Institution for Social and Policy Studies. New York, Oxford: Oxford University Press, 161–184.

Young, James Sterling (1966) *The Washington Community, 1800–1828*. New York: Harcourt, Brace & World, Inc., A Harbinger Book.

Zagorin, Adam (1994), "The Sins of a Sainted Bank", *Time,* 144(8(August 22): 54–5.

Zakaria, Fareed (1994) "Culture is Destiny, A Conversation with Lee Kuan Yew", *Foreign Affairs*, 73(2)(March/April): 109–126.

Zhilin, Aleksandr (1995) "Criminal Financial Dealings Dramatically Increased in Russia", The World Bank, Transition Economics Division, *Transition, The Newsletter about Reforming Economies*, 6 (11–12) (November– December): 9–10.

Zinman, John (1978) *Reliable Knowledge: An exploration of the grounds for belief in science,* Cambridge, London, etc: Cambridge University Press.

Zuckerman, Mortimer B. (1998) "A Second American Century", *Foreign Affairs* 77(3)(May/June): 18–31.

Index

About the Author

Andrew Martin Kamarck is the retired director of the World Bank's Economic Development Institute (World Bank Institute) and the founding director of the Bank's central economics complex. He was educated at Harvard with degrees in economics SB (summa cum laude), MA and Ph.d. in Political Economy and Government.

In 1939, Kamarck joined the International Section of the Federal Reserve Board but was borrowed by the Secretary of the Treasury for war work. A reserve officer, he entered active duty in 1942 as instructor at the Field Artillery School.

In 1943, Kamarck was posted to the Allied Control Commission for Italy, in charge of the Banca d'Italia in southern Italy and, then in Rome, IRI (Instituto per la ricostruzione industriale) which controls much of Italian finance and industry. In December 1944, he was released from the Army, given the assimilated rank of Lieutenant-Colonel, was assigned as Chief of US Financial Intelligence in Germany. In Berlin, he became Deputy-Director of the Control Council's U.S. Finance Division and U.S. Deputy on the Allied Finance Directorate for Germany.

Back at the Treasury in 1946, Kamarck chaired the Staff Committee for the cabinet National Advisory Council for International Monetary and Financial Problems (NAC). This committee set the financial, fiscal, foreign exchange and monetary policy guidelines for the Marshall Plan. The final estimates of US aid were coordinated by a State and Treasury committee, which he also chaired.

Following on two years in Italy as US Treasury Representative, and Chief of the Marshall Mission's Finance Division, Kamarck became the World Bank's Economic Adviser on Europe, Australasia and Africa. In 1964/65 he was Regents Professor at UCLA, returning to the Bank as Director of a new Economics Department. In 1971, he was Research Associate at the Harvard Center of International Affairs, returning to the Bank as Director of the Economic Development Institute (EDI). He was responsible at one time or another for writing, supervising or reviewing economic studies that in total covered most of the members of the Bank.

On retiring from the Bank, Kamarck served for eight years as Visiting and Associate Fellow of the Harvard Institute of International Development.

He has written four books:*The Economics of African Development*, with French, Swedish, Portuguese and Spanish eds; *The Tropics and Economic Development,* with French and Spanish eds; *La Politica Finanziaria degli Alleati*; *Economics and the Real World.*

He is the co-author of 17 books on a range of economic subjects. He is listed in *Who's Who in the World* and *International Who's Who.*

Kamarck lives with his wife, Margaret, an artist, on Cape Cod.

For Product Safety Concerns and Information please contact our EU
representative GPSR@taylorandfrancis.com
Taylor & Francis Verlag GmbH, Kaufingerstraße 24, 80331 München, Germany

www.ingramcontent.com/pod-product-compliance
Lightning Source LLC
Chambersburg PA
CBHW070354270326
41926CB00014B/2548